# Universal Emancipation

NEW WORLD STUDIES

A. James Arnold, *Editor*

J. Michael Dash, David T. Haberly, and Roberto Márquez, *Associate Editors*

Joan Dayan, Dell H. Hymes, Vera M. Kutzinski, Candace Slater, and Iris M. Zavala, *Advisory Editors*

# Universal Emancipation

## THE HAITIAN REVOLUTION AND
## THE RADICAL ENLIGHTENMENT

Nick Nesbitt

New World Studies
*A. James Arnold, editor*

University of Virginia Press
Charlottesville and London

University of Virginia Press
© 2008 by the Rector and Visitors of the University of Virginia
All rights reserved
Printed in the United States of America on acid-free paper

*First published 2008*

9 8 7 6 5 4 3 2 1

Library of Congress Cataloging-in-Publication Data

Nesbitt, Nick, 1969–
   Universal emancipation : the Haitian Revolution and the radical Elightenment / Nick Nesbitt.
      p. cm.   — (New World Studies)
   Includes bibliographical references and index.
   ISBN 978-0-8139-2802-9 (cloth : alk. paper) — ISBN 978-0-8139-2803-6 (pbk. : alk. paper) — ISBN 978-0-8139-2776-3 (e-book)
   1. Haiti—History—Revolution, 1791–1804. 2. Liberty. 3. Enlightenment—Influence. I. Title.
   F1923.N47 2008
   972.94′03—dc22

2008022937

# Contents

| | | |
|---|---|---|
| | Acknowledgments | vii |
| | Introduction | 1 |
| 1 | Saint-Domingue and the Singularization of Enlightenment | 9 |
| 2 | The Idea of 1804 | 41 |
| 3 | Penser la Révolution Haïtienne | 81 |
| 4 | Beyond Jacobinism: Hegemony and Universalism in the Haitian Revolution | 129 |
| 5 | Toussaint Louverture, the *Moun andeyo,* and the Transcendental Conditions of Political Autonomy | 153 |
| | Conclusion: Remembering 1804 | 179 |
| | Appendix: Chronology of the Haitian Revolution (1791–1804) | 199 |
| | Notes | 207 |
| | Works Cited | 241 |
| | Index | 257 |

# Acknowledgments

IN A PROJECT ranging over five years and innumerable sites of research and discussion, more debts have been incurred than I can possibly hope to acknowledge here. This book began through an invitation from Deborah Jenson to contribute to the volume of *Yale French Studies* she edited. In the ensuing years, her research, criticism, and collegiality have been a major inspiration in giving this project the form it has progressively taken on. At Cornell University, a fellowship at the Society for the Humanities and the Department of Romance Languages offered a nurturing home for this work in its incipient versions. There, I benefited from the congenial criticism of Bret de Bary, Susan Buck-Morss, Jacques Coursil, Richard Klein, Mitchell Greenberg, and Barry Maxwell, who took the time to welcome me into their inspiring community.

My good friends and colleagues at Miami University submitted much of this material to the incisive critical spirit of the wonderful community that is our Department of French and Italian. Their understanding and generosity as I improvised in the face of life's hurdles during these years has left me with a sense of gratitude and debt that these pages can only hint at. While at Indiana University, I found exciting and munificent interlocutors in Jeff Isaac, Aurelian Craiutu, Jerome Brillaud, Eileen Julien, Doyle Stevick, Oana Panaite, Bill Rasch, and Sarah Knott, while at the European College of Liberal Arts in Berlin, Costica Bradatan and David Durst contributed substantially to the betterment of this work. At the University of Aberdeen, my new colleagues at the Centre for Modern Thought and the School of Language and Literature, and Alberto Moreiras, Chris Fynsk, and Michael Syrotinsky in particular, cultivated this research in its final stages.

Other colleagues and friends who generously gave time and attention to this work include Laurent Dubois, Kaiama Glover, Pim Higgenson,

Lydie Moudileno, Martin Munro, Donald Moerdijk, Daniel Maximin, Charles Forsdick, Chris Bongie, Valerie Loichot, Madison Bell, Edwidge Danticat, Peter Hallward, Richard Watts, Marcel Dorigny, Jeremy Popkin, Dawn Fulton, Abiola Irele, and Alec Hargreaves. At the Collège de philosophie and Tulane University, Jean-Godefroy Bidima has continued to be an inspiration and tireless interlocutor in developing our shared vision of a Black Atlantic Critical Theory.

At the University of Virginia Press, A. James Arnold and Cathie Brettschneider have kept faith in this book in its long gestation, and helped immeasurably in its progress. I also wish to extend my thanks and gratitude to the two anonymous readers whose perceptive comments and suggestions were enormously helpful in revising my manuscript. I would like to thank *Yale French Studies* for granting generous permission to reprint material that appeared in the article "The Idea of 1804" (107 [Spring 2005]: 6–38), and Lexington Press for permission to reprint portions of my contribution to *Memory, Empire and Postcolonialism: Legacies of French Colonialism* (ed. Alec Hargreaves, 2005, 37–50). Earlier versions of material incorporated herein appeared as well in *Critique, Carribean(s) on the Move—Archipiélagos literarios del Caribe, Small Axe,* and *Research in African Literatures.*

Finally, this book would never have been possible without the care, critique, and sustenance of Eva Cermanova.

Universal Emancipation

# Introduction

THE HUMAN right to be free from enslavement inspired the eighteenth-century Age of Revolution, which spoke widely of the injustices of "slavery" and "servitude," while, paradoxically, chattel slavery was maintained and defended as an actual social institution throughout the Atlantic world. On January 1, 1804, however, the former slaves of the French colony of Saint-Domingue took the decisive step of universally abolishing slavery unconditionally and immediately upon achieving independence as the new nation of Haiti. Acting decades in advance of the North Atlantic powers, they turned the abstract assertion of a human right to freedom for all citizens into historical fact and created a slavery-free society, without discrimination other than that one be human and present within the borders of this new state. This book will explore the implications of this fundamental event of modern human history, the invention of *universal* emancipation (as opposed to, say, the emancipation of white, male, adult property owners).

Living in a different time, our concerns are inevitably different from those of earlier historians of the Haitian Revolution such as Victor Schoelcher and C. L. R. James; yet my claim is that the Haitian Revolution continues to be, as it was for these distinguished predecessors, of vital importance in thinking about the urgent problems of social justice, human rights, imperialism, torture, and above all what Hannah Arendt identified as the eternal and preeminent problem of political thought: human freedom and its relation to the sociopolitical structures we choose to give to our communities.

In Saint-Domingue this struggle for freedom took the form not of the defense of personal choice, thought, or an inner freedom in an unfree world but specifically of what Arendt would describe as "the freedom to call something into being which did not exist before, which was not given, not even as an object of cognition or imagination, and which, therefore, strictly speaking, could not be known," in other words, a freedom of active creation (1986, 151). Though individuals had on occasion imagined universal rights as a pure abstraction, no society had ever been constructed in accord with the axiom of universal emancipation. The construction of a society without slavery, one of a *universal* and *unqualified* human right to freedom, properly stands as Haiti's unique contribution to humanity.

Though in this sense the Haitian Revolution constituted a drastic leap forward beyond other contemporary political structures, it stands in another light as the culminating, most progressive event of the Age of Enlightenment. If recent historical revisionism has effectively demolished the prejudice that there was either a single movement identifiable as the "Enlightenment" or that such a movement was the product of a single nation (that is, France, England, or the Netherlands), better understanding of the political philosophy of the Haitian Revolution should help to undo what remains perhaps the last shibboleth of Enlightenment Studies: that, as Tzvetan Todorov claimed in his exhibition notes to a 2006 exhibition at the Bibliothèque de France, "The thought of the Enlightenment was the work of Europe" (11). Even so insightful a historian of ideas as Jonathan Israel maintains a similar faith in a "single European Enlightenment" (140).[1] Instead, this book will explore the many ways in which the Haitian Revolution, an ocean away from Europe, both was inspired by Radical Enlightenment ideas and, in turn, fundamentally transformed this transnational, world-systemic historical process.

The declaration of Haitian independence in 1804 can in a certain sense be understood as the political climax of what Israel has called the "radical" (as opposed to a "moderate") Enlightenment. The latter was typified by politically conservative thinkers such Fontenelle, Newton, Locke, Leibniz, and Wolff, all of whom pursued the Cartesian derivation of knowledge solely from mathematic-based human reason, while simultaneously attempting to avoid critique of the established political and religious orders of the day.

In contrast, a long tradition of transnational radical thought—extending across Europe from Van den Enden and Spinoza in the 1760s to thinkers including Radicati, Mandeville, La Mettrie, and Diderot—constructed a critique of human knowledge and society that affirmed the indivisibility and inalienability of sovereignty. It was not, however, until 1804—following upon the Jacobinist initiative—that an entire nation constituted itself in consonance with such a critique, structuring a society so as to affirm the constituent power and rights of all human subjects. Haiti was in this sense the first nation to realize the full political implications of the Spinozian critique of constituted authority and the call for a society in which all human subjects retain their self-moving constituent power (*natura naturans*). The former slaves of Saint-Domingue were conscious participants in this Radical Enlightenment, directly influenced by French thinkers such as Diderot (via Raynal's *Histoire des trois Indes*) and the Jacobin articulation of the undivided "Rights of Man," while further radicalizing in turn an Enlightenment that refused to address Africans as full subjects of human rights.

If my project here has been to draw together some of the diverse historical and intellectual threads that were woven into what we now call the Haitian Revolution, it seems unquestionable that the most immediate factor in turning what began as one more in a long series of New World slave revolts for better working conditions into a struggle for the universal abolition of slavery was the publication of the French *Déclaration des droits de l'homme et du citoyen* in August 1789. Though I will argue that other components—from the thirteenth-century Mandé Declaration of Universal Human Rights ("Charte du Mandé") to Vodun and the Catholicism Toussaint Louverture imbibed from his Jesuit benefactors in the decades before 1791—contributed to this process, the testimony of the rebel slaves themselves unequivocally supports such a conclusion.

In July 1792, to cite only the most explicit example, they wrote to the General Assembly of Saint-Domingue of "the fortunate revolution which has taken place in the Motherland, which has opened for us the road which our courage and labor will enable us to ascend, to arrive at the temple of Liberty, like those brave Frenchmen who are our models and whom all the universe is contemplating" (Bell 2007, 39–40). Though one should no doubt read such a statement as bearing some degree of flattery aimed at placating its metropolitan *destinataires,* there would no doubt have been better ways to ingratiate themselves, had they chosen to, with the *grands blancs* plantation owners in Paris who wished to maintain the slave-based labor system underwriting their wealth. Refusing such compromises, and less than a year after it had begun, these supposedly ignorant former slaves had unequivocally transformed their revolt into a revolution unique in world history.

Similarly, Toussaint Louverture described to the increasingly proslavery French Directory in 1797 how "the French Revolution . . . changed my destiny as it changed that of the whole world" (cited in Bell 2007, 59). No mere imitation of the events in France, the Haitian Revolution quickly came to exceed its model in its commitment to human rights, and this radicalism would come in turn to transform events in Paris by 1794. The chapters that follow will interrogate this process of radicalization in its causes, forms, limitations, and implications, tracing the dense networks of impulse and induction at work in what was truly a world-systemic process.

My resolution here is to seek to recover what 1804 might have become (or became only in the sheer exteriority to our world of the Haitian rural peasantry, the *moun andeyo*). It is to discern this promise to modernity, to recover for our now postmodern, univocal world of sheer immanence and political alienation, the historical remnants of a sign previously visible to the world only as terror, chaos, and dysfunction, a sign that two centuries after its appearance still can illuminate the path before us in a twenty-first century in which more humans are enslaved than at any other time in human history. Contrary to the hand-wringing of the Western media, if there was a "failure" of the Haitian Revolution, it lies not, as is generally thought, on the side of Haitians who would have "betrayed" its ideals. No country has ever remained *more* faithful in its awareness and actual constitution to the image of its revolutionary founding and the potential freedom of all humans. Instead, that failure has been our own repeated inability or refusal to follow through on Haitian democratization.

The localized Haitian destruction of the global slaveholding regime and the institution of a political system of undivided human rights should rightfully have shamed the United States and France. Instead, it terrified them. The Haitian Revolution called into question the world-system of slave-based agricultural capitalism that had developed from the sixteenth to the eighteenth centuries. Slavery (and serfdom in Eastern Europe) was central to the development and functioning of this system, and the total, immediate abolition Haitians first implemented in 1793 was indeed shocking for the North Atlantic powers. The failure of the Haitian Revolution has instead lain, for the past two centuries, on the other side, on *our* out-side (speaking as a U.S. citizen), in our failure to properly interpret (if not our active repression and/or destruction of) this image of emancipation that should rightfully have obliterated chattel slavery throughout the world in the years immediately following 1804.

In the single year of 1787, the slaves of Saint-Domingue had produced 131 million pounds of sugar for the North Atlantic world's consumption (Dayan 201). The colony's enormous resources and profits were seized in the course of a single night's uprising on August 21, 1791, and every slaveholding nation knew the same could happen again anywhere, anytime. While the plantations would continue to function to an important degree in the relative calm of Toussaint's domination from 1796 to 1802, what *was* destroyed in a single night was the system that organized that production regime around slave labor. The former slaves decisively refused and demolished all forms of slave labor, and proceeded to invent an unheralded social system that successfully refused the reimposition of surplus-based wage labor, no matter which successive leader tried to reimpose it from 1795 to the present (Polverel, Toussaint, Christophe, the U.S. Marines in 1914 . . .).

Despite the overwhelming inertial resistance of the socialized world to its own transformation, events *consistently* occur that break free of the weight of any given situation. This book, then, constitutes an attempt to elucidate and to remain faithful to the historical singularity of figures such as Toussaint Louverture, to refuse the *ressentiment* of an always-ready-at-hand retort, to refuse the ever-renewed jouissance of the automutilation of hope in a world putatively without transcendence.

*Universal Emancipation* is an attempt to understand the Haitian Revolution, in both its historical singularity and its uniqueness along with its vital relevance to the present. The singularity of Haiti is so often posed to us in negative terms—as the singular poverty and abjection of what the media see only as "the poorest country in the Western hemisphere"—that it requires no small effort of imagination and understanding to see to what degree the uniqueness of Haiti is precisely the opposite: the world-historical invention and imposition since 1804 of an egalitarian freedom unknown in the North Atlantic. This rural society *andeyo* (outside) the North Atlantic world-system has long remained invisible to an external world dedicated to economic development at all costs and the liberal-bourgeois system that has achieved near total hegemony in the two centuries following 1804. Though its existence has become increasingly imperiled in recent decades, the stateless egalitarian society that arose from the Haitian Revolution nonetheless functioned for a century and a half in radical exteriority both to the dominant Creole culture of exploitive modernization within Haiti and to the general process of North Atlantic (and now global) modernization as a whole. All the while, it has remained an unassimilable, indigestible political product of the dialectic of Enlightenment both within and without Haiti. A central project of this book, then, will be to trace a genealogy of this postcolonial conflict between the forces of modernization and an antimodern, egalitarian society. It will show how the Haitian Revolution created entirely new subjects of modernity, subjects who despite their shared antipathy to the slave-based economy of the North Atlantic world they overthrew, nonetheless possessed often radically different visions of how the process of universal emancipation was to be implemented.

In the 1790s, on this distant colonial periphery of the European world, there arose a radical, progressive, and cosmopolitan politics that allied a diversity of political thinkers in defiance of reigning divisions of nationality, race, class, and gender. In assembling these postcolonial fragments of the transnational event that has come to be called the Radical Enlightenment, my intent is to look to this past to contribute to an archeology of our contemporary transnational public sphere. This book constructs a constellation the aim of which is to transform our understanding of what is politically and historically possible by examining the unfulfilled promise contained in this shattered, incomplete project of Enlightenment *countermodernity*. Essentially, such a transformation requires thinking beyond a North Atlantic–centered vision of modernity, as well as the disciplinary boundaries that found its epistemology. This is a process that has become not only possible but of utmost urgency since 1989 and the post-9/11 rise of a global politics of terror, fundamentalism, and cultural exceptionalism (of both West and East). In looking to this history, we can find not icons of the ineluctable march of historical progress, but images of an unfulfilled promise of social justice and human dignity that are perhaps only today becoming decipherable in the world beyond their site of origin.

The lesson the Haitian Revolution holds for us today is simple: it is to move beyond regimes of difference and to refuse the neutralization of political claims under the banner of liberal tolerance. In place of difference (what were called "special" [that is, proslavery] laws in Saint-Domingue, Jim Crow and apartheid in our own), we should enlist all such claims for cultural and juridical distinction into the political struggle for universal equality and emancipation.

The first chapter places the Haitian Revolution within the context of both the Radical Enlightenment and the American and French revolutions, while introducing the general claims for its singularity that will be developed in detail in subsequent chapters. Chapter 2, "The Idea of 1804," examines the events in Saint-Domingue itself in the context of the Radical Enlightenment. The chapter focuses particularly on the role of the Saint-Domingue revolution in the creation of a global public sphere of debate in the Atlantic world, a public sphere that, I argue, extended far beyond the bourgeois European social groups where European thinkers such as Kant sought to limit it. Instead, debate over the parameters of universal emancipation took place across the entire network of the early-modern capitalist world-system, while the materials of its self-fashioning extended back in time as far as thirteenth-century Mali.

Chapter 3 pursues the analysis of this system of knowledge production in the transnational Radical Enlightenment to consider a number of its geographically dispersed conceptualizations of an inalienable human right to freedom: the long tradition of European natural rights theory and its culmination in the 1789 *Déclaration des droits de l'homme et du citoyen*, as well as the Kantian and Hegelian critiques of slavery. Chapter 4 brings the Gramscian concept of "hegemony" to bear on the Saint-Domingue revolution, focusing on its recent articulation by Ernesto Laclau as a theory of "populist reason." I argue that the concept of hegemony shows the Haitian Revolution to have been a violent social struggle to redefine the content of an abstract universal signifier: *liberté*. The chapter proceeds to examine in detail the historiographic evidence of this struggle for symbolic hegemony in Saint-Domingue, charting the protean meanings expressed in the earliest years of the revolution by the French/Kreyol concept I dub *liberté/libete*. The analysis of the Haitian Revolution as a creative process of subjectification, of the invention of new, unheralded, and scandalously inadmissible subjects of enlightenment, thus takes the critique of the Kantian/Habermasian public sphere elaborated in chapter 2 a step further: I argue that not only did the coordinates of this sphere lay far beyond the North Atlantic world but that participation in public debate over the meaning of "freedom" in the Enlightenment world was not undertaken by static, preexisting subjects who had simply to agree to formal rules of debate; rather, this cannibalization of public-sphere rules and rhetoric was a generative self-fashioning of new subjectivities, forms of being-in-the-world that are only today becoming intelligible in an (outside) world long unable to "digest" their fullest political implications.

Chapter 5 examines Toussaint Louverture's politics of universal emancipation as a peripheral epistemology in the Radical Enlightenment. It concludes by discussing the limitations of Toussaint's implementation of emancipation and his decision to reconstruct an independent Saint-Domingue by forcible (albeit paid) plantation labor. I argue that the simple, indivisible fidelity to universal emancipation shared by the entire subaltern population of Saint-Domingue nonetheless quickly revealed a primary contradiction between the developmental, wage- and surplus-based model of labor shared by all the modernizing elites from Toussaint and Sonthonax to Christophe, and, in contrast, an unyielding strategy of resistance within the *Bossale* (African-born) community, the *moun endeyo*.

The latter successfully refused the construction of all forms of forced labor and the transcendental state apparatuses that would impose and enforce them. The book's final chapter then turns to the legacy of the Haitian Revolution and its construction of a universal, egalitarian model of human freedom, in search of the lessons it may hold for our early twenty-first century, where we find ourselves once again torn between a will to defend universal human rights and the exploitation endemic to the nascent world-system of empire.

Not a historiography of Saint-Domingue, this is a particular study of the events of 1791–1804.[2] It is a history, yes, but the history of an idea (universal emancipation) focusing on the site (Saint-Domingue) of its first world-historical articulation. As such, in the pursuit of this idea, I was drawn across time, space, and cultures. In the drive to elucidate a concept that cannot—by its own definition—be limited to any single locality or field, the reader will find here a strongly interdisciplinary spirit. I primarily invoke historiography and political philosophy, but also, at various moments, literature, linguistics, anthropology, musicology, and film. My hope is that scholars of these disciplines will find within these pages spurs to fuller elucidation than I can offer here of the materials and questions I present, and I will be happy if the variegated constellation I have arranged strikes the imaginations of others in ways I cannot envision.

# 1 Saint-Domingue and the Singularization of Enlightenment

IT IS ONLY today, two hundred years after its conclusion on January 1, 1804, that we are beginning to decipher the radical message of the Haitian Revolution. Unlike the earlier American Revolution, it was, as Patrick Bellegarde-Smith has pointed out, one of the few revolutions in history that truly overthrew and eradicated one social form (the slaveholding plantocracy) in a process in which "swift, violent and radical change occur[ed] in the political, economic, social, and cultural conditions of the country" (xviii). Less happily, newly independent Haiti also demonstrated to the world the first instance of what would later be called neocolonialism, where ruling elites (both mulatto and black) united with the military and a merchant class to create an instable balance of power (Trouillot 1990, 57). This depended upon the taxation of both agricultural exports and tertiary imports and a corresponding systematic underdevelopment of local productive forces, all at the expense of the excluded majority.[1]

The development of the first postcolonial state apparatus in Haiti, a phenomenon new to Atlantic modernity, came at the expense of all but a tiny minority. After 1804, following the failed attempts of Dessalines, Christophe, and Boyer to forcibly reimpose plantation labor (only Christophe's violent regime had some short-term success in this), the Haitian state quickly reconstructed itself to fulfill a single task: it became a mere "agent" for the extraction and redistribution of surplus profit on foodstuffs (Trouillot 1990, 71). Both the unfinished project of decolonization and the actuality of neocolonial imperialism imply that attention to the Haitian Revolution and its aftermath is of most pressing concern if we are to understand the origins and classic forms of decolonization and neocolonialism that continue to confront our twenty-first century.

However important these problems may remain, the course of this thirteen-year revolution contains a further, more radical dimension that has only gradually become apparent, after the failure of socialism and the looming degeneration of liberal democracies into citizen surveillance machines. We have seen two hundred years of totalitarianism and genocide, fascist and so-called socialist states that sacrificed the process of democratization and the autonomy of human subjects to industrial "productionism"; two hundred years of nationalist states that merely sacrificed their citizens *tout court* in genocidal hysteria.

At the same time, Western liberal democracies have fostered a culture of consumption to compensate for popular disenfranchisement, as oligarchies of the elite make their own decisions regarding war, the environment, and social justice in the name of those they are supposed to represent. After the collapse of socialism and the rise of neonationalisms, as we confront reactionary Western political elites that eagerly sacrifice the rights of their subjects for the chimera of impregnable fortress-states, the assertion of the universal rights of all humans is suddenly a most pressing and basic concern.

A *positive* idea of human rights, understood as the capacity of individuals and collectivities to exert control over their existence and development, has suddenly taken precedence in the contemporary era in which human rights have achieved hegemony over the concept of the political (Gauchet). This positive notion of human rights moves beyond the merely negative safeguards that were called human rights in the English and American traditions. It is only after the political and human disasters of the last century that the North Atlantic world has begun, however hesitantly, to move toward the idea of a universal right of all human beings to freedom as the positive capacity for self-determination on a global, and not merely local, scale. In fact, human rights are increasingly understood to be the primary criterion in evaluating political regimes. Economic development and even democracy, both of which can and often do sacrifice the rights of individuals, are only *means* of achieving universal human rights.[2]

This attempt to ground a society not upon economic freedom or representative democracy, but instead upon the most basic universal human rights, was first successfully articulated two hundred years ago in the Haitian Revolution. The events in Saint-Domingue brought to fruition the unfulfilled promise of the French Revolution to found a state in which positive rights applied equally to all citizens, without exception.[3] It marked true progress in human existence—if one understands such progress not as the perfection of means of production or increases in material wealth, but rather as humans' increasing success in resisting terror, suffering, and fear.[4] Furthermore, it initiated (though never stabilized) a

## 11  Saint-Domingue and the Singularization of Enlightenment

uniquely progressive democratic order of transnational scope.[5] Haiti sent the world a message few in 1804 could hear: freedom did not mean leaving landowners alone to enjoy their property, human or otherwise.

The Haitian Revolution moved beyond mere national and civil rights, those of the "citoyen" of 1776 and 1789, to press the universal claims of the rights of "Man" (Knight 394). On those few occasions when domestic and international pressures allowed the embattled Haitian state an imperial foreign policy in the nineteenth century, the nation acted to abolish slavery when and where it could. In 1822 President Boyer successfully invaded Santo Domingo and abolished slavery in the Spanish colony (Trouillot 1990, 48). From the moment of its creation in 1804, Haiti presented freedom to the world as an absolutely true logic, one that must be made, in turn, universal reality: no humans can be enslaved. Until the much later creation of Liberia and Ethiopia, Haiti stood as the world's sole republic of free African peoples in a slaveholding world-system, an "international anachronism," in Trouillot's telling phrase (57).

This new state announced that freedom can exist only when we create a global society whose structures and laws allow for the full and unimpeded development of our possibilities as living individuals. This pronouncement was shocking and inadmissible in a system of global colonialism grounded and dependent on the enslavement of a portion of the human population. The idea of the Haitian Revolution was so scandalous that enormous efforts were made to silence it, to falsify it, to demonize, in short to reduce Haiti as both idea and reality to no more than the "poorest country in the Western Hemisphere." Haiti was immediately quarantined and pauperized into the forced dysfunction of a postcolonial state hamstrung by the terrified slave-holding powers that then controlled the globe.

In hindsight, however, as we look back across two hundred years of Haitian independence at a succession of despotic regimes, systemic economic underdevelopment, and social injustice, one might question the utility of a revolution that paved the way for these historical (under)developments. Perhaps all those timorous French Enlightenment thinkers, from Condorcet to l'Abbé Grégoire, were right: a too rapid freedom granted to slaves "unprepared" for liberty could only lead to chaos.[6] In Saint-Domingue, like Paris of 1793–94, there was violent brutality perpetrated on both sides, though it was likely the "horrors" of Rochambeau's "white terror" that were by far the most brutal (Dayan 186). An entire society was literally reduced to ashes by 1804 in the name of a single imperative: universal emancipation.[7] For those who had known the suffering of slavery before 1791, however, nothing else mattered in the face of this categorical imperative, not property, not happiness, not any other good. To focus only on the visible, subjective violence of this struggle is to ignore the immeasurably greater systemic violence of slavery that deformed and destroyed every aspect of the lives of millions of Africans.

Such hand-wringing over the violence of the Haitian Revolution is refuted by the simple fact that the situation of black Haitians after 1804, in terms of labor, living conditions, freedom of movement, sexual exploitation, and cultural production, was substantially changed for the better (Blackburn 1995, 96). The former slaves of Saint-Domingue rightfully authorized and legitimated their own struggle, without awaiting accreditation from any master. The subjective violence of their struggle destroyed the most violently exploitative and destructive system (North Atlantic slave labor) the world has yet known, one that directly claimed the lives of some ten to thirty million Africans. Because of this total revolution, hundreds of thousands of Haitians in fact avoided the vicious reprisals that fell upon blacks in Guadeloupe when Napoleon reinstated slavery there in 1802. Moreover, this gain is quantifiable: they avoided precisely forty-six years of enslavement (1802–48). Who else but those concerned could judge what this progress was worth? The slaves of Saint-Domingue, who knew slavery firsthand, decided for themselves that, faced with its imminent reimposition, nothing else mattered, that they would never return to the world of chattel slavery.

### The Buttressing of the American and French Slave Regimes

If the French and American revolutions had first articulated an abstract recognition of universal human rights, the Haitian Revolution brought to bear a simple truth denied by these earlier political sequences: the freedom of the few cannot be predicated upon the enslavement of the many. Haitians did not simply reproduce the 1789 *Déclaration des droits de l'homme et du citoyen* by transplanting this foreign bird to tropical climes; they demonstrated human freedom precisely in their unique transformation of this empirical object. The dehumanizing experience of enslavement impelled the slaves of Saint-Domingue to alter the immanent meaning of the universal declarations of 1776 and 1789, making the Haitian Revolution the most accomplished political event of the Age of Enlightenment.

While the American and French revolutionaries, following John Locke, often spoke of the injustices of "slavery," few understood this critique to include all citizens, unequivocally. The vocal critics of slavery in the

## 13  Saint-Domingue and the Singularization of Enlightenment

North American English colonies such as James Otis, Benjamin Rush, and Benjamin Franklin were a tiny minority in the colonial public sphere (Frey 49; Davis 1975, 113). While the second half of the eighteenth century witnessed the creation and global spread of an abolitionist culture, in the 1760s and 1770s this was primarily a moral and religious phenomenon that would only subsequently be politicized in Saint-Domingue (1791) and France (1794).

The American revolutionaries in particular were often more concerned with enlightenment as a passage from "barbarism" to "civility" and mastery of gentlemanly social behavior than with the problem of (positive) freedom (Gordon S. Wood 192–98).[8] The American Revolution was primarily a revolution for the equality of nonslaves, where liberty meant primarily freedom from unjust taxation and military conscription. It began as a tax revolt among a group Davis has called "conservative *criollos*," and as such addressed only citizens who had the privilege to pay taxes; it was never intended by colonial leaders to call into question North American social and class relations.[9] The revolt of 1776 was above all a call for the freedom of property owners, those who defended, in the words of the 1772 Boston declaration, "the Rights of the Colonists . . . to life, liberty, and property" (cited in Zuckert 60). Similar assertions of the basic right to property are to be found in virtually all such American declarations of rights from the period: the Declaration and Resolves of the First Continental Congress (1774), George Mason's draft of the Virginia Declaration of Rights (1776), and the Pennsylvania, Delaware, and Massachusetts declarations of rights (1776, 1776, 1770).[10]

In the winter of 1791, when revolutionary leaders in Saint-Domingue began to call for the immediate, universal abolition of slavery, there existed no available model for such political claims in the Atlantic world. In the United States, only a very few cautious, hesitantly granted gradual-emancipation laws had been promulgated at the time; all of these subordinated the immediate interests of slaves to the defense of the rights of property owners (Davis 1975, 28, 87–89, 334). Vermont, often cited as the first nation in world history to abolish slavery, was in fact no different.[11] Its 1777 constitution explicitly specified the abolition of slavery, but only for adult males over twenty-one and women over eighteen:

> I. That all men are born equally free and independent, and have certain natural, inherent and unalienable rights, amongst which are the enjoying and defending life and liberty; acquiring, possessing and protecting property, and pursuing and obtaining happiness and safety. Therefore, no male person, born in this

country, or brought from over sea, ought to be beholden by law, to serve any person, as a servant, slave or apprentice, *after he arrives to the age of twenty-one Years, nor female, in like manner, after she arrives to the age of eighteen years, unless they are bound by their own consent.* (italics added)[12]

The northern states' gradual emancipation acts were in addition addressed only to a tiny minority of their population, and never posed the danger of overthrowing an entire socioeconomic structure, as was the case in the American South as well as in Saint-Domingue. Moreover, the 1777 Articles of Confederation expressly limited states' rights to emancipate slaves brought within their territory by masters from slaveholding states, rendering the scope of all northern state initiatives decidedly less than universal on this count as well (Blumrosen 153).

American abolitionist groups such as the Quakers were deeply imbricated in colonial economic and social networks, and their calls for abolition were frequently tempered by a respect for the continuity of English and colonial profitability (Davis 1975, 237–51). Religious leaders such as the Garrisonian John Cooper were few and far between in arguing (in 1780) that "if we keep our present slaves in bondage, and only enact laws that their posterity shall be free, we save that part of our tyranny and gain of oppression, which to us, the present generation, is of the most value" (cited in Davis 1975, 296).

British-American slaves themselves, of course, were quick to assert their natural right to freedom as early as 1770, setting a precedent for the slaves of Saint-Domingue: "We have in common with all other men," stated one published appeal, "a natural right to our freedoms without Being depriv'd of them by our fellow men as we are a freeborn Pepel and have never forfeited this Blessing by aney compact or agreement whatever."[13] But while the American Revolution must be understood as a "triangular process" fought between pro- and anti-independence whites and some half million African slaves, it was the slaves of North America who can truly be said to have been the losers of the American Revolution (Frey 45).

The contradictions of the American Revolution encompassed the conflicting postulation of a right to "life" (implying sovereignty over one's body) and an equally abstract and unconditional right to property. If the rights of life, liberty, and property offered a vision of "personal sovereignty" (Zuckert 66), when left unqualified, such a model failed to address (or even recognize) the problem of the relation of that self to an other, considered the former's "property" in a slaveholding society.[14]

## 15  Saint-Domingue and the Singularization of Enlightenment

English and American antislavery theorists tended to equate "freedom" not with human perfectibility (as would French theorists such as Rousseau, Robespierre, and Grégoire), but with the external, objective rights of legal status and property ownership. David Brion Davis has gone so far as to claim that "the success of emancipation [in the eyes of many abolitionists] would depend not on the Negro's capacity for liberty, but on finding a substitute for the labor discipline of slavery" (1975, 306).

In fact, the empirical result of the American Revolution was that in the period from 1790 to 1807, and in the face of growing American popular opposition to slavery, more African slaves were imported to the United States than during any time in the colonial era. From 1776 to 1820, the slave population in the United States actually *tripled* (Davis 1975, 122). As a legal and political *enabling* of slavery, the institution of the United States of America (most explicitly in the three-fifths clause of the 1787 Constitution that legalized slavery in the southern states) stood directly and reactively opposed to what would be accomplished in Haiti in 1804.[15] Rather than beginning to institute even a gradual movement toward emancipation, the constitution they ratified afforded American slave owners immensely improved privileges and powers. They were assured of legal autonomy within the federal system, and garnered increased power through their own political "representation" of their slaves.[16]

In revolutionary France, slavery would not be proscribed until 1794, when it had already been formally abolished in Saint-Domingue since August 1793, having first been overthrown in the two years prior to that. Prior to 1789, French abolitionists such as Condorcet and Grégoire had called only for a gradual emancipation over a period of multiple generations. Though often celebrated for his defense of the "Rights of Man" and his attacks on the institution of slavery, Grégoire's vaunted "universalism" appears decidedly parochial in comparison with the calls for universal abolition that would emerge from Saint-Domingue after 1791. Though Grégoire became a highly vocal critic of slavery from the late fall of 1789 until his death in 1831, he explicitly and repeatedly refused to endorse universal, immediate abolition, calling instead for a gradual "preparation" of slaves for a freedom defined by the norms of Euro-Christian utilitarianism. Grégoire was admittedly nearly alone in his struggle to place (gradual) abolition at the center of post-1789 debate. His speeches and writings strove to confront slave owners with the Declaration of the Rights of Man, and he challenged them to "get out of it if they could." He attacked planters for their violent treatment of both free blacks and slaves, and he repeatedly described the possibility of slave revolt, making the radical assertion that all people had the right to insurrection against their oppressors (Dubois 2004a, 83).[17] When abolition did occur in 1794, however, Grégoire judged it to be "a disastrous measure"; instead, the *abbé* thought abolition should have occurred gradually, and he instead fought for immediate abolition only of the slave *trade* (cited in Brière 36).

Though he was in the political avant-garde in his 1789 defense of the civil rights of mixed-race colonial citizens, Grégoire paternalistically decreed black slaves unprepared for freedom at that time. Their cause, he proclaimed, "has nothing in common with that of the [free] mulattos. One must not rush into anything ... and give political rights to men who do not know all their duties" (cited in Sepinwall 96). In calling only for partial (immediate) and gradual (universal) abolition, and like nearly all his fellow white abolitionists in England and the United States, Grégoire ultimately sided with the slaveholding social system itself. To call for an abolition that would be implemented decades or generations in the future is necessarily to defend the system of slavery in the present. Rather than basing his judgment of slavery upon an axiomatic principle of universal right (as would Robespierre and Toussaint), Grégoire worked instead to assure the undisrupted continuity of the existing society he lived in by minimizing the inevitable economic and social disruptions that would come with abolition.

Though Grégoire's views on slavery evolved significantly over his long public career, the Bishop of Loir-et-Cher showed a systematic and unhesitating readiness to judge and speak in the name of others. This included his criticisms of Jewish particularism, a lifelong tendency to misogynist denunciations of women as immoral, frivolous, and malicious, efforts to "enlighten" the poor masses while reinforcing their subaltern status, as well as his condescension toward the Haitians he corresponded with after 1804. Grégoire continuously subjected the groups for whose rights he struggled to such paternalist arrogance. Moreover, he predicated the eventual extension of universal rights to these excluded populations upon the erasure of any singular, differential cultural traits (Sepinwall 196).

In the Parisian Assemblée Nationale, when calls for immediate abolition did arise, they were actively sidelined and silenced by those interested in maintaining the status quo. Fully 15 percent of the Constituent Assembly of 1789 actually owned property in the French colonies (Blackburn 1988, 167). The colonial policy of the National Assembly between 1789 and 1791 was systematically designed to protect the interests of Metropolitan property owners, and this defense was managed by a so-called "triumvirate"

## 17 Saint-Domingue and the Singularization of Enlightenment

of three representatives: Adrien Duport, Alexandre Lameth, and Antoine Barnave. Together, they ensured that the call for the defense of the Rights of Man would not impinge on the rights of colonial property owners in the years immediately following the fall of the Bastille. Their defense of the new revolutionary order subordinated the rights of slaves to those of the commercial and plantation bourgeoisie to create a strong counterweight to both the Royal and the Third estates (Blackburn 1988, 178). On March 8, 1790, the Committee on the Colonies headed by Barnave made explicit this refusal to universalize the Rights of Man: "The National Assembly," it pronounced, "does not intend to make any innovations in any of the branches of commerce between France and the colonies, whether direct or indirect; it puts colonists and their property under the special safeguard of the nation" (cited in Blackburn 1988, 179). This colonialist triumvirate repeatedly managed to silence debate over slavery and the rights of the enslaved prior to the summer of 1791 by the tactic of submitting various reports and then calling for their adoption without discussion (186). With such "defenders" of the Rights of Man in power in Paris, the slaves of Saint-Domingue would manage to bring the question of their equal human rights into political debate in 1791 only by extraordinary means.

One pamphlet from 1789, "The Slavery of the Blacks Abolished or the Means to Improve Their Situation," reveals the contradictions of metropolitan abolitionism in the uncertainty of its title. It begins by openly calling for the abolition of slavery in light of the Declaration of the Rights of Man and states that "God has created all men free." Consequently, "slavery should only continue to exist for criminals condemned according to the laws," and it then goes on to argue that "liberty ought to be restored to that unfortunate class of beings, our brothers though of different color, whom European greed has kidnapped annually for nearly three centuries from the coasts of Africa and condemned to an eternal captivity, hard work, and harsh treatment" (reproduced in Hunt 102). The author then immediately "qualifies" this call for emancipation, however, in the name of "the political interests and property rights that would be infringed if freedom was suddenly restored to the Negroes of our colonies": the infringement of property rights trumps the human rights of "the Negroes"; slavery should in fact *not* be abolished, but rather, starting in some unspecified future "epoch," it should be limited to a period of ten years' enslavement (102). This was the customary order of priority in the French Revolution: the rights of those qualified to speak in the assembly systematically superseded those of excluded Others.

The voices of abolitionists were few and isolated, and the plantation landowners' Club Massiac skillfully reduced the Société des Amis des Noirs to political inefficacy. Any attempt to dominate this hegemonic struggle was drowned in the sea of colonial interests dominating the French Assembly.[18] In March 1790 the assembly formed a colonial committee for Saint-Domingue unconstrained by the Declaration of the Rights of Man, the mission of which was to represent the planters' particular (that is, slaveholding) interests. Though Mirabeau attempted to speak out against the motion, his denunciation of this act was violently shouted down. The assembly rushed to a vote with no discussion, and the law was quickly passed. "The colonies," Laurent Dubois observes, "were safe from universalism" (2004a, 85).

If one accepted the notion that African slaves were human, the promulgation of the *Déclaration* in 1789 necessarily engendered an enormous contradiction between the universal norm of freedom and the fact of actually existing slavery in France's colonies.[19] All those benefiting from the slaveholding system, including not only whites but also mulattoes and even free blacks, studiously avoided invoking the cause of human rights in their fight for representation. Most often, in the early years of the revolution when the National Assembly was still trying to maintain slavery in the face of the first mulatto and slave revolts, the *Déclaration* remained a white elephant never mentioned by anyone in the voluminous debates. To do so would immediately have drawn the speaker, no matter what his position, into enormous logical contradictions.

A letter from the Provincial Assembly of Saint-Domingue to "83 départements du royaume" rejecting the legal attribution of rights to colored and free black citizens defended this position in terms of the huge economic loss that (they argued) would result from the elimination of slavery: "The colony of St. Domingue has no doubt that if the intention of France is to impose upon it [the rights of the free men of color] by arms, it would sooner or later manage this. What, though, would be the result? The annual loss of two hundred million francs, the loss of its commerce and production, the destruction of its navy, and ruin and disaster in the site where the most flourishing culture on the globe had brought you to the first rank of the European political powers and which was the key to your opulent society."[20]

If the English, French, and American bourgeois revolutions all served to create the structural conditions for the protection of individual liberties of economic choice and property, the particularity of the Haitian Revolution was to redress the imbalance they had introduced between

Fig. 1. Drawing of indigo cultivation from the *Encyclopédie* of Diderot and D'Alembert, ca. 1760, depicting the colonial mode of production based on slavery. (Author's collection)

equality and liberty in favor of the latter. The Haitian constitutions of 1801 and 1804 invented the concept of a postracial society. Though Article 4 of the Constitution of 1793 granted citizenship to any adult foreigner who resided in Metropolitan France for a year (Habermas 1998, 509), the French Revolution instituted an assimilationist version of nationalism that predicated social unity upon the erasure (rather than tolerance) of communitarian difference. By the time the French Assembly finally got around to extending the principles of its 1789 declaration to slaves, the abolitionist movement had been eviscerated amid the Terror, and the 1794 act was merely recognition of a fait accompli, designed to preserve French influence in what had been its most profitable colony in 1789 (Davis 1975, 148).

The Haitian Revolution could not look to the liberal model of society imported from England and North America for a viable political alternative to metropolitan France's continued defense of slavery from 1789 to 1794. This was true not simply because of the formal emphasis that had been placed upon individual (negative) liberties at the expense of universal freedom in the Anglo-Saxon political sphere. Rather, the liberal model *presupposed* individuals to be free, autonomous subjects who merely need to be left alone to go about their business, a pseudo-universalist claim that Marx would later critique as the self-serving ideology of a dominant social class. The former slaves who drove the Haitian Revolution to its culmination in a novel constitution and state knew from experience that all humans are *not* free; they took human autonomy not as an a priori given, but strove to enact it as a social, human accomplishment, an ongoing construction that was itself only instantiated in the process of giving form to an emancipated society.

## The Singularization of the Enlightenment

The idea of general emancipation progressively came to determine the Haitian Revolution in a process I am calling singularization. In this development the specificity of the events in Saint-Domingue arose from a complex historical matrix, including vernacular remnants of African human rights charters, news of the French and American revolutions and their declarations of independence and the rights of man, the brutal experience of New World slavery, and Afro-American religious experience (Vodun). To speak of a "singularization" of the Radical Enlightenment implies that in its relation to the Age of Enlightenment, Saint-Domingue was neither a mere subordinate tributary or backwater, where Euro-American ideas of the Rights of Man took on a "tropical" flavor, nor entirely isolated from North Atlantic ideas and history. Instead, the Radical Enlightenment idea of a universal and natural right of all humans to freedom adopted an unforeseen character in Saint-Domingue when slaves, who had previously been excluded from this vision, claimed those rights as their own in an event at once singular in its localized destruction of the plantation regime and universal in its address to all human beings.[21]

The Haitian Revolution offers perhaps the most compelling argument that the intellectual and historical climate of the second half of the eighteenth century must be understood as a variegated complex of multiple "enlightenments," which nonetheless share a common concern for the universal problem of human freedom. As I will argue in greater detail in subsequent chapters, the Haitian Revolution serves to disprove the notion that there was any single "Enlightenment project" (abolition was actively excluded from discussions of freedom from 1774 to 1792 in North America and Paris, but not in Saint-Domingue) as well as the current received wisdom that a putatively monological "Enlightenment" thought erased the singularity of individual cultures and people beneath abstract universal moral principles. In theory, I will show that this erasure is contradicted in the moral philosophy of Enlightenment thinkers such as Diderot, Robespierre, Toussaint, and Kant, while in its political practice Saint-Domingue sustained the singularity of the experience of slavery in its relation to a universal moral imperative.[22] The events in Haiti from 1791 to 1804 demonstrate that debate over the complementary notions of human freedom, universals, singularity and multiplicity, and political autonomy extended far beyond the geographical limits of Western Europe, and with singular and dramatic consequences for the content of that debate.

## The Spinozian Foundations of the Haitian Revolution

The Haitian Revolution constitutes an intensive political development of what Jonathan Israel has called the "Radical" Enlightenment. The latter stands in contrast to a more moderate philosophical movement that sought to accommodate itself to existing power structures of church and state, while continuing to elaborate the humanistic, mathematical modeling of a law-based natural world initiated by Galileo and Descartes. The thinkers of this moderate Enlightenment, such as Newton, Leibniz, and Locke, sought to preserve a transcendent realm of divine action unhindered by the laws of Nature. This had the advantage of enamoring them of kings and popes alike, since it provided an implicit (and often explicit) ontological justification for the analogous division of society between those entitled to freely make sovereign decisions, and a subaltern multitude alienated from such constituent power.

In contrast, the Haitian Revolution is the culmination of a radical strand of Enlightenment political philosophy that acted upon Spinoza's revolutionary proposition: to avoid insofar as possible the alienation of constituent power to representative bodies and to "always preserve the natural right in its entirety" (cited in Israel 259). It was in Saint-Domingue, building upon the auspicious beginnings of the American and French revolutions and the direct influence of thinkers such as Rousseau, Diderot (via Raynal), Mirabeau, and Robespierre, that this proposition was first put into practice without prejudicial distinctions of race, gender, age, or property. My argument is thus not only that we should understand the Haitian Revolution as (among many other things) a development of the Spinozian Radical Enlightenment but, reciprocally, that the political implications of the Radical Enlightenment were most fully articulated between 1793 and 1804, in the propositions and actions of the former slaves of Saint-Domingue.

To trace this chain of influence from Holland, through France to her New World colonies, is a difficult yet essential endeavor for the history of political philosophy. The influence of Spinoza in the French Enlightenment was at once all-encompassing and almost entirely indirect. Though his fundamental propositions would influence virtually every Enlightenment thinker, in France, as Paul Vernière has observed, he had virtually no disciples before the revolution. Spinoza's system "exploded" into European consciousness, but only in the multiple, anonymous fragments that various eighteenth-century thinkers would plunder in their own name (Vernière 329). Though—with the exception of La Mettrie—even the most radical sought to distance themselves from association with his name, Montesquieu, Voltaire, Diderot, and d'Holbach were all intimately familiar with his thought, both directly and through the neo-Spinozian clandestine literature that circulated throughout the century (330). Diderot in particular, in his increasingly materialist philosophy after 1750, was undoubtedly the most visibly Spinozian of the philosophes (Proust 290). He seems, however, to have absorbed the majority of this Spinozianism indirectly, principally through his reading of the atheist, libertarian *abbé* Jean Meslier, who was responsible for the first coherent and original materialist system in French intellectual history (Vernière 367–70; Proust 276–77).

In its turn Spinozian political philosophy propelled the radicalization of the Haitian Revolution via its reinscription within the political philosophy of Diderot, Rousseau, and the Jacobins. Spinoza's proposition that human rights are universal, indivisible, and inalienable is the logical outcome of his fundamental axioms: the universe consists of a single, universal substance, and movement and the capacity for self-determination is inherent in matter itself (*natura naturans*), not instilled by an external First Mover.[23] Though for Spinoza all existent Beings (*natura naturata*) have necessarily been determined in their existence, a Spinozian political "ethics" would strive to maximize the capacity for self-determination that is a universal, immanent potential in all natural beings. In this, Spinoza stood far beyond moderate Enlightenment theorists of inalienable natural rights such as Hobbes, who derived inalienable natural rights from the mere imperative to preserve physiological life.

Instead, Spinoza argued that natural right must protect and cultivate not only biological life but also any being's fullest, unrealized possibilities (what he called its "essence") (Lazzeri 25, 33). The basis of Spinozian right is the infinite, open-ended productivity of beings who constantly singularize themselves as expressive beings. Human nature is implicitly for Spinoza—as it would be explicitly in Rousseau's "perfectibility"—no unchanging constant but is instead in continuous transformation. Though

## 23   Saint-Domingue and the Singularization of Enlightenment

not all (and perhaps even a tiny minority of) humans live freely, in conformity with reason ("man does not always have the power to reason and to be always at the peak of human freedom"), Spinoza maintained that every human being is capable of expressing himself with maximum freedom. Only when "reason is most powerful" will one "also [be] most fully possessed of one's own right" (Spinoza 1958, 273, 275, translation modified).[24]

The (logical) claim that Substance is inherently self-moving, and must (ethically) strive to create the maximal conditions of possibility for the self-determination of its infinite modalities, leads inevitably (for those existentially concerned with such matters) to the conclusion that slavery, as the most brutal and dehumanizing alienation of this inherent potential, must be overthrown and destroyed by any means necessary. Slavery, as the systematic, institutionalized attempt to deny the expression of human singularity, is an immanent fact of nature (insofar as society, for Spinoza, is not opposed to nature, but is merely one of its modes). It must, nonetheless, be overthrown. In Spinoza's political logic, the natural right of the slave owner disappears before the nascent desire, force, and understanding of the slave: "One individual is subject to the right of another as long as he is subject to the other's power. He is independent as long as he is able to repel all force, and take what vengeance he pleases to avenge any harm against him" (Spinoza 1958, 273, translation modified).

If the rule of natural law is universal, holding true without exception, the political domain cannot stand in exception to this ubiquity.[25] Just as it holds universally for the physical world, in the domain of social justice and right, the rule of law must apply indivisibly to all rational beings. Spinoza was unequivocal on this point: "All men," he stated in the *Tractatus Politicus,* "have one and the same nature; it is power and culture which misleads us" (cited in Israel 271). Spinoza was not the first to call for a true democracy in which all would rule without distinction and qualification; he was, however, the first to deduce such an injunction systematically from the very simplest of ontological presuppositions. The magnificent systematicity of this vast ontological edifice, in which such political deductions formed only one small facet, scandalized the constituted European powers for at least 150 years (1650–1800).[26]

As a concept of the Radical Enlightenment, universal emancipation must above all be understood as what Spinoza called an "adequate idea." While moderate Enlightenment thinkers sustained Descartes' distinction between logical clarity and actual reality, Spinoza's concept of the adequate idea was not so much a *rejection* of the Cartesian *idée claire et distincte* as the fulfillment of its inherent promise. The Spinozian *adequate idea* is not defined by the correspondence between subject and object, as a correct (mental) representation of an object, but rather as the essential expressive force of an idea (Deleuze 1968, 118). The adequate idea moves beyond merely superficial, abstract classifications such as race toward "common" or general ideas such as universal emancipation from servitude (256). The formation of such common ideas is in fact for Spinoza the point at which a being passes from passivity to activity: "The formation of common ideas marks the moment in which we take formal possession of our power to act" (259).

While the clear and distinct idea merely describes the effectivity of a being in its externality, the adequate idea, in contrast, expresses the cause of an idea (Deleuze 1968, 119). As an existential and ethical problem, human freedom calls not merely for a clear and distinct (encyclopedic) understanding of its nature but also for an adequate (ethical) idea of its real conditions of realization. This in turn calls not for the inward isolation of the Cartesian reflective self, but for the expressive actualization of a politics. Only in (political) society can reason become active and fulfill its real potential: "The man led by reason is freer in society, where he lives according to common decree, than in solitude, where he only obeys himself" (Spinoza 1999, 452).

To understand the events of the Haitian Revolution as such a spontaneous, self-moving *singularization* of the Spinozian Radical Enlightenment implies that the Haitian Revolution be understood not merely in its *difference from* the French and American revolutions, but rather in both its *singularity* and its *commonality* with other revolutionary moments in the Age of Enlightenment. The Haitian Revolution was not the negation of 1789; no less did it find its transcendental foundation in the *Déclaration des droits de l'homme*. The extension of universality through the early modern world occurred via a series of nodal points spread throughout a transnational network. In this process the requisite conditions for the social construction of human rights were extended—and adapted—from one "laboratory" site to another.[27] This extension of universalism was not the unfolding embodiment of a metaphysical essence, but the productive expression of an immanent potentiality, the potentiality to universalize the sociohistorical conditions for emancipation from a small number of "laboratories" (Athens, Mali, Philadelphia, Paris, Saint-Domingue) to encompass the modern world-system in its totality. The self-differentiation of these events occurred as an ongoing historical project and not through a purely internal and unrelated ontological expression of difference. The

## 25  Saint-Domingue and the Singularization of Enlightenment

challenge confronting contemporary interpretation of the Haitian Revolution is to grasp how these events came to construct their singularity in relation to other nodal points in this network.

The Haitian Revolution demonstrates not only the falsity of any monological understanding of the Enlightenment but also, paradoxically, its truth. The specificity of Saint-Domingue in the eighteenth century was determined by the universalist and globalizing structure of capital that expanded beyond Europe to create sugar production facilities that incorporated humans into its machinic assemblies. The Haitian striving for a singularization of political subjectivity was simultaneously a dialectical negation of slavery, violence, and global capital. As Haitians strove for a political singularization of their experience, they could not simply pull themselves out from this world by their bootstraps. Like all of us, only more so, Haitians have not been free to fashion their identities in any way they wanted, in abstraction from either the global plantation-slavery complex or the North Atlantic politico-military-capital machine that has worked to isolate and actively destroy Haitian independence from 1804 to the present day. The process of Haitian singularization is only comprehensible as existing in tension with the determinate conditions that impelled and governed its emergence. To claim univocally that the Enlightenment was not one but multiple, indeed to claim that any singularity exists without external relation "with another thing ... [that is] all that it is not," is to ignore and cover up the monological universalism of modern capital, to remain only on the surface of its diverse implementations and effects.[28] The violent *erasure* of difference that was slavery and the plantation accompanied, or, rather, dialectically compelled, the attempt in the late eighteenth century to recover a realm for free human action within a world of necessity. The progress toward a real, instantiated humanity that occurred in the Haitian Revolution is inseparable from the progress it made in the cultivation of singularity.

The concept of singularization I am describing originates in Spinoza's concept of singularity. For Spinoza, though the universe is constituted of a single substance with no transcendent element (God in the Judeo-Christian/Cartesian understanding), the immanent world is made up of an infinity of related, determinate beings, what Spinoza calls the modes of the single universal substance. Each of these beings in turn possesses its own singularity in an infinity of relationships with all other beings: "Each singularity [*Quodcunque singulare*], in other words each thing that is finite and has a determinate existence, cannot exist ... unless it is determined to exist and function by another thing, which itself is finite and has a determinate existence . . . and thus to infinity" (Spinoza 1999, 63). For Spinoza, the singularity of any and all finite objects cannot be understood in isolation, but only when any single element is comprehended in relationship to the infinitely extended system of determinate beings. It was Spinoza, long before Deleuze or Edouard Glissant, who initiated for the modern world this concept of a single, universal substance in which the infinite modalities of beings nonetheless retain their differential specificity (Macherey 131, 196).

Contemporary neo-Spinozians such as Deleuze and Negri describe what Deleuze called "internal difference," Deleuze and Guattari *haecceity* ("a perfect individuality lacking nothing" [261]), and Badiou, Negri, and Hardt the "singular" and "singularity." Despite their differences, all of these notions share an indebtedness to Spinoza's definition of a "substance":[29] "By substance I understand what is in itself and is conceived through itself, that is, that whose concept does not require the concept of another thing, from which it must be formed" (84). I do not, however, share the faith of contemporary Spinozians such as Hardt and Negri that singularity is always already present in the "Multitude." Instead, in analyzing events such as the Haitian Revolution, we should take our cue instead from Spinoza's oft-repeated political realism, one that always addressed humans both as they are (mired in violence and conflict) and as they can be: that is, capable of, but still lacking a fully reasonable or enlightened existence.

I wish to argue that the Haitian Revolution—and the gradual development of the political thought of Toussaint Louverture in particular—shows that the awareness of both our singularity and our common relations with other singular beings must always be constructed in a historical process at once reflective (a becoming conscious of our singular universality) and politico-historical (that we might—without erasing our singularity—enter into common relations with others based on a shared concern for freedom and equality). Universal emancipation, when it constituted in Saint-Domingue an *adequate* (and not merely clear and distinct) idea, moved beyond the idealist Cartesian clarity of earlier Enlightenment condemnations of slavery to become a historical event. The Haitian Revolution thus marked the point in modern political history in which the expressive potential of humans in their infinite singularity (and not taken as a genus or totality) emerged from within the finitude of determinate circumstances to encompass the infinite (as real universalism).[30]

This historical event is an example of the process of becoming-singular Deleuze first described in *Différence et répétition:* "Instead of a thing that distinguishes itself from another thing [for example, Haiti from France, 1804 from 1789, Toussaint from Napoleon], let us imagine something that distinguishes itself": the Haitian Revolution as something like the self-becoming into dignity of the Haitian subject (43). Against Deleuze's otherwise absolute notion of singularity, however, awareness of one's singular relation to the universal must occur in time and space, as a *process of singularization*.[31] No one is a singularity a priori; as humans who must conquer autonomy and self-understanding, we all must work to singularize ourselves as both individuals and communities.

To describe such a process of singularization as it occurred in Saint-Domingue between 1791 and 1804 will entail not a search for origins, for the miraculous appearance of a singular truth born fully formed in a moment of godlike invention, but instead the charting of the processes through which a symbolic field of social understanding (the Radical Enlightenment) was transformed in practice.[32] An archeology of what I will call *liberté/libete* (underlining the phonetic, conceptual, and historical proximity of the French and Kreyol signifiers)[33] will ask how a radically singular meaning came in Saint-Domingue to be attributed to a term that was only identical to the French "liberty" of 1789 in its purely abstract form (as an empty signifier).[34] To follow the singularization of the Radical Enlightenment concept of human freedom in the global public sphere that emerged in the early modern period means no more than this: that in any of its singular instantiations (in Spinoza, the Black Atlantic Enlightenment, Diderot's *Encyclopédie,* or the discursive theory and practice of Rousseau, Robespierre, or Toussaint), we must attend to the singularity hidden by the identity of a common signifier. Rather than following the movement of some self-same, perfect idea in its furtive geographic and historical distribution, as in Mornet's classic study *Les origines intellectuelles de la révolution française,* I would like to track instead the articulations of this discontinuous field. But to do so will require simultaneously delineating the ground of emergence of any such singularity; beginning from the empty form of the signifier (*"liberté"*), such an analysis must both describe the system of its dispersion throughout the Atlantic world and account for the very *possibility* of any such redistribution and redefinition in both historical and ontological terms.

One value of a philosophy such as Alain Badiou's is to reorient our thought away from a defense of localized, communitarian politics to questions of universal truth, to singular events, and to what Badiou terms a "politique d'émancipation" (1998). But if the Haitian Revolution constitutes a singular event in human history, it was not a miraculous epiphany, the undetermined break with being of a decision to revolt that bears "its intelligibility within itself" (15). The truth of the Haitian Revolution was no absolute and undetermined rupture with historical being; though long underappreciated in Western historiography, its archival resources are rich and varied, and await further investigation (Geggus 2002). Its singularity can only become clear in mediated relation with all that it denied. In 1797 Toussaint Louverture declared to the Directory, "We renew [our oath] to bury ourselves under the ruins of a country revived by liberty rather than suffer the return of slavery. . . . Do [you] think that [those] who have been able to enjoy the blessing of liberty will calmly see it snatched away? . . . [I renew my oath to defend] the rights . . . of humanity, for the triumph of liberty and equality." Toussaint constructed this universal imperative, this politics of emancipation, not from divine inspiration, but from diverse elements such as a personal knowledge of the dehumanization of slavery and the 1789 *Déclaration de droits de l'homme et du citoyen*. The difficulty of interpreting the Haitian Revolution is to grasp the coexistence of these two dimensions in their determinate relation with other historical factors, along with the explosive appearance of a novel political structure within the continuity of human experience.

## Exploding the Enlightenment Order of Knowledge

The Haitian Revolution testifies to both a radicalization and a comprehensive demolition of the epistemology that dominated the Age of Enlightenment. It brought to bear the slaves' highly evolved ability to link moral and political judgment in an effective politics. Before 1791, political decisions regarding slavery in the United States and France had often judged the institution of slavery by relative, practical criteria. John Adams's refusal to condemn the southern institution of slavery during the first session of the Continental Congress in 1774 ("I constantly said in former times to the southern gentlemen," he recalled later in life, "'I cannot comprehend this object. I must leave it to you. I will vote for no measure against your judgments'"), for example, enabled the compromise with southern slavery that would culminate in the institution's full legalization in the Articles of Confederation of 1777 and the 1787 Constitution (Blumrosen 88, 154).[35] In essence, the refusal to judge slavery an unconditional wrong and to vote for its institutionalization in 1787 ensured prosperity for northern whites in an area freed from the economic competition of unpaid black laborers. This compromise was advantageous for all parties, save for the slaves who had only the most compromised and partial representation in the likes of George Mason,

Jefferson, Franklin, and Adams. To a one, whenever push came to shove, these representatives all placed their own property and political interests before those of American slaves.

Without invitation or accreditation to do so, the slaves of Saint-Domingue asserted their unconditional right and capacity to exercise the universal human faculty of judgment when faced with the likely continuation of Atlantic slavery that held them captive. After their initial uprising in August 1791, these now-former slaves, the great majority of whom were of course illiterate and without "formal" education, put to the test the Enlightenment faith in human reason as a universal possession of the human species, "the same for all thinking subjects, all nations, all epochs, and all cultures" (Cassirer 1968, 6). They enacted the Enlightenment proposition that there in fact exists a structure of reason that grounds and allows for the appearance of any singular manifestation of empirical acts of judgment across cultures and epochs, a potentiality defined by the *Encyclopédie* as "this natural faculty that God has granted men, to know the truth, whatever direction [*lumière*] it may follow, and in whichever fashion it may be applied" (*"Raison"*).[36]

Insofar as the empirical, local, and personal experience of slavery informed their acts of judgment, the Saint-Domingue revolutionaries operated within the Enlightenment belief that all knowledge arises from empirical sensation. This understanding of human reason was fundamentally antisystematic, categorically rejecting the (Cartesian) deductive derivation of knowledge from a master theory or system grounded in the mind's immediate intuition of truth. Instead, following Newton, Enlightenment thinkers understood truth to arise from the analysis of an empirical situation or *expérience*.[37]

In interpreting the concept of *liberté/libete* autonomously, Haitians necessarily brought the lived-through experience of slavery to bear upon a concept. They proceeded not according to dogmatic, alien principles (the North Atlantic doctrine of liberty for white, male property-holders), but instead rejected such authority to proceed as if a universal order of right were discernible in the world, if only one could abstract and extract the notion of that order from singular empirical experience. Quite simply, a Parisian bourgeois revolutionary (even an "enlightened" one like the Abbé Grégoire) knew little of slavery, viewing it only as a reified abstraction: as the suffering of an abstract Other or the monetary profit margin extracted from colonial slave labor. In turn, the experience of these former slaves, like any other, was itself limited (remaining largely oblivious to the exploitation of women, to religious intolerance, to democratic exclusion);

and yet their political intervention progressed beyond the North Atlantic parochialism of 1776 and 1789 and its compromises with property, pointing the way toward the more systematic inclusionism of much later documents such as the 1948 Universal Declaration of Rights.

New World plantation slavery was a universe of utterly amoral destruction and devastation whose only contemporary analogue, Joan Dayan has argued, was the mechanical bestialization of Enlightenment reason recorded in the writings of Sade. Two centuries before the moral self-satisfaction of Euro-Americans would be shattered by the rise of totalitarianism and the Holocaust, the bestial world of the plantation forced slaves to find within themselves the capacity to analyze and judge their world without the traditional tenets of morality. New World slave owners were not affectless Eichmanns who only refused to exercise their universal faculty of judgment, but, rather, quite actively tortured and bestialized as a colonial power whose actions were defended by the state and rule of law that promulgated the *Code Noir*.

Thrown together without regard for cultural and geographic origins, cut off from much of the substance of their ancestors' traditions and moral communities, the slaves of Saint-Domingue were obliged to move beyond the moral desolation of their world to undertake creative acts of judgment with whatever materials they might find at hand, including the surviving shards of African human rights traditions and the Catholic, Masonic, Enlightenment, and Vodun moral codes that circulated more or less freely throughout colonial Saint-Domingue. Vodun in particular, as Carolyn Fick has commented, "was one of the few areas of totally autonomous activity for African slaves. As a religion and a vital spiritual force, it was a source of psychological liberation in that it enabled them to express and reaffirm their self-existence" (1990, 44–45). The abstract concepts of *liberté* and *égalité* that floated overseas to Saint-Domingue in August 1789 were not ossified universal precepts under which various empirical phenomena were to be subsumed, but just the opposite. These monstrous concepts were explosive destroyers of social customs and habits, whose meaning was quite unfixed and novel. (Did they include the poor? Free *gens de couleur*? Slaves? Women? Jews?) Only concerted acts of communitarian, intersubjective political judgment, and not the forcible imposition of an ossified truth, could decide such questions and lead to the destruction of the abjection of the subjects of slavery, both Master and Slave. The caustic force of this concept destroyed putatively universal Enlightenment-era habits of thought that had made the right to property an absolute and, in consequence, slavery a necessary evil enshrined to the greater glory of economic expansion.

In consonance with Enlightenment thought, the Haitian assertion of universal right—as an operation of situation-based judgment made by a political community—enacted a radical historicization of truth. Truth was no longer to be taken as a divinely engendered "innate idea" preceding all experience (as for Descartes, Leibniz, and Malbranche); instead, truth became the coefficient (that is, the constant that is a measure of a property of a substance) of the human power (*potentia*) to consciously shape and order social life itself. To destroy the systematic violence of plantation slavery, the truth of universal emancipation *necessarily and unavoidably* took the form of a violent shattering of an entire social world. To paraphrase Žižek, the desire for infinite justice necessarily appeared to the participants in that world as ultimate barbarity (2008, 56). Haiti radicalized in the violence of destruction and creation Cassirer's assertion that "the whole eighteenth century understands reason . . . not as a sound body of knowledge, principles, and truths, but as a kind of energy, a force which is fully comprehensible only in its agency and effects" (13).

The Spinozian axiom of the immanent self-moving and self-defining capacity of beings (*natura naturans*), first postulated philosophically, increasingly came to animate the political sphere throughout the Atlantic world as the effort to construct regimes that would maintain and maximize the inalienable sovereignty of all subjects in line with the dictates of reason.[38] In Spinoza's view, the true idea is not encapsulated in an abstract universal. As the vaguest and least concrete of ideas, "the lowest degree of the power of thought," the abstract universal must be superseded by the power of thought to understand any singular thing (Deleuze 1968, 146). From there, thought gradually extends its power from one singularity to another, potentially to encompass the totality of the immanent universe.

Enlightenment reason was fundamentally critical, violently eradicating the authoritarian, tradition-based order of knowledge it was born into, to inquire instead into truth from within any given situation: each marginalized, "peripheral" subject of enlightenment in Saint-Domingue in essence observed that "I have lived through the experience of slavery; I therefore categorically refuse my exclusion as a human subject from this loudly proclaimed 'universal' *liberté/libete*. What then does this deduction imply for my own actions and existence in the world I find myself in today? Clearly, the uncompromising destruction of that order and the construction in its place of a regime of universal emancipation." This implicit act of judgment followed Spinoza and his moderate and radical followers alike—Locke ("All ideas come from sensation"), Condillac ("Pleasures and pains . . . [are] the sole source of our enlightenment"), and Helvétius ("Every idea and every judgment may be reduced to a sensation")—in rejecting all dogma, doctrine, and master discourses as a basis for knowledge, to depart instead from empirical experience.[39] Furthermore, the Haitian revolutionaries implicitly followed Helvétius in giving absolute priority in the development of knowledge to the sensation of pain and its experiential affect: suffering. They are at one with Aimé Césaire in deriving the expressivity of their Negritude ("Haïti où la negritude se mit debout pour la première fois") from the common experience of slavery ("la negritude . . . mesurée au compass de la souffrance").

Departing from the analysis of their situational being-in-the-world, these subjects of enlightenment proceeded to articulate a political philosophy in the Atlantic public sphere and to forcibly construct a sociopolitical structure that conformed to these insights. The spirit of the Radical Enlightenment in Saint-Domingue refused the ontological weight of the factual ("you are a slave, a beast of labor, and the plantation is your destiny") to confront that empirical sense data with the categorical notions of *liberté* and *égalité*. This subject understood the plantation *system* precisely as a totality requiring total destruction, and proceeded beyond eternal (Newtonian) *natural* law to affirm, following the logic of 1789, the political, historical *constructability* of human right.[40]

The Haitian Enlightenment both conformed to and broke with the North Atlantic Enlightenment affirmation of a unified order of knowledge. Logically, human right was understood in the age of revolution to be grounded by the ontological proposition of *liberté/libete*. Politically, the Haitian Revolution ultimately reaffirmed Jacobin centralism, insofar as all impulses toward an anarchistic construction of social relations would be reterritorialized by the sovereign leader (Toussaint, Polverel, Dessalines, Christophe . . .). On the other hand, the Saint-Domingue revolutionaries refused to view their position in the political totality of the 1790s as a mere subsumption of elements (to a sovereign Parisian center), and instead affirmed the singular power of a progressive process of individuation. This activity took the shape of a universal political process that, in Cassirer's words, formed "the common ground of the entire series" of the Age of Enlightenment: universal emancipation (83). In contrast to the paternalistic refusal of (cultural, racial, linguistic) difference of North Atlantic politicians such as the Jacobin Abbé Grégoire, the

Haitian Revolution initiated a process of internal differentiation of a multitude of singularities, as they affirmed the autonomous capacity to singularize themselves that results from the constituent internal force of self-determination (*natura naturans*).

In all these senses, the Haitian Revolution confirmed and radicalized the Enlightenment affirmation of an immanent order of knowledge whose ontological ground is understood to arise from human experience, reason, and action within the natural realm. The sequence of events from 1791 to 1804 enacted a drastic and utterly singular break with the Enlightenment order of knowledge, however, on the level of the *transmission* of knowledge. The conception of enlightenment itself was fundamentally ambiguous. On the one hand, a range of Enlightenment thinkers celebrated the human capacity for autonomous reflection: Rousseau and Condorcet stressed the constituent process of an individual's becoming-autonomous (as "perfectibility"), William Godwin critiqued "the system of political imposture [that] divides men into two classes, one of which is to think and reason for the whole, and the other to take the conclusions of their superiors on trust," and Kant famously defined Enlightenment as the subject's emergence from self-incurred immaturity (cited in Kramnick 476). On the other hand, the metaphor of "enlightenment" implied a hierarchical order of knowledge, in which the knowing, "enlightened" master illuminates a subaltern subject entrapped in the cavern of ignorance. The *Dictionnaire*'s definition of education clearly reveals this fundamental bias: education is not the subject's self-directed coming-to-knowledge, but is instead "the care that one takes to nourish, to raise, and to instruct children" (see "Education").

Such elitism was fundamental to Enlightenment theories of knowledge, all of which reaffirmed this structural inequality in the transmission of knowledge.[41] Locke, in "Some Thoughts Concerning Education," viewed education as a matter of "how to breed" children, such that their "awe and respect be grown familiar, and there appears not the least reluctance in the submission and ready obedience of their minds." For the Condorcet of the *Esquisse d'un tableau historique des progrès de l'esprit humain,* though the *capacity* for enlightenment was universal, it went without question that the "French and Anglo-Americans" were "the most enlightened, the freest and the least burdened by prejudices" of the world's peoples. In Europe, one found "enlightened men" benefiting from "the superiority of our knowledge," while elsewhere one encountered the "barbarism of African tribes" and "the ignorance of savages." Knowledge itself would thus be "propagated," thought Condorcet, from an enlightened center to be passively "received" in such dark regions of ignorance. To attain this truth, as perfect, unchanging, and timeless as the purest mathematical axiom, "all that [the unenlightened] need to do is to follow the expositions and proofs that appear in our speeches and writings."[42]

For the Abbé Grégoire, those subaltern groups the bishop judged to be in need of "regeneration" were to submit to a process directed by an enlightened elite. The poor were to submit to "the paternal solicitude of the government," and Jews were to be "corrected" and "civilized," their cultural singularities erased in order to "dissolve them into the national mass." Women, whom he denounced as incorrigibly conceited, immodest, and dissolute, should be denied the "universal" rights of "Man," and the black blood of African slaves was to be Europeanized by racial miscegenation. In turn, the putative ignorance of Africans on every continent would be erased by paternalistic education: "In their native land," Grégoire wrote between 1796 and 1799, "the Africans are unaware of all the advantage they can draw from their soil and their climate for their own use and that of others. They are without instruction and without knowledge of useful arts. As for their like in our colonies, who have become our fellow citizens and brothers, are they not abandoned to a profound ignorance? Do they not have an urgent need for moral and physical instruction?"[43] Even the author of *Emile* saw education as a transmission of wisdom from master to disciple, in which the child would be led "to see the light that you offer as a guide" and eventually be "imbued with the laws of the State and the precepts of the general will" (cited in Kramnick 232, 234).

The slave and free black populations' reception and judgment in Saint-Domingue of the events of 1789 and the Declaration of the Rights of Man and Citizen utterly negated such a model of education and enlightenment. Despite all the nuances in these theories of education and judgment, from Locke's view of children as human-animals to be "bred," to Rousseau's compassionate insight into childhood experience, all stood agreed that a radical divide exists between the enlightened and the unenlightened. Consequently, no matter what the modality of enlightenment (whether as violent training or compassionate guidance of the learning subject's desire), a deep division was constantly renewed in North Atlantic Enlightenment thought between the ignorant and the enlightened subject, between *maître* and *élève*. The Haitian Revolution would never have occurred had these slaves simply acquiesced to the dominant order of knowledge, had they turned to a *maître* who would all-knowingly *interpret* a text such as the

1789 *Déclaration* to them. The various Parisian and *grand blanc maîtres* repeatedly strove to reinscribe their subjects' subordination, benevolently describing to them the logical reasons why this document did not apply to them, why they were not ready for freedom (Condorcet, Grégoire), or why their enslavement was necessary for the greater good of the French economy (the Barnavian triumvirate and the planters' Club Massiac). Rather than affirming the slaves' universal faculty of autonomous judgment, such *maîtres,* whether pro- or antislavery, all attempted in the years following 1789 to reinscribe a structure not of self-enlightenment, but of perpetually renewed *abrutissement*.[44]

The slaves and free blacks of Saint-Domingue constructed a system of knowledge that utterly destroyed the hierarchical model of all-knowing master/ignorant disciple. They never stopped to wonder whether they were subhuman or if instead the faculty of human reason was universal; they simply proceeded upon the latter assumption. They presumed that all humans share an equal intelligence, and that inequality lies only in the energy and attention devoted to its expression. They proceeded immediately to make use of their faculty of reason as a tool for their emancipation. They needed no *maître* to tell them how to proceed toward this emancipation; their own experience of slavery and the plantation gave them this knowledge and forced them to reject all socially anointed "masters."

Never having read a word of Spinoza—though inspired indirectly by the intellectual climate descended from his thought—the former slaves of Saint-Domingue proceeded in exact consonance with the axioms of the *Ethics*. Humans do not need to be prepared to think by already enlightened masters, Spinoza asserted in a radical critique of Cartesian "first principles." Instead, it is simply our experience of being-in-the-world that, always already, *"homo cogitat"*: "man thinks" (Spinoza 1999, 94). Though our faculty of thought must constantly grow and extend its capabilities, all humans are thinking beings, and for Spinoza there exists no demarcation between the enlightened and the unenlightened, but rather an infinite gradation in each human's capacity to use the fullest powers of her thought.[45] These former slaves knew immediately that they were capable of all that any human is capable of; a mere word, text, or document allowed them to exercise, sharpen, and extend their faculty of judgment. They had only to pick up an idea one day after 1789 when they went down to the docks of Cap du roi, talking to a French sailor or having someone read them a posted announcement of the Rights of Man, and to refine that tool of revolutionary France's denial of civil rights (to slaves, women, Jews) into their own concept of universal emancipation.[46] These former slaves needed no interpreter; they had only to observe, compare, combine, evaluate, and act. This activity was possible anywhere on earth; indeed, it was not in the halls of the Sorbonne or the National Assembly, but only on the so-called periphery of the modern world-system in 1791 that this truth of 1789 could be most fully comprehended.

Two acts preserved in the archives define the archetype of this improvisational, nonhierarchical epistemology: a plantation owner's 1791 description of an anonymous rebel slave caught bearing "pamphlets printed in France, filled with commonplaces about the Rights of Man and the Sacred Revolution" (Parham 34),[47] and Sonthonax's decision to post the Declaration of the Rights of Man and Citizen publicly throughout Saint-Domingue at the moment of abolition in 1793, where they could be read (and thus heard) by any and all. A text, a document placed directly between two intelligences, bypassing all "enlightened" interpretation for the uninitiated, announced to those able to interpret it properly the creation of a slavery-free society. When the 1789 *Déclaration* arrived in Saint-Domingue, it impelled a new configuration of knowledge, one constructed between two ignorant subjects (the *Tiers état* and the slaves of Saint-Domingue), both of whom desired to construct their own emancipation without the interposition of any *maître interposé*. No abstract Cartesian cogitation, their political improvisations were infused with the experience of suffering. The judgment of this document in Saint-Domingue was no passive witnessing of a pure, unchanging truth, but instead the invocation of an unheralded power to translate a North Atlantic language these slaves did not speak into their own experiential idiom, the desire to express their insight into the categorical need to destroy plantation slavery in the language of the Rights of Man.

This "translation" was literally a "bringing across" of knowledge from one world to another, the power to bring past experience of injustice and corporal suffering directly to bear upon what a group of slaves sought to know and judge: a *feuille,* a posted announcement proclaiming the universal rights of man. The sequence of the Haitian Revolution from 1791 to 1804 could follow no master plan; it was from beginning to end the most brilliant political improvisation of the globalized Radical Enlightenment. These former slaves systematically followed through the political implications of a new model of knowledge: just as in their epistemology they refused the interpellation of all *maîtres,* they judged themselves politically apt to govern without any interposition of authority, of those "entitled" to rule by virtue of their birth, sex, property, nationality, or race. The Haitian Revolution scandalized the North Atlantic Enlightenment powers because it was essentially an affirmation of true democracy: the proper and logical right of anyone, absolutely anyone, to rule. The scandal of the Haitian Revolution is to have affirmed the right to rule on the part of those with absolutely no qualification beyond their human capacity to judge and act autonomously.[48] Like all master improvisers in the Black Atlantic tradition, they structured their improvisation from the formal coordinates of a preexisting Standard (the *Déclaration*), but refused simply to reiterate the same *esclavagiste* refrain rehearsed in Paris or Philadelphia, improvising instead a political elegy to freedom and equality whose message would be heard around the world.

### The Traumas of Historiography

Our understanding of the process of revolution is distorted by the imperative we have inherited to critique the deformalization of law that occurred in the French Revolutionary Terror (1792–94). In the wake of a tradition characterized by the thought of François Furet, all revolutions since 1789 have increasingly come to be read in the reflected light of the cold blade of the guillotine. The self-proclaimed Terror of Robespierre and Saint-Just predicated the success of the revolution after 1792 upon the annihilation and destruction of all opposition, of all differences and dissent that asserted itself in contrast to their desire to found a monological General Will.[49] In the words of Saint-Just to the Committee of Public Safety: "Our goal is to create an order of things such that a universal inclination toward goodness be established; such that all factions suddenly find themselves flung upon the gallows" (cited in Weber 109). Under the Terror, all citizens were increasingly subject to the Jacobin accusation of having subverted the revolution, whether actively or through their passive lack of zeal.

This menace was the result of a deformalization process culminating in the laws of 22 Prairial that, on June 10, 1794, suspended the rights of the accused; in the Grande Terreur that followed, some fifteen hundred citizens were guillotined in seven weeks. It is quite right to critique such a destruction of rights and of the rule of law and justice along with its accompanying attempt to destroy all dissent in the name of an abstract universal under the Terror.[50] Moral universalism, however, has been so conflated with this critique, we have so come to equate any and all fidelity to a universal moral imperative with the implementation of Terror, that we overlook the fact that in this respect the Terror of 1792–94 was precisely the *betrayal* of the moral imperatives of 1789.

The trauma of the French Terror that has gripped the dominant classes of Western societies since that time has rightfully sensitized us to the dangers of combining moral absolutism with absolute power. But we are also left unable, from within this trauma, to recognize the difference we purport to cherish: when all revolutions are interpreted a priori as paths to Terror, their particularities and (necessarily partial and fallible) striving for social justice can easily be overlooked. It is all too easy to condemn the subjective violence of the guillotine and to ignore the much greater violence of systemic injustice, whether ancien régime, *esclavagiste,* or capitalist. We are led to ignore, for example, the simple fact that the Haitian Revolution enacted the only successful and relatively complete land reform in the Americas until well into the twentieth century, such that Haiti stands virtually alone today following this "peasants' victory" that established a nation of autonomously controlled "minifundia" landowners (Trouillot 1990, 39; Lundahl 1979).

Why have Haitians been repeatedly obliged to assert their radical insurgency against constituted power in the face of a nearly continuous state of crisis since 1791? Only a critical analysis of the multiple, ambiguous, and contradictory forms of constituted power in that nation over the past two centuries, rather than its absolute vilification, could begin to supply an answer. In the two centuries since its foundation, the Haitian elite has developed a system of exploitation and violence that has systematically undermined popular sovereignty.[51] At the same time, the Haitian peasantry, effectively excluded from political life, successfully protected its hold on small-scale private land ownership until well into the twentieth century, effectively blocking the elite from that source of autonomous economic subsistence. The result of this unique course of historical events has been double: a mass-based revolutionary victory since 1804 (measured in terms of autonomous control of land and labor) combined with an extreme form of political alienation, in which the citidan elites, defeated in the domain of labor, instead worked to extract their surplus profits much farther down the production chain, in the customshouses.[52]

If Haiti has too often in its post-1804 history witnessed the disintegration of legal order, one must resist any fetishization of an imposed rule of law or its conflation with the notion of justice. Striving for the rule of law must always remain a *means* to achieving social justice, always subordinate to the process of democratization. The rule of law must always coexist alongside the possibility of civil disobedience. Nonetheless, the rule of law remains a *necessary* element in the process of democratization and the striving for social justice.[53]

Democratization, in light of the Haitian Revolution, should nonetheless emphatically not to be understood as Schumpeter's "achievement of substantial agreement" among dominant elites following a period of authoritarianism (cited in Fatton 1). "Democracy" in Haiti has rarely if ever meant more than such power-sharing that founded order upon the active disenfranchisement of the rural *moun andeyo*. In the "democratization theory" of contemporary political science, such processes of agreement necessarily imply the systematic exclusion of the multitude, justified ideologically as "'insulation' from popular pressures preventing the rise of 'extremist' demands, and the triumph of the 'political center.'" Robert Fatton, in his critique of "democratization theory" in light of Haitian politics, rightly concludes that "in the paradigm's view, democracy cannot tolerate too many popular pressures; it cannot be too democratic" (2). Instead, a true process of democratization implies not only, as Fatton concludes, "a participatory structure of governance where rulers are accountable to citizens and where the economic sphere comes under popular control" (7) but, quite simply, the increase in governance of those without entitlement.[54]

In events such as 1804 and Jean-Bertrand Aristide's democratic triumph of 1991, a Benjaminian "flash" occurred in which the progress of universal human emancipation became a localized, concrete reality. The event of 1804 denied the brutal rule of arbitrary force and subjugation, abolishing slavery immediately and unconditionally, launching the global process of decolonization that continues unfinished today. While the multitude necessarily drives the process of democratization, Haitian history shows that the difficulty lies in sustaining such evenemential, momentary increases in the process of democratization. As Fatton rightly concludes, the problem of democratization is most crucially one of resisting the dissolution and co-optation of the process by the more organized and financially secure dominant classes. The model for this resistance can perhaps be found in the development of peasant democratic forces that occurred after 1986 in groups such as Tet Kole Ti Peyizan Ayisyen.[55]

The Haitian invention of decolonization and universal emancipation was a momentous rupture, one that obliterated the slaveholding logic of eighteenth-century global capital. It was the production of a concrete universal, the construction of immanent human potentialities and unknown worlds that remain largely an unfulfilled promise today. As we witness radical and exponential increases in our world in the mediated powers of constituent subjectivity, imperfectly instituted in the Internet, in the furtive construction of a global democracy subject to the rule of universal laws such as the banning of offensive wars and the total elimination of slavery and nuclear weapons, we can no longer have the faith of Kant that humanity is progressing irreversibly despite its local and temporary setbacks. If even a few years ago some could confidently predict the demise of the nation-state, we know today that progress is all too reversible, that genocide, nuclear annihilation, and the destruction of the rule of law are all too real threats; we see with each passing day how fragile even the smallest progressive steps remain. And yet, to examine the Haitian Revolution in its historical specificity is to bear witness to the fact that progress occurs, that a world-system based upon an obscene degree of human exploitation and suffering can and has been destroyed and replaced by more just relations. Perhaps the only hope we can maintain is that as long as we continue to exist, as long as we can keep from wiping ourselves out in offensive global explosions of violence that know no limits, human consciousness and desire will continue to possess a definite orientation, an orientation to truth and justice. This was the potentiality that allowed Haitian slaves to understand themselves as subject to a universal process of emancipation in the face of everything the actually existing world told them. This orientation unleashed in the events of 1791–1804 propels us into the future and toward the difficult construction of a universal freedom first given historical concretion in the Haitian Revolution.

## 2  The Idea of 1804

> Penser la pensée revient le plus souvent à se retirer dans un lieu sans dimension où l'idée seule de la pensée s'obstine. Mais la pensée s'espace réellement au monde. Elle informe l'imaginaire des peuples, ... dans lesquels se réalise son risque.
> —Edouard Glissant, *Poétique de la relation*

> La politique n'est pas faite de rapports de pouvoir, elle est faite de rapports de mondes.
> —Jacques Rancière, *La mésentente*

TWENTY YEARS ago, in an essay commemorating the bicentennial of the French Revolution (originally entitled "The Idea of 1789"), Jürgen Habermas had to argue for the continued relevance of an event that, after intensive investigation over the course of two centuries, seemed increasingly irrelevant as the generation of May '68 settled into the comfort of *Mitterandisme*.[1] In comparison to the French Revolution, we know comparatively little of the Haitian Revolution, despite the fact that it has never receded from public consciousness throughout the African diaspora. It has remained to an important degree "silenced" and "unthinkable" in Western discourse, as Michel-Rolph Trouillot has argued, since the moment it began to unfold in 1791 (1995). A search of the Cornell library database on the historiography of the French Revolution reveals over 350 Library of Congress subject headings alone, and well over 7,000 individual volumes. A similar search for Haiti reveals twelve subject headings and a grand total of 235 volumes (many of them duplicates) on the events of 1791–1804.[2] What are the causes of the revolution and how did it proceed? Certainly, the archival resources on Saint-Domingue exist; the fault lies with a scholarly tradition—with the exception of indigenous Haitian scholarship—that has only recently begun to devote the attention to the revolution that its singular importance in Western modernity demands.[3]

Writing in 1988, Habermas renewed Kant's identification of the world-historical importance of the French Revolution in the *idea* it put forward:

"There seems to be only one remaining candidate for an affirmative answer to the question concerning the relevance of the French Revolution: the ideas [of] ... democracy and human rights [that] form the universalist core of the constitutional state that emerged from the American and French Revolutions" (1998, 465). In light of Habermas's lapsus (the all-too-common failure to consider the Haitian Revolution alongside the American and French), I think it is essential to pursue the question of the *idea* of the Haitian Revolution: Did the Haitian Revolution play a unique role in the development of "the ideas of democracy and human rights" in the Age of Enlightenment, or were events there a mere echo of those in the North Atlantic world? The hegemony of a Euro-American-dominated historiography would lead us to view the Haitian Revolution as a mere tropical mimicry of its better-known French and American cousins. In fact, when we confront the question of emancipation, these earlier events appear distinctly parochial and limited: the Haitian Revolution stands among the greatest events of the Age of Enlightenment because—as the preceding chapter showed—it was the first to implement, as early as 1791, not the freedom of a certain class or race, nor the civil rights of a "constitutional state," but the program of *universal* emancipation that we today call human rights.[4]

## The Political Philosophy of the Haitian Revolution: From the Singular to the Universal

How is it possible to conceive the specificity of the Haitian Revolution in relation to the absolute, universal claims of the 1789 *Déclaration des droits de l'homme et du citoyen* that were among its most important motivating factors? What were the historical factors and intellectual trends in the eighteenth-century Atlantic world that may have contributed to the articulation and politicization in Saint-Domingue of the concept of universal emancipation? Rather than holding the Haitian Revolution to some abstract, external definition of the universal, we can, at least provisionally, attempt to address it within its own historical horizon. Various cultural materials undoubtedly contributed to the conceptualization of the universal in revolutionary Saint-Domingue. In the case of Toussaint and other Catholic participants in the revolution, a devout Christian faith may have served as an initial template; the Pauline tradition of Christianity allows for only one principal to define its possible range of subjects: that one be a human being.[5] Yet this ahistorical, transcendental truth of the Christian faith was used to justify, as the conversion of "savages," the brutally exclusionary operations of colonialism and at times even slavery itself. Christianity called for forbearance and submission to the dominant order in this world, and obeying one's worldly masters, in the words of the Bible, "with fear and trembling, in a singleness of [one's] heart, as unto Christ."[6]

Only a radical fidelity to the lived experience of slavery, to an experience so brutal and dehumanizing that it simply could not await divine retribution and the afterlife, could motivate the transformation of this transcendental abstraction into the immanent universalism of human rights. Toussaint's devout Catholic faith formed a conservative element of his character in consonance with the moderate, Christian tradition of Enlightenment thinkers such as Newton and Locke.[7] In placing Toussaint squarely within the Radical Enlightenment tradition described by Jonathan Israel, however, my claim is that Toussaint's Catholicism, though an essential dimension of his character, was always superseded in political decisions regarding slavery by the Radical Enlightenment tradition that defended human rights universally and immediately. This line of thought refused any compromise with the actual political powers of the slave-based world-system, as well as any separation of those rights from individuals themselves, male or female, child or adult, black or white.

Undoubtedly, certain elements of African and Taino cultures surviving in 1791 influenced the universalism of the Saint-Domingue revolution. Vodun in particular contributed to both a nascent Haitian conception of a universal right to freedom and a corollary awareness of a specificity of the experience of suffering and exploitation under slavery.[8] John K. Thornton has explored the possibility that the events in Saint-Domingue were significantly determined by the political ideology of the Kongo kingdom in Central West Africa. Not only, Thornton points out, were some half of the slaves in 1791 Saint-Domingue African-born; of those, half again may have been sold out of the Kongo nation itself. Fully 60 percent of the slaves in the Northern Province of Saint-Domingue appear to have hailed from this region (185).

These slaves were captured and sold as a result of the civil wars that had divided the Kongo nation throughout the second half of the eighteenth century, and Thornton makes the further claim that this ongoing African conflict over the nature of political sovereignty "can be seen as a source of revolutionary Haiti's ideology" (186). Thornton's argument is scrupulously researched and persuasive. It is helpful primarily in documenting a previously unconsidered African origin of the incipient revolt of 1791 and in its accounting for the astonishing military prowess of the rebel slaves. Thornton shows how the societies of the Kongo region had been extensively militarized by these ongoing civil wars, and the author draws the logical conclusion that the *Bossale* (African-born) slaves of Saint-Domingue brought these military skills and experience with them.

Nonetheless, Thornton's analysis appears to be relevant only to the very earliest stages of the Haitian Revolution, and he makes no claim that Kongolese political philosophy can account for the post-1791 universalist radicalization of the Haitian Revolution that constitutes its most significant historical feature. Revealingly, Thornton focuses primarily upon the declaration of the rebel leader Macaya from 1793, in which the latter refused the overtures of the commissioner Etienne Polverel with the words "I am the subject of three kings: of the King of the Kongo, master of all the blacks, of the King of France who represents my father; of the King of Spain who represents my mother" (cited in Thornton 181). As Thornton shows, conflicts in the Kongo had never addressed the question of universal human rights or their political implementation within a democratic polis. Instead, the Kongolese civil wars focused on the nature of monarchic sovereignty. These wars never raised the possibility of overthrowing a king but instead called for the ameliorative and gradualist reform of African monarchy: "Unlike the conqueror king of the centralized state, the new founder [of the early-eighteenth-century Kongo nation] needed to be a more republican sort of ruler, one who recognized the rights of numerous families and local powers and ruled by consensus and consent" (190).

If the role of ideology in the Kongolese wars centered on monarchic reform alone, it thus can be said to have progressed no further in the direction of democratization than did, say, France in the summer of 1789. Thornton draws attention to the self-description of early rebel leaders such as Jeannot as "kings," and concludes that these rebel-kings "in the early days of the revolution may represent a tentative movement in the direction of a local limited monarchy based on African ideological views." Had it been achieved, such a regime, while bearing no devotion to universal rights, would certainly have been "less authoritarian" than the slaveholding plantation regime it would have replaced (210). One could say much the same of France after the États Généraux had there been no *prise de la Bastille,* to say nothing of Varennes. While Thornton's argument helps explain the rebels' devotion to the French and Spanish monarchies in 1791–93, it offers no evidence of an African origin for the concern for universal human rights that so distinguished the ideology of the Haitian Revolution from Toussaint's first public declaration in August 1793 ("I want liberty and equality to reign in Saint Domingue") to Haiti's world-historical, unqualified abolition of slavery in 1804.

## Mali, 1222: Foundations of Universal Human Rights

It is nonetheless true, however, that Toussaint and his colleagues did not have to look to the North Atlantic, late-eighteenth-century world to find a model for a universal declaration of human rights. In 1222, some five and a half centuries before 1789, at a time when northern Europe had hardly begun to emerge from the Middle Ages, the first universal declaration of human rights was promulgated on the periphery of what was at the time the "First" (Islamic) World. In present-day Mali (Dakadjalan) in that year, the founder of the Mandé Empire, Soundiata Keïta, came to power. The context bore a number of striking similarities to eighteenth-century Saint-Domingue. As Islam had expanded westward since 622 AD, it had brought with it a general regime of slavery that tore Africans from their homeland in the wake of wars of conquest. In response, the fundamental and non-negotiable political goal of Soundiata Keïta was to eliminate the threat of slavery for his people (Cissé 3).

Upon Soundiata's successful expulsion of the Arabic slave traders, in late 1222 he inaugurated the new Mandé nation with a charter, which has since become known as the Charte du Mandé.[9] While the charter is an oral document that has been handed down in varying forms, it clearly demonstrates the circulation of a public discourse on universal human rights in thirteenth-century West Africa, and the version of the text transcribed and published in 2003 is extraordinary in the formulations it offers of these rights.

This version of the Mandé Charter calls not for the preservation of the rights of the Mandé hunter caste, nor even for the rights of the Mandé people as a whole. Rather, centuries before such *civil* rights would even be *theorized* in the West, the Mandé Charter founded a society based upon the universal and unqualified rights of all human beings to be free from enslavement. As with the French "Liberté, Egalité, Fraternité," and the American "Life, Liberty, and the Pursuit of Happiness," the Mandé Charter begins with a preamble asserting, "The Mandé was founded upon understanding and harmony, love, freedom, and fraternity" ("Manden sigila bèèn ni kanu le kan, ani hòòrònnya ni bandenya"). The charter then proceeds to its fundamental, world-historical proclamation: "Every human life is a life" ("Ko nin bèè nin"). Though my claim is necessarily speculative, this radical formulation of undivided rights, the categorical axiom that no life is any less dignified than another, that, as the charter states, "one life . . . is no more respectable than another life, just as one life is worth no more than another life," this universal truth statement appears to have survived the centuries and the Middle Passage, and to have entered the Haitian lexicon in one of the most common of all Kreyol proverbs. Jean-Bertrand Aristide famously chose it for the title of his own autobiography: "Tout moun se moun," or "Every person is a person," and all are strictly identical in their nature and rights.

The consequences to be deduced from this axiom of Black Atlantic culture are thus applicable to all human beings, as the Mandé Charter goes on to state in its seven short paragraphs: "Every life being a life, . . . none shall henceforth place the bit of slavery in the mouth of his fellow man to sell him." The Mandé Charter was the first declaration that—like the much later declarations of 1776 and 1789—was not simply an abstract moral statement (such as the Decalogue), but founded instead an emancipationist political regime and nation. Moreover, the very raison d'être of this nation lay in its creation of a regime of limited, delegated sovereignty in which natural rights would remain with individual subjects themselves. Though both human rights and their denial were for the Mandé universal facts, ("The slave is shorn of his dignity throughout the world"), it was the political power of this new Mandé state that allowed the declaration actually to be realized amid a world-system founded upon slave labor: "The essence of slavery is extinguished this day, 'from one wall to another,' from one frontier to another of the Mandé." Though, like the founders of the Haitian state in 1804, the Mandé could not eliminate slavery universally, this did not stop them from either perceiving its universal character or implementing through the assertion of political sovereignty a general abolition limited only by geographic extension.

Finally, the Mandé Charter announced the much later conceptualizations of human rights in the Age of Enlightenment in its derivation of those rights, not from object-based property relations, but from fundamental human dignity. Humans are not to be reduced to the objectivity of their mere biological, physical being, what the Charter calls "man as an individual made of flesh and bones, of marrow and nerves, of skin covered with hair, and who nourishes himself with food and drink." Rather, humans are distinguished for the Mandé by their "soul" or "spirit."

The Charter defines this human dignity or "spirit" in proto-Spinozian terms, as the human being's expressive capacities: the human spirit "lives from three things: seeing what it wishes to see, saying what it wishes to say, and doing what it wishes to do." Freedom of movement, freedom of expression, and freedom of action. As long as the practice of these three freedoms "respects" the "laws of the Fatherland," their expression is to be absolutely unlimited by the state. In this sense, the Mandé were centuries ahead of such putatively enlightened thinkers as Leibniz and Locke, who would seek to limit such rights of expression in deference to the state.

Toussaint and his colleagues presumably knew the Mandé Charter only through the Kreyol proverb that appears to have derived from it, one that can have played no more than an indirect role in the events of 1791–1804. The primary factor in the passage from localized, personal, or communitarian ameliorative justice to an unqualified immanent and revolutionary universalism was rather the Enlightenment thought embodied in the French *Déclaration des droits de l'homme* of August 1789. The Enlightenment universalism this document embodied could be simply defined as that of a truth claim operating via human reason independently of any experience. What was the nature of a universally true idea for Enlightenment thought? It was Spinoza who first formulated this Enlightenment concept of a truth derived independently of the empirical, as what he called the *verum index sui*, a self-indexing truth. It is the Spinozian concept of the "adequate idea" that most accurately accounts for the universal character of both the 1789 declaration and the concept of emancipation that Saint-Domingue contributed to the Radical Enlightenment.

For Spinoza, an idea is true not because of a correspondence between a concept and an empirical object, but because the idea stands before reason in its full and sufficient *adequacy* (Alquié 28). It is not always clear how Spinoza can distinguish true from falsely adequate ideas (is the essence of a sick body to be sick or to heal; of an enslaved body to labor or free itself?); in the end Spinoza's doctrine of natural right simply tells us that if a body can free itself (from sickness or enslavement) to attain greater perfection, it has the right to do so.

To arrive at a truly adequate idea, then, one must forsake above all enslavement to one's own imagination (say, to imagining the pain of the master's whip and choosing to continue to work). It is not empirical or imaginative conditions that determine truth for Spinoza, but rather the quasi-mathematical necessity of a perfectly true idea (that all triangles are plane figures with three sides and three angles, or, less obviously, that humans should by nature be free) acts to reorient human activity within any given empirical situation. An idea is only truly adequate when we conceive it actively from the power of our own understanding (*Ethics* 4, appendix). An apparently external necessity must come to be grasped in its purely internal, eternal truth.

Though in other respects (such as the distinctions between phenomenal and noumenal worlds, and the empirical and pure reason) Kant refused

Spinoza's uncompromising univocity, he nonetheless maintained something of it in his concept of *allgemeine Erkenntnisse*. He defined this most clearly in the first version of the introduction to the *Critique of Pure Reason:* We apprehend "true universality [*wahre Allgemeinheit*]," Kant tells us, through "universal cognitions [*allgemeine Erkenntnisse*]." These "must be clear and certain for themselves, independently of experience. . . . For if one removes from our experiences everything that belongs to the senses, there still remain certain original concepts and the judgments generated from them, which must have arisen entirely a priori, independently of experience, because they make one able to say more about the objects that appear to the senses than mere experience would teach . . . and make assertions contain true universality and strict necessity" (1997, 127–28). This last sentence could stand as an abstract formulation of precisely what occurs in Haiti, where emancipation is *forced* to occur as a "strict necessity" whose truth is independent of all (prior) experience.[10]

It seems fair to say that none of the actors of the Haitian Revolution had read Spinoza or their contemporary Kant. But it is only against such an intellectual background of adequate, universal truths that we can understand both the theoretical and historical meaning of the texts they *did* read, texts such as the French and American declarations of "truths" that "we hold to be self-evident" or the French assertion of "universal" rights of man. Above all, a single figure was responsible for bringing the transnational political philosophy of the Radical Enlightenment to Saint-Domingue. Through this political theorist, Radical Enlightenment thought spread from Spinoza's *Tractatus*, through its appropriation in Rousseau's *Contrat social* and the *Déclaration,* to reach the shores of the European periphery of Saint-Domingue and Toussaint Louverture via the political philosophy of Maximilien Robespierre carried to Saint-Domingue in the newspapers, journals, and migrations of the period.

## Robespierre and the Politics of the Adequate Idea

The political thought of Robespierre, which Toussaint absorbed in regular doses in his daily reading of the French political press that he had begun well before 1789 (a point I will return to below), strove to articulate a Spinozian politics of pure deduction.[11] An eminently reflective politician, Robespierre systematically attempted to deduce his practical responses to the ever-changing daily circumstances of the revolutionary situation in reference to a series of guiding *adequate ideas* (to borrow Spinoza's term), ideas that he sustained in unswerving, "incorruptible" fidelity to the ever-shifting context of the years 1789–94. In one of his last speeches, "On the Principles of Political Morality" (February 5, 1794), Robespierre articulated this deductive methodology as he strove to bring the period of revolutionary Terror of the past year to an end, and to inaugurate a new, democratic political order based upon "certain rules . . . in light of principles" (Robespierre 2000, 288–89).

These eternal and universal principles of a democratic polity are simply put: "the peaceful enjoyment of freedom and equality; the reign of this eternal justice whose laws have been engraved, not upon marble or stone, but in the hearts of all men, even in that of the slave who forgets them, and of the tyrant who denies them" (289). These laws, then, are the transcendental laws of a universal (human) nature. They precede and ground the institution of any particular society. These laws are not for Robespierre positive constructs of human will. Instead, they have been passively "engraved" there by a higher power that Robespierre does not identify: perhaps the transcendental Christian God of Descartes, Locke, and Newton, perhaps Spinoza's Substance, or the immanent, naturalist expressive force of Diderot. Robespierre is too much the politician to lose himself in such metaphysical subtleties.[12] Like Spinoza's *Ethics,* his is a practical political ethics that simply begins *in media res,* stating axiomatically what we *must* believe and bring to bear upon our actions if we are to be free.

Like Spinoza before him, Robespierre believed that only one form of government is capable of realizing these principles: democracy. This form of government is to be derived neither numerically, as the simple presence or aggregate of the multitude in a single formless congregation (abstract direct democracy), nor by the infinite subdivision of the multitude into isolated, contradictory "fractions" (290). Instead, Robespierre defined democracy in perfectly Spinozian terms: democracy is simply "a state in which the sovereign people, guided by the laws that are its product, does on its own all that it can [*fait par lui-même tout ce qu'il peut bien faire*]" (291). Robespierre's extraordinary formulation renders all formal questions secondary and deductive; democracy is whatever form of government humans can imagine and implement that allows a "people" to preserve their full sovereignty.

Above all, Robespierre's definition makes the analytic of democracy a matter of Spinozian *potentia*. A democracy is the political structure that allows individuals to realize or *do* ("faire") "all that they can." Democracy is simply a state that allows the full development and expression, without division, subtraction, or alienation, of what Spinoza called the "essence" of any singular being. The delegation of sovereignty is *only* to be resorted to insofar as the complexities of modern society prevent the realization of these capacities by isolated individuals. Though this axiom is for both Spinoza and Robespierre universal and timeless, its realization is necessarily historical: one can only "do" all one is capable of within a given historical, existential situation. Thus, Robespierre's approach, no less than Spinoza in the *Tractatus politicus*, is practical, realist, and dialectical, striving to mediate the postulates of universal reason and the particularities of daily political practice through the thousand some day-to-day speeches he formulated.

From this small number of premises, Robespierre proceeded then to explore the "immense consequences to be drawn from [these] principles" (292). Such principles, he argued, offered the citizens of his democracy-to-come "a compass that can direct you amid the storms of every passion ... [,] the touchstone by which you can test all your laws, all propositions that are made to you. In comparing them with this principle ... you can give to all your actions the coherence, the unity, the wisdom, and the dignity [required of a true democracy]" (293).

From his earliest interventions in the French Revolution, Robespierre demonstrated with unswerving fidelity the practicality of this orientation to truth. From the earliest months of 1789, he oriented his acts of practical judgment in reference to the single imperative of undivided, universal freedom and equality. On October 22, 1789, and again in April 1791, Robespierre (joined by Grégoire) argued against the class-based division of society into the politically "active" and subaltern, disenfranchised "passive" citizens based upon the required payment of a "*marc d'argent*" equivalent to one day's labor. Robespierre's argument was a pure and uncompromising deduction of undivided equivalency: "All citizens, whoever they may be, have the right to the fullest degree of representation [*ont droit de prétendre à tous les degrès de représentation*]. Nothing is more in conformity with your Declaration of rights, before which all privileges, all distinctions, all exceptions must disappear" (25). From his minoritarian position in 1791, he articulated a politics of dissidence that attempted to hold the representatives of the French *peuple* to their legal directives with uncompromising rigor.[13] "The constitution establishes that sovereignty resides in the people, in all the individuals of the people. Each individual therefore has the right to contribute [*concourir*] to the law by which he is obligated. . . . Otherwise, it would not be true that all are equal in rights, that each man is a citizen." Centuries before the Czech philosopher and dissident Jan Patočka would formulate the concept, Robespierre undertook the systematic attempt to conduct a politics based upon the imperative that one "live in Truth."

Robespierre stood practically alone against the all-encompassing claims to property rights that arose in the eighteenth century among thinkers such as Locke, Pufendorf, and Lord Kames, the latter of whom put forward the claim that it is "a principle of the law of nature . . . that men be secured in their possessions honestly acquired" (cited in Herman 95). Emeric de Vattel condified this conceit in his 1758 *Le droit des gens ou principe de la loi naturelle,* where he put forward the claim that "the cultivation of the soil is an obligation imposed upon man by nature." Vattel's influential treatise promoted the imperialist destruction of his era, brazenly comforting his readers in their genocidal proclivities: "Those peoples . . . who, though dwelling in fertile countries, disdain the cultivation of the soil . . . deserve to be exterminated like wild beasts of prey."[14] In contrast to such exhortations to brutality, Robespierre's politics of equality grounded its axiomatic prescriptions in the concrete experience of human suffering and inequality:[15]

> These people [*gens*] of whom you speak, [Robespierre continued in his attack on the voting requirement of a *marc d'argent*], are apparently men who live, who subsist in society, without other means. . . . Yes, the hagard clothes that cover me, the humble shack where I claim the right to retire and live in peace; the petty salary with which I nourish my wife and children; all that, I admit, are hardly lands, castles, and horses; all that may perhaps be called nothing, in the eyes of luxury and opulence, but it is something for humanity: it is a property doubtless as sacred as the brilliant domains of the rich. (2000, 79)

Robespierre, virtually alone with Toussaint Louverture and Babeuf in the Age of Enlightenment, thus redefined property from the unqualified, absolute, and naturalized right that it had been in the American Revolution and for the Girondins and Thermidorians of his own time and place, to a *qualified* right dependent upon that of human freedom (80). Consequently, Robespierre's proposition to the National Assembly in 1791 was to reject the requirement of a *marc d'argent* and to affirm instead that "all the French, that is to say all people [*hommes*] born and living in France, or naturalized there, must enjoy in fullness and equality the rights of the citizen" (93). The first human right, he argued, one that comes before any (partial) right to property, is the right to exist (183).

Such applied rigor characterized the totality of Robespierre's practical interventions in the unfolding revolution. He defended the civil rights of comedians and Jews (December 23, 1789) based on the principle that "every citizen who has fulfilled the conditions of eligibility that you have prescribed [in the declaration of the Rights of Man] has the right to participate in his government [*fonctions publiques*]" (30). The National Guard, whose mission was in Robespierre's estimation to defend the Rights of Man, was to be strictly nonprofessional, composed by the citizenry in its totality, without distinction between "active" and "passive" classes (53). Finally, like Spinoza and Kant before him (and unlike so many other figures of the Moderate Enlightenment so ready to accommodate their thought to the demands of political power), Robespierre defended a total freedom of the press, the freedom to express *all* ideas that do not "formally" (that is, clearly and explicitly) incite to crime or disobedience of the law. Otherwise, he argued categorically that "each citizen has the right to publish his opinion without being exposed to any form of retribution" (110).[16] The single, enormous blind spot in the political logic of Robespierre, however, was the rights of women. Political (if not human) rights were quite literally and indefensibly limited in Robespierre's politics to those of the numerically lesser half of humanity, in stark contrast to contemporaries such as Condorcet, Etta Palm d'Aelders, and Olympe de Gouges.

This deductive political philosophy of Radical Enlightenment figures such as Robespierre was at once theoretical and practical. Theoretically, it received its fullest determination in Spinoza's political ethics, Rousseau's social contract, and Kant's practical philosophy, while politically Robespierre (and Toussaint in his wake) sought to orient his concrete practice in light of his apperception of the dictates of reason. No clear line of demarcation is available to distinguish these two realms. To call the former "philosophers" and the latter "politicians" would in effect collapse into abstract academic categories an array of elemental resonances that to an important degree overwrote all prior distinctions of nationality, language, and social situation. Instead, there existed a continuum of reflective politics in the Radical Enlightenment. The problem of the "self-evident truths" of natural law preoccupied historically, politically, and philosophically engaged individuals across all divisions of Atlantic society of the eighteenth century, from the isolation of Spinoza's retreat from public life to the battlefields of the Parisian Commune and Saint-Domingue.

The Enlightenment faith in what Jefferson called the "self-evident" truth of a human right to freedom received its purest demonstration in Saint-Domingue. While the experience of slavery made human suffering an unsurpassable reference for Toussaint and others, from another perspective the plantation, through its various forms of ultraviolence, constituted a systematic, if vain, attempt to obliterate every intimation of universality from the slaves' mental life, indeed, to keep them from thinking at all.

This it could never accomplish, of course. But empirical experience of the plantation told the slaves of Saint-Domingue that they were subhuman, devoid of free will and reason, subject only to the will of an external master. One could say that the empirical world of the plantation told them nothing of a universal right to freedom. That idea had to arise from the resources of their own rational reflection. It was not suffering, I would argue, but only the contact of suffering, enslaved individuals with a previously existing idea (Enlightenment-era universal right), as Spinoza had originally claimed, that engendered a subsequent adequate idea (universal emancipation).

In a sense, the Declaration of the Rights of Man appeared from beyond the empirical experience of suffering offered by daily life in Saint-Domingue (arriving suddenly, on board vessels from another world). Though they could not have derived their novel insights without a prior experience of slavery, the declaration addressed itself not to the slaves' *experience* (in the world of the plantation where slavery was a legal and daily fact of life) but to their faculty of reason, a faculty that could recognize the universality of its truth *independently of all experience*.[17] Instead of admitting to the particular "fact of nature" that made up their daily experience (their suffering and the slave-masters' attempt to reduce them to sheer animality), in their revolution they strove to act in accord with reason, to, as Kant famously put the matter, "act in such a way that [they could] will that [their] maxim become a universal law": that slavery be abolished, universally and without exception. More precisely, slavery had meant the attempt to reduce humans to mere means (of the mechanical, bestial production of sugar). Instead, they sought to "use humanity always . . . as an end [that is, the realization of universal freedom], never merely as a means" (Kant 1996, 57, 80).

To claim that the notion of a "universal reason" is a "European" category that does violence to other forms of human thought by branding them "mythical" ignores the specificity of the notion of a universal human freedom. The faculty of reason has no racial or geographic a priori content; on the contrary, it is manifested precisely in the singular, *nonhierarchical,* and *transcultural* creative acts of all human beings, whether European or not.[18] In too quickly judging a putative "Enlightenment" supposition of universal human reason to be *mere* violent imposition, such an "anti-universalist" viewpoint remains blind to the singularity of an event such as the Haitian Revolution, a singularity that finds its most adequate contemporary explication in the Enlightenment conceptualization of human freedom.[19]

In affirming their own reasonableness, by conceiving of themselves as rational subjects of a universal imperative to abolish slavery, the slaves of Haiti transformed the European understanding of reason; by no means did they passively acquiesce to its definitions. The Declaration of the Rights of Man was not "intended" to apply to Africans, anymore than was the American Declaration of Independence. After the first major defeat of Napoleon by his equals in strategic and rhetorical genius, by those far his superior in ethical comportment and insight, that is to say by Toussaint Louverture and the Saint-Domingue multitude that brought their revolution to completion, the concept of reason could no longer exclude the African diaspora to the same degree.[20] By this measure, these African slaves, and not the procolonialist French Assembly, were the reasonable beings who recognized themselves in the universal abstraction of the rights of man and acted to transform the very concept of "reasonable being" accordingly.

What processes can account for the radical displacement and reconfiguration of abstract, universalist concepts of the Radical Enlightenment such as right, reason, and emancipation, and the historical emergence of a space in which this theoretical universality became embodied in 1790s Saint-Domingue? Some historians have argued against the fundamental role of the French *Déclaration* in the earliest period of the Haitian Revolution. Michel-Rolph Trouillot has claimed that in 1791 the slaves of Saint-Domingue already "had their own program" calling for the amelioration of working conditions rather than "an abstractly couched 'freedom'" (1995, 103). Carolyn Fick has demonstrated that such autonomous demands, which owed little or nothing to Jacobinism, persisted throughout the 1790s as an important factor in the successful drive to independence. Trouillot asserts that "the claims of the revolution were too radical to be formulated in advance of its deeds" (88). Was, as Trouillot seems to imply, a universal human right to freedom from slavery simply an explanation appended to unconscious actions after the fact? Or did a universal, categorical imperative to strive for a world without slavery regulate slaves' actions—at first obscurely, later explicitly—from the very beginning, insofar as they perceived themselves immediately in their singular, open, and constructive human freedom and possibility?

I think Trouillot's claim fails to acknowledge the degree of pure practical reason at work in each and every conscious human action. "*Every* use of reason with respect to an object [that is, practically]," Kant wrote, "requires pure concepts of the understanding (*categories*), without which no object can be thought" (1996, 249; my emphasis). The slaves of Saint-

55   The Idea of 1804

Fig. 2. Drawing of a sugar refining mill from the *Encyclopédie* of Diderot and D'Alembert, ca. 1760, showing the "bestial" mechanics of production. (Author's collection)

Domingue, a Kantian could argue against Trouillot, acted as rational human beings (and not following a mere unconscious instinct) to attain their goal of ending slavery from the night of their first, unimaginable (for Europeans), consciously planned and well-organized revolt in August 1791, despite the fact that this project would not until 1793 be explicitly formulated in accord with a universal moral principle.

In this view, the philosophy of freedom articulated in Saint-Domingue was unquestionably a philosophy of praxis, rather than an act of purely rational abstraction. While Kant's *Critique of Pure Reason* (1781) had demonstrated that the attempt to conceptualize freedom *in purely rational terms* necessarily ends in logical antinomies, and that pure freedom itself is nonexistent, Kant thought that the development of human freedom could still remain the ground of philosophical reflection if one separated "pure reason" from what he termed "practical philosophy." In the latter, a priori universal precepts "determining choice" guide empirical human decisions and actions:

> The concept of *freedom* is a pure rational concept, which for this very reason is . . . a concept such that no instance corresponding to it can be given in any possible experience, and of an object of which we cannot obtain any theoretical cognition; the concept of freedom cannot hold as a constitutive but solely as a regulative and, indeed, merely negative principle of speculative reason. But in reason's practical use the concept of freedom proves its reality by practical principles, which are laws of a causality of pure reason for determining choice independently of any empirical conditions. . . . On this concept of freedom . . . are based unconditional practical laws. (1996, 376)

What the former slaves of Saint-Domingue formulated after August 1791 was precisely such an "unconditional practical law": the practical imperative to eliminate slavery unconditionally. Moreover, they followed this imperative more completely and without reservations than any other political community in the Age of Enlightenment. How they did so is one of the most fundamental processes a history of ideas in the Black Atlantic Enlightenment can hope to describe.

### The Universalization of the Rights of Man and Citizen

From 1791 to 1804, the Haitian revolutionaries—not just Toussaint, but, as Carolyn Fick has demonstrated, the whole multitude of Haitian slaves—fought to institute an emancipatory social structure that would allow for the free development of all human beings. If the French *Déclaration* enfranchised white, male, adult property owners who could afford to pay a discriminatory *marc d'argent*, it accomplished this enfranchisement by negating the civil rights of women, slaves, and others. Nonetheless, its universal prescription was rightly understood by the enslaved of Saint-Domingue to interpellate them as subjects to a politics of emancipation. In Saint-Domingue in 1791, the abstract universal concept of emancipation became a more concrete universal, as hundreds of thousands of former slaves invented and instituted the global movement of decolonization that had remained a mere *idea* in post-1789 Paris. "Philosophy," as the Abbé Grégoire put the matter in a letter of June 8, 1791, to the mulattoes and free blacks of Saint-Domingue, "has enlarged its horizon in the New World. . . . One day the sun will shine only upon free men in your lands" (10, 12).

In a few short years the ideology and events of the French Revolution utterly transformed the slaves of Saint-Domingue into both citizens of France and subjects of a global culture of the Enlightenment, as C. L. R. James first recognized. Though many participated in this process, Toussaint

## 57   The Idea of 1804

Louverture was the articulate voice of this transformation. Toussaint quickly dominated and reconfigured the grounds of struggle for freedom from what they had meant in 1789 Paris. Toussaint repeatedly based his and his colleagues' actions on the universal rights put forward in 1789. For Toussaint this was not a struggle for mere civil rights or negative, individualistic rights (as in the American Revolution), but for the universal right of humans to be free from slavery. "The liberty that the [French] republicans offer us you say is false," he wrote to Jean-François to explain his rallying to the French Republic in 1794. Once the French Republic had abolished slavery, there could be no ambiguity possible: "We are republicans and, in consequence, free by natural right. It can only be Kings whose very name expresses what is most vile and low, who dared to arrogate the right of reducing to slavery men made like themselves, whom nature had made free" (cited in James 155).

Toussaint's letter of 14 Brumaire (November 5), 1798, written as the Directory abandoned the advances of the revolution and prepared the way for Napoleon, stands as one of the great documents of the Age of Enlightenment and Revolution.[21] Justly celebrated by James, this letter eloquently testifies to the Black Atlantic dispersion and active reconfiguration of the Radical Enlightenment ideal of human autonomy grounded upon universal natural rights. Toussaint begins by expressing his astonishment that the Thermidorian "liberticides" in the French Assembly could "threaten us with the return of slavery." The letter testifies to Toussaint's gift for a particular form of rhetorical persuasion. Toussaint flatters his readers by confronting them with their own self-idealization: these "wise legislators who have decreed the Liberty of Peoples" should never allow such "detestables projects" as the reimposition of slavery to go forward.

Toussaint bases his resolve to defeat these goals upon a sole criterion: that liberty (understood as the continued abolition of slavery after 1794) should continue to exist in Saint-Domingue: "I swear to do so, by all that Liberty holds sacred. My fidelity to France, the recognition that all the blacks hold for her, oblige me to affirm to you . . . the oath that we renew to bury ourselves beneath the ruins of a Country awoken [*ravivé*] by Liberty, rather than allow the return of Slavery."

In such phrases Toussaint strictly avoided making any of his claims in reference to local privileges or rights (of class, race, nation). Instead, any action the Directory takes should, he argued, be addressed to the blacks of Saint-Domingue as members of the human species: "Do not allow," he wrote, "that brothers, that friends be sacrificed to men who wish to reign over the ruins of the Human Species [*l'Espèce humaine*]." Though

Toussaint welcomed all "French Republicans" to return to the island, he made clear, four years before Napoleon would send French troops with explicit orders to reinstate slavery, that he would resort to military force to repel anyone, French or otherwise, hoping to reinstate human bondage in the colony: "We shall always repel from us those foolish enough to limit the Rights the Constitution guarantees us."

Toussaint maintained that the reimposition of slavery was not a matter of local concern for a small Caribbean community of Africans at the boundaries of the known world. The Declaration of the Rights of Man had become a reality for the slaves of Saint-Domingue, and Toussaint affirmed unambiguously that its universal prescription of a right to freedom based on reason ("principle") grounded their actions. Toussaint's closing lines constitute one of the great articulations of the Enlightenment faith in human reason, freedom, and universal rights:

> Do they think that men who have enjoyed the Blessings of Liberty could stand by while these were taken from them? They bore their chains as long as they knew no state happier than that of Slavery.... But no, ... the same hand that broke our chains will not enchain us again. France will not revoke her principles.... She will not allow her sublime morality to be perverted, the destruction of those of her Principles that so honor Humanity.

In conclusion, Toussaint based the will to resist such an eventuality upon the knowledge and reason shared by all his colleagues, the result of the process of enlightenment in which he had participated firsthand since 1789:

> But if, to reestablish servitude in St. Domingue, this were the case, I declare to you that this would be to attempt the impossible: we have known how [*nous avons su*] to confront danger to obtain our Liberty, and we will know how [*nous saurons*] to confront death to conserve it.... [I shall] cease to exist ... before the Land of Liberty is profaned and soiled by the Liberticides, before they can tear from my hands ... these arms that France has confided in me for the defense [of the] Rights of humanity, and for the triumph of liberty and Equality.

## Reading, Writing, and Authorship in Enlightenment Saint-Domingue

These Enlightenment ideas did not spring miraculously formed into Toussaint's mind. Fluent in both Kreyol and French, he actively dictated and rewrote all of his letters with a team of French secretaries until they forged them into the prose of the Enlightenment. Nor was Toussaint the passive pawn of these French secretaries. Deborah Jenson has shown how he actively managed public perception of the events in Saint-Domingue as a veritable "spin doctor" of the Age of Enlightenment. Already in the first months of the uprising in 1791, the French captive of the rebels, Procurator Gros, expressed his amazement at how minutely his captors were following events in France since 1789. Toussaint in particular was a voracious reader of French papers such as the *Moniteur*, and interviews with him appeared there in turn throughout the second half of the 1790s (Jenson 5). He boasted to his rival Chanlatte in 1793 of how well-informed he (Toussaint) was and how often he "received news from France" and "New England" (Bell 2007, 29, 86).

To the degree early-modern communication networks would allow, Toussaint avidly followed every turn of events in revolutionary North America and France. An article in the French paper *Le Publiciste* from 1798 describes how Toussaint, "to follow the course of events . . . [,] wrote to a European philanthropist, to whom he sent the funds necessary to subscribe to French newspapers."[22] In a letter of August 14, 1794, to Étienne Laveaux, Toussaint begged his mentor to send him printed descriptions of the revolutionary events in France: "Having promised me the newspapers describing the exploits of our brave republicans, please use this occasion [to send them]; I have a burning desire to know of their valorous courage." In his next letter an impatient Toussaint reminds Laveaux, "You had promised to send me the most recent news that you have received; undoubtedly you have forgotten this" (Laurent 126, 136).

The contemporary account of one French witness (himself a white plantation owner hostile to Toussaint) is particularly revealing as to how this largely illiterate former slave actively transformed himself into a prominent figure and public intellectual of the French Revolution: "I saw him in few words verbally lay out the summary of his addresses [to his secretaries], rework the poorly conceived, poorly executed sentences; confront several secretaries presenting their work by turns; redo the ineffective sections; transpose parts to place them to better effect; making himself worthy, all in all, of the natural genius foretold by Raynal" (cited in Jenson 8). Incredibly, Toussaint would dictate as many as three hundred letters in a single day (Bell 2007, 197).

While one of the great figures of the Enlightenment, unlike any of the other great theorists of liberty of the Enlightenment (Paine, Jefferson, Franklin, Raynal, Grégoire, Robespierre, Danton . . .), Toussaint had lived the formative years of his life as a slave, and this experience allowed him, alone in the 1790s, "to defend the freedom of the blacks without reservation" (James 198).[23] In the *Bulletin Officiel de St. Domingue* of February 12, 1797, Toussaint issued a public declaration that recalled the experience of slavery he shared with his audience, calling on his fellow citizens to unite around "the sacred cause of liberty.... Let us unite, and we shall die free rather than live as slaves!" Always aware of the rhetorical effect of his words, in much of his correspondence with France, Toussaint flattered his readers, calling them the "architects" of the slaves' liberty, while in other statements he explicitly figured the blacks' freedom from slavery as their own achievement.

The implications of this autonomous achievement were for Toussaint clearly of universal consequence for the slaveholding Atlantic world-system. In an address to the army he commanded on May 18, 1797, he described "the sacred fire of liberty that we have acquired" not as a local libertarian predilection, but as a universal project that must encompass all humankind: "Let us go forth to plant the tree of liberty, and shatter the chains of those of our brothers still held by the shameful yoke of slavery. Bring to them our rights, the imprescriptible and inalienable rights of the free man.... [We must] break the barriers that separate nations, and unite the human species in a single brotherhood."[24]

In articulating this project of a universal, transnational regime of human rights in the 1790s, Toussaint was not passively parroting ideas imported from France and forced upon him. Before Toussaint, the Rights of Man had not, with rare, tentative exceptions, been understood to extend to African slaves. In the face of this repressive partiality, Toussaint used the public sphere of the Enlightenment with tactical genius to redefine the notion of universal right.

Toussaint's interjections into the Enlightenment public sphere are a key element in a variegated knowledge-system spread across the entire Atlantic world, one that actively debated the nature of human freedom from Salamanca to St. Marc, Königsberg to Les Cayes, Timbuktu to Tiburon. The modalities of this debate varied, from the political speeches and letters of Robespierre, Toussaint, and Abbé Grégoire, to the writings of Diderot and Raynal, the logical treatises of Condorcet and the academic philosophy of Kant and Hegel. This field of debate and knowledge production must furthermore be understood to have included the symbolic interventions of illiterate slaves who autonomously exercised their faculty of judgment in order to illuminate the universal implications of the natural rights tradition in ways unthinkable for the North American or Parisian political class. This world-system of symbolic exchange and

## 61 The Idea of 1804

debate possessed its own division of labor, with various members expressing themselves via the particular modes of their field, from the rhetorical flourishes of Robespierre's speeches to the Kantian and Hegelian philosophical master discourses. For all these distinctions of form and content, a comparative, systemic analysis of the knowledge-system of the Atlantic Enlightenment can elucidate without prejudice the various possibilities opened up by each modality within this diversified structure. Though they left no systematic "critique," it was not, for example, Condorcet or Kant, but the former slaves of Saint-Domingue, largely illiterate and formally uneducated, who exercised the most highly developed faculty of judgment in the Enlightenment debate on slavery and freedom.

The Abbé Grégoire, like Condorcet, had defended the need to end slavery gradually, and commentators such as Louis Sala-Molins have rightly taken them to task for this restriction.[25] Similarly, Joan Dayan describes "how the making of enlightenment man led to the demolition of the unenlightened brute [under the *Code Noir*], how the thinking mind's destructive proclivities dominated a passive nature or servile body" (204). Such a description, for all its justice, neglects the degree to which those bodies were able to refuse "passivity" and "servility." What has remained underappreciated is the role the concept of human rights may have played for the slaves Grégoire wrote to in Saint-Domingue, assuring them that "[slaves] are born and remain free and equal. The irresistible march of events and the progression of enlightenment lead all peoples shorn of their freedom to recover this inalienable property" (12). In the end, one could reply to Sala-Molins, it mattered little whether Grégoire and Condorcet thought slavery should be abolished gradually or immediately. It was their ethical idealism that was unambiguous, and it was heard in Saint-Domingue. This process, what Srinivas Aravumudan has called "Tropicalizing the Enlightenment," was not one of mere passive mimicry, but instead one in which the slaves of Saint-Domingue actively restructured contemporary debate on universal human rights.[26]

Little attention has been paid to Haitian participation in this global discursive sphere.[27] Not only, I think, because its traces can be hard to ascertain. Attention to the role of ideas in the revolution has been perceived as implying an inferior position of passive reception, when in fact such a view misses perhaps the most significant and singular aspect of this revolution.[28] We no longer live in the intellectual world of Negritude, that of James and Aimé Césaire, when in the 1930s these authors found it necessary to affirm the value of African civilizations before their systematic devaluation by the West. As students of the work of Herskovitz and Mintz, of Richard Price and Robert Ferris Thompson, the legacy of their anthropology (as well as of Negritude itself) should encourage us to consider the ideas of the European Enlightenment not as the threatening *negation* of African cultural survivals in the Americas, but as one more (essential) element in the complex mix of cultural materials contributing to the construction of Haitian modernity.

The radical transformation of France after 1789 did not *determine* the appearance of the Haitian Revolution; instead, the Declaration of the Rights of Man was a key element in creating what David Scott has called the "conditions of possibility," the ontological ground that allowed for a local rebellion's increasing articulation in terms of universal human rights. In this sequence of events, rebel slaves "appropriated the modern concepts and institutions [they] found around them and creatively turned them to their own purposes" (107, 114). "In other words," Scott concludes, "the alternative modernity being made by Toussaint Louverture and his colleagues was not a prior choice they made as preconstituted subjects waking up in the middle of a world they found as objectionable and in need of change; it was a choice partly constituted by that modern world and, therefore, a choice partly constructed through its conceptual and ideological apparatuses" (115).[29]

Carolyn Fick's *The Haitian Revolution from Below* gives a perfect example of a tendency to overlook evidence pointing to the importance of Enlightenment ideology in the development of the Haitian Revolution. As she mounts her compelling case for a revolution driven by the Haitian masses, and not their nominal leaders, she quotes from the diary of a young plantation owner named Parham. Returning from France to his plantation in 1791, he captures an anonymous rebel slave. Fick quotes from the diary at length, yet she passes over in silence what to me is its most astounding aspect. The slave "met death without fear or complaint. We found in one of his pockets pamphlets printed in France, filled with commonplaces about the Rights of Man and the Sacred Revolution" (Parham 34). The planter disdains these pamphlets as mere "commonplaces," while they are not even noticed by Fick. Yet such random traces are the only testimony we have to the enormous role the concept of universal human rights played in the Haitian Revolution, and to the active, original role Haitians played in the globalization and realization of an Enlightenment that started an ocean away in the elite salons and revolutionary clubs of Paris.[30]

Any inquiry into these "beginnings" of the Haitian Revolution must necessarily remain a partial and unfinished investigation. David Geggus lists a few of the many causes of the revolution in Saint-Domingue in *Haitian Revolutionary Studies:* the "grouping [of slaves] in large units . . . , the involvement of the ruling class in war or internal struggles . . . , economic depression . . . , urbanization . . . , high concentrations of the recently enslaved . . . , maroon activity . . . [and] emancipationist rumors" (59–62). Geggus, like Carolyn Fick, distinctly underplays the admittedly "perplexing problem" of the influence of ideas on the revolution because it is so hard for historians to quantify.

In distinct contrast to this historiographic trend, Aimé Césaire, in his 1959 study *Toussaint Louverture,* located the origins of the Saint-Domingue revolution in the former slaves' immediate understanding of the full implications of the French Revolution: "To have awaited the abolition of slavery as a spontaneous gesture of the French bourgeoisie, under the pretext that abolition was a logical implication of the Declaration of the Rights of Man, would have been . . . to ignore that the bourgeois revolution's own historical task was only carried out when they were pushed on by the people with a sword at their back. What is astonishing is that the black masses so quickly understood that they should expect nothing from Paris and that they would only definitively achieve what they would have the courage to conquer for themselves" (171).

Like Eugene Genovese a generation after him, Césaire identified the specificity of the Haitian Revolution in its transformation from one of many New World slave *rebellions* that looked back to a lost African past, into a progressive, modernist revolution at the hands of Toussaint. "As soon as Toussaint joined in, [the rebellion (*l'émeute*)] became a revolution. And this meant . . . becoming conscious of one thing: that, beyond individuals, it was a system that had to be destroyed. The goal, the only valid goal, could be none other than freedom, universal freedom" (196). The Haitian Revolution, Césaire tells us, was fundamentally a *transformation in consciousness,* consciousness of universal freedom as a categorical imperative, and only secondarily a complex and contingent series of events. Precisely what Kant had called, in 1784, "enlightenment": leaving our self-incurred minority and the acceptance of external authority for that of our own reason. In 1795 Toussaint wrote: "Brothers and Sisters, the moment has arrived in which the thick veil that obscured the light must fall" (Césaire 228).

Beyond all the contributing factors such as Vodun and an African natural rights tradition (*Charte du Mandé*), Christianity, and the enormous disproportion between slaves and masters in colonial Saint-Domingue, the determining factor that turned these events into "the call for a new . . . [,]

more advanced society" was the mere "idea" of a universal right to autonomy (Genovese 82). This idea developed in Saint-Domingue via the slaves' active participation in a global discursive community. While this community arose long before 1791, and thus decisively informed these slaves' own subjectivity as subjects of the New World plantocracy, they in turn radically transformed the parameters, geographic distribution, and limits of this global public sphere.[31]

This influence was no linear filiation, from an enlightened and reasonable France to its savage colony. On the contrary, this study is an attempt to argue against any simple, inevitable, linear progression leading from 1789 to 1804, from France to Haiti. The Haitian Revolution testifies to the radical *discontinuity* obtaining between these two realms; the Haitian Revolution exploded into an Occidental consciousness unprepared to address, and even to comprehend, the sweeping claims of its transformation of the concept of human freedom. It belies the tendency Roger Chartier, glossing Foucault, has described of official historiography to "dissolve the singular event in an ideal continuity" (16). The "pursuit of origin," of any event, Foucault wrote, "is an attempt to capture the exact essence of things . . . and their carefully protected identities, because this search assumes the existence of immobile forms that precede the external world of accident and succession" (1977, 142). Such an essential, platonic essence for a concept such as liberty, unchanging through its worldly instances, is precisely debunked by its transformation in Saint-Domingue.

At the same time, this study is also an attempt to address the universal ontological foundation that allowed for the appearance of such a singular event; despite all necessary Foucauldian skepticism regarding the "search for 'origins,'" the open and untotalized signifier *liberté* did in fact travel across the globe in the Age of Enlightenment to become the creolized concept *liberté/libete,* an abstraction that subsequently took on radically distinct forms in its various localized instantiations (140). A Foucauldian historiography of radical singularities and episteme has no ground to account for the emergence of such a singularity.[32] In contrast, one might figure this study as a search, not for the essential and immortal "origins" of the Haitian Revolution, but rather at once for what Foucault calls the (multiple, singular) "beginnings" of any event ("liberating a profusion of lost events"), along with what Foucault never accounts for: the ontological foundations allowing for the contingent appearance of any such singular beginnings (146).

If Yves Benot begins his outstanding study *La révolution française et la fin des colonies* with precisely the question I wish to ask of the

Haitian Revolution—"What can an ideology accomplish?" (7)—he is ultimately unable to provide a substantial answer for Saint-Domingue itself because his inquiry tends to focus on the production of ideas in Metropolitan France, while Benot implicitly understands the revolutionary Haitian slaves to be mere *actors*.[33] On the one hand, Benot argues, "The Revolution in France brought the ideal of liberty and equality to the entire world, and thus to the slaves themselves." On the other hand, Benot comments that these same slaves "imposed" the 1794 Abolition not through an active reformulation of an ethical doctrine, but through the (implicitly preconscious) "act" of *soulevement* (19, 8). Beyond a few tantalizing glimpses (138–40), Benot never demonstrates a process of reflection to have taken place among the slaves of Saint-Domingue themselves. Attention to archival sources, however, reveals many such traces of autonomous reflection in Saint-Domingue on the content of universal rights.

## The Black Atlantic Public Sphere

The former slaves of Haiti were in fact active participants in a transnational discourse on human rights. This debate over slavery and its possible abolition appeared only in the second half of the eighteenth century, with the development of a secular, international public sphere. Julius Scott's 1986 study of the dispersion of Enlightenment ideas in the Atlantic world first revealed to scholars many of the vectors of this process:

> In the oral cultures of the Caribbean, local rulers were no more able to control the rapid spread of information than they were able to control the movements of the ships or the masterless people with which this information traveled. The books, newspapers, and letters which arrived with the ships were not the only avenues for the flow of information and news in Afro-America. While written documents always had a vital place, black cultural traditions that favored speech and white laws that restricted literacy gave a continuing primacy to other channels of communication. . . . In cultures where people depended upon direct human contact for information, news spread quickly and became part of a shared public discourse. (115)

The "public sphere" of the Enlightenment must be understood to have extended far beyond the salons of literate bourgeois European society where Habermas first identified it, to include both printed sources and the traces of the predominantly oral culture of Saint-Domingue slaves (Habermas 1962). This participation in an oral-based public sphere of discourse on human rights was not limited to linguistic expression: a fuller exploration of this sphere than I can offer here would address such nonlinguistic expressive and communicative practices as song and dance, religious expression (Vodun), shared experiences of bodily suffering on the plantation (torture, rape, murder), and the destruction of families and the bonds of care and responsibility.[34]

The public sphere, in Habermas's typology, refers to a specific social space that appeared in the Enlightenment, one separate both from the family and private life and from organized politics. This was a "public of private people making use of their reason" (51). In this space, members of society could come together to discuss issues of mutual interest without the constraints and limitations of political life, and were thus free to critique existing political power.

What Habermas isolated, bracketed, and subsequently neglected to describe, a so-called "plebian public sphere" distinct from the "liberal" sphere he chose to investigate, was in Saint-Domingue neither separate nor fully subordinate to the dominant one (xviii). Habermas's analytical bent, which hoped to isolate and define a category (the "bourgeois") in purity from all "plebian" contamination, in effect reproduced on the level of scholarly analysis a homologous sociohistorical process that had excluded slaves from the discussion of universal rights in the Age of Enlightenment. Simply put, contra Habermas, it is impossible to understand the public discussion of universal human rights in the period of the French Revolution without analyzing how the enslaved "plebian sphere" forced members of the metropolitan "bourgeois" republican sphere to reorient their debate, and subsequently actually to abolish slavery in 1794.

Such a reconception compels any analysis of the Radical Enlightenment to overcome the economic bias of "world-system" theory that tends to locate superstructural processes (such as intellectual debate) in a putative "center," while locating infrastructural economic processes such as slave labor on a corresponding "periphery." Instead, one must understand the Enlightenment public sphere of intellectual debate not as a centralized, European phenomenon, but instead as a widely dispersed and formally variegated component of the entire early-modern world-system. Saint-Domingue had by 1789 certainly become one of the fundamental and central production sites in the transnational system of agricultural capitalism described by Wallerstein (85). From the perspective of the twenty-first-century information-based global system, it is now obvious that, already in the eighteenth century, the "public sphere" (understood as a diffuse network of communication and struggle over representation) was itself a world-system, with its own consecrated divisions of labor ("enlightened" versus "unenlightened" spheres, oral versus written methodologies, and so on) that was an essential component in the more or less smooth production, extraction, and reproduction of surplus capital for the North Atlantic powers.

Attention to the unfolding of the Haitian Revolution forces us to reconceive the very notion of a "public sphere" in a manner radically different from its articulation by either Kant, Hegel, or Habermas.[35] Both Kant and Habermas make an absolute distinction between communicative action in a (bourgeois) public sphere and action for political or social change, which they limit to the most gradualist, representative delegation of authority to a political elite or bureaucracy. While I will in the following chapter examine in detail Kant's problematic ban on the right of a people to revolt, Habermas also sanctions any concrete striving for social change not delegated to a representative bureaucracy: "Democratic movements emerging from civil society must give up holistic aspirations to a self-organizing society" he states in a moment of neo-Thermidorianism (1996, 372). As such, what had appeared in his 1962 study to be a mere methodological decision (to separate the bourgeois from the plebian public spheres) had come by the publication of the monumental *Between Facts and Norms* (1992) to constitute a fundamental limitation for any notion of the public sphere, a concept Habermas constrained to the most narrowly defined norms of rational communicative action.

The positive contribution of *Between Facts and Norms* to the ongoing debate on the public sphere was to move beyond any monological notion of a single, all-encompassing European bourgeois public sphere, to adopt a vision of plural, highly differentiated realms. "In complex societies, the public sphere consists of . . . a highly complex network that branches out into a multitude of overlapping international, national, regional, local, and subcultural arenas" (373). All of these provinces nonetheless continue for Habermas to be overcoded by a single "universal public sphere" characterized by the author's highly normative model of communicative action (374).

Kant had distinguished absolutely between, on the one hand, participation in the marketplace, open to all (including not only minors and women, but also "a domestic servant, a shop clerk, a day laborer, or even a barber"), and, on the other, participation in a rational public sphere, open only to those able "to use [their] understanding without direction from another" (1996, 295, 17). Despite the clarity of this directive, Kant fails to hold his judgment to its unambiguous prescription. The former, mere "passive citizens" are to be barred from status as active members of society free to make and judge laws; the latter status, however, is limited by Kant *not* (as one might logically assume following his argument in *What Is Enlightenment?*) to anyone who demonstrates their autonomous ability to reason, but to the same arbitrary, empirical, and restricted category that so compromised the revolutionary initiatives of 1776 and 1789: that of adult male property holders (Montag 136).

Habermas's dismissal of the "plebian" public sphere echoes the elitism of Hegel, whose conception of the public sphere he critiques. Hegel's 1820 *Philosophy of Right* offered an unambiguous and strikingly original defense of the Haitian Revolution, understood by him to demonstrate the universal right of slaves to overthrow the system that enchains them.[36] In his ideal image of the state, however, Hegel defended the need for a strong bureaucratic class to orient its decisions, simultaneously denigrating the capacity of the masses, informed by the strong functioning of a public sphere of discussion, to sustain this function. While he defended and celebrated freedom of the press and public discussion (*Philosophy of Right* §315), public opinion for Hegel could never be any more than that, mere *opinion*, "the site of *particular* and irresponsible decisions."[37] In contrast to Kant's defense of the public sphere as the guarantor of a free society, Hegel criticized this claim as mere ideology (in anticipation of Marx) and discounted its inherent progressive potential, which Habermas would seek to recover (though only for the "bourgeois" public).[38] Similarly, one might say of Habermas himself that his analytical excision of the plebian sphere, while initially paying lip service to the possibility that it might have functioned as a realm "of enlightenment," "demotes" it to function, silently, as the mere subjective corroboration of the bourgeois public sphere.

While Habermas silences the "plebian" sphere and excludes it from political practice, Hegel's analysis is similarly infected by the view that the "rabble" (*Pöbel*) in modern society remains subject to the mere "contingencies of public opinion, with its ignorance and perverseness, its false information and its errors of judgment" (§317). Public opinion, for Hegel, remains forever cut off from participation in universal truth, a truth accessible in this view only for a scientifically trained bureaucratic elite. Ineluctably, "the people [*ein Volk*] is deceived *by itself.*" This is precisely where the Haitian Revolution he analyzes elsewhere so insightfully (but as a mere imperfect *moment* in the march to universal freedom) stands as a radical demonstration that, in Saint-Domingue, *all* members of society (insofar as slavery and the plantation determined social life in Saint-Domingue in its totality) were *actually and already* (nonidentical,

## 69  The Idea of 1804

antagonistic) participants in the understanding and realization of a universal truth. Those slaves whom Enlightenment thinkers thought unfit to grasp the universal concept of freedom actually and explicitly demonstrated their understanding when they acted to make the *Déclaration* live up to its own universal claims.

Habermas's analysis of the public sphere sustains and absolutizes these Kantian and Hegelian biases.[39] The public sphere, whether single or multiple, is for Habermas to exclude all forms of what he calls "the pressure of the street [*Dem Druck der Strasse*]" (Montag 133). In Habermas's paternalist exclusionism, all "processes of opinion-formation" (through communicative action in the public sphere) are furthermore to be "separated from putting those dispositions into action" (1996, 362). As citizens of any democracy putatively founded on the autonomous sovereignty of its members, it is astounding to hear Habermas reassure his readers that "the communicative structures of the public sphere *relieve* the public *of the burden of decision making,* the postponed decisions are reserved for the institutionalized political process" (362; emphasis in original). Two decades earlier, in his trenchant and virulent critique of Czechoslovak bureaucratic socialism, the dissident Václav Havel knew what such paternalist celebrations of representative government really meant: "Avoid politics if you can; leave it to us! Just do what we tell you, don't try to have deep thoughts, and don't poke your nose into things that don't concern you! Shut up, do your work, look after yourself—and you'll be all right!" (Havel 62).

Echoing the blinkered reductionism of Fukuyama's so-called end of history, Habermas presents a world in which triumphant representational liberalism has become the only free and democratic social structure imaginable: "A robust civil society can develop only in the context of a liberal political culture and the corresponding patterns of socialization." Any attempt to institute an alternative modality, he assures us, would be to return to the atavistic primitivism of "populist movements . . . that blindly defend the frozen traditions of a lifeworld endangered by capitalist modernization" (371).

The events of the Haitian Revolution waylaid such an absolute banning of the "plebian" multitudes from participation in a transnational public sphere. For Habermas, "speaking from the street" with the intent *directly* to transform society stands as the absolute negation of communicative reason, not only of a "bourgeois" public sphere but also of *any* possible public sphere conceivable (Montag 141). The articulate defense in Saint-Domingue of all humans' unqualified right to universal emancipation from slavery negated such elitism, to demonstrate that, in the Age of Enlightenment and beyond, it was in the fields and towns of this peripheral colony that such a universal truth was most fully articulated. The year 1804 demonstrates the utter absurdity of the Kantian, Hegelian, and Habermasian visions of a multitude devoid of truly autonomous communicative reason. The creation of the nation of Haiti tried to *communicate* in the most logical and striking terms to an astounded world of slaveholding nations an idea that would take many decades for them to understand. This was a strictly logical argument of pure, undivided, and unqualified human rights, to which argument it was in fact *those putatively enlightened nations* who responded only with the most extreme violence (naval blockades, refusal of diplomatic recognition, extortion of payments, military occupation).

The Habermasian notions of the public sphere and communicative reason have been the object of intense and often dismissive criticism by critics such as Judith Butler and Peter Sloterdijk. Whether underscoring the "provincialism" of Habermas's Eurocentric viewpoint, or, more significantly, the inherent violence and intolerance of a process that forces participants to agree to certain ground rules and norms so that communication might proceed, such criticism is fundamental to any decentered, transcultural understanding of the public sphere.[40] Taking into account such critiques, there was, moreover, a historical example of a subaltern group participating in a transnational public sphere of the Enlightenment unknown or invisible to Kant, Hegel, or Habermas. This participation occurred not through the passive acceptance of an externally imposed transcendental definition of a concept such as *liberté*, but instead as a hegemonic struggle to *redefine* the very content of that notion as *liberté/libete*, through what Ernesto Laclau has called a process of "radical investment" (2004, 135). No doubt, in such situations as that of Saint-Domingue, this hegemonic fight over the content of the symbolic in a public sphere of debate leaves unexplored many other registers at which the struggle for emancipation occurred (most obviously, that of corporeal affects such as pain and suffering). Still, it is clear enough that such a hegemonic struggle did occur, and should be analyzed if we are even to begin to understand the importance of the idea of human rights in the development of the Haitian Revolution.[41]

What were the characteristics of this more inclusive transnational, subaltern "public sphere"? Historians such as Roger Chartier and Arlette Lafarge have drawn a picture of intense activity in the "plebian" sphere in revolutionary France, where, in Farge's words, "information gusted through [Paris] scattering gossip and rumours as readily as important news. People learned from what they saw or heard . . . ; opinions were modulated by news, and although news might be forgotten, the will to know and to have some grip on affairs remained" (60). While these authors have portrayed a domain operating alongside and in *reaction* to the bourgeois public sphere, the particularity of the "plebian sphere" in Saint-Domingue is that it explicitly and precisely did not "remain oriented toward the intentions of the bourgeois public sphere," as Habermas claims occurred for the French "plebeians."

Instead, Haitian slaves joined the discussion on universal freedom without an invitation, while drawing conclusions and insights that were antithetical to those of all other constituencies in both France and Saint-Domingue. These conclusions led directly to the destruction of the slave-based labor system in Saint-Domingue. Implementing the radical implications of Vodun culture and the experience of slavery, they reoriented debate and refused to allow the question of emancipation to be sidelined by the interests of those who dominated them. As Seyla Benhabib puts the matter (discussing the bourgeois public sphere's exclusion of women and their concerns from public debate), the Haitian slaves demonstrated that "the struggle over what gets included in the public agenda is itself a struggle for justice and freedom. . . . All struggles against oppression in the modern world begin by redefining what had previously been considered private, nonpublic, and nonpolitical issues as matters of public concern, as issues of justice, as sites of power that need discursive legitimation" (1992, 79, 84). Through the slaves' forced incursion into this discussion, an enlarged public sphere was formed that cut across all levels of society. Their incursion into the bourgeois democratic public sphere forced the discussion on universal freedom to include other, nonbourgeois publics.[42]

### Globalizing the Enlightenment: The Public Sphere of Discourse in Saint-Domingue

When news of the French Assembly's declaration first spread to the colonies, these putatively inhuman slaves were able immediately to ask exactly the right question: *who* is the subject of these "universal" human rights? If the answer—"We are!"—was obvious, if not to their "owners," to them and to us, they simultaneously perceived the contradiction between this insight and their own suffering and juridical and social exclusion. The news of the French Revolution came to Saint-Domingue in part via the huge influx of French sailors constantly arriving there, bringing news from Europe as interpreted from those sailors' predominantly exploited, proletarian standpoint. In 1789 alone, "710 vessels brought 18,460 mariners to the booming French colony" (Scott 50). This nomadic maritime community constituted a quasi-"enslaved" underclass formed by the violence of subaltern life onboard seagoing vessels, a life of forcible conscription, utter subordination, and strict, often arbitrary discipline.[43] Peter Linebaugh and Marcus Rediker, in their study of the revolutionary ideas of a transnational Atlantic proletariat, describe how the ship "provided a setting in which large numbers cooperated on complex and synchronized tasks, under slavish, hierarchical discipline in which human will was subordinated to mechanical equipment, all for a money wage. . . . The ship was . . . not only the means of communication between continents, but also the first place where working people from those different continents communicated. All the contradictions of social antagonism were concentrated in its timbers" (150). Sailors on shore in Port-au-Prince outnumbered both the white and free colored citizenry. These sailors, often remaining on the island for weeks and months, interacted extensively with the *petit blanc* and urban slave population of Saint-Domingue as they set up stalls on the wharves to barter goods they had brought from overseas (Moreau de St. Méry 1053, 315).

Linebaugh and Rediker describe in detail the complex multicultural and transnational environment of the New World waterfront and wharves and its role in the spread of revolutionary ideas in 1740s New York: "The docks and taverns, like ships, were places where English, Irish, African, Native American, and West Indian persons could meet and explore their common interests. The authorities could not easily circumvent the flow of subversive experience, for a port city was hard to police" (181). What is true today in Haiti was equally so in the Age of Enlightenment: "One of the most striking characteristics of Haitian everyday life is the ubiquity of market-places and traders." In colonial Saint-Domingue "up to 15,000 slaves traded on market day . . . in the Negro market in Cap-Français" (Lundahl 1979, 124). Undoubtedly, these transnational Atlantic sites were crucial in the development of an awareness of a common, universal concern for freedom. Both the ships and waterfront communities of the New World thus offer early-modern instances of an Atlantic multitude, neither a "people" united by a single common racial or cultural identity, nor an indistinct "mass" or "mob"; instead, these were singular individuals, each with his or her own identity and background, cares and concerns, yet their singularity persisted within the common concern for freedom that united them.

## 73  The Idea of 1804

Of course, news also arrived in Saint-Domingue in the form of print. One British traveler described the feverish excitement that greeted the unloading of a mailbag in a West Indian port:

> On the packet making the harbour it caused a crowd not unlike what you may have seen at a sailing or rowing match upon the Thames. Each wishing to be first, and all eager to learn the reports, the vessel was beset on every quarter before she could come to anchor, and the whole bay became an animated scene of crowded ships and moving boats. Many who could not go to the packet as she entered the harbour, repaired on shore to be ready, there, to meet the news. The people of town, also, thronged the beach in anxious multitudes. All was busy expectation. Impatience scarcely allowed the bags to reach the office. (cited in Scott 129)

In addition to such overseas sources of information, newspapers printed in the French West Indies sprung up, including forums solely devoted to reprinting news of the revolution and the debates of the assembly, thus multiplying the effective distribution of information exponentially, while assuring that within weeks of the start of the revolution, its events were known in Saint-Domingue.[44] "European books concerning liberty," wrote one administrator soon after the fall of the Bastille, "are circulating in St. Domingue" (Pluchon 43). In a letter of September 25, 1789, the governor general of Saint-Domingue, de Peinier, wrote to the navy secretary in France that "the news of what has happened in Paris and in the kingdom through July 20 are known through a multitude of brochures [*imprimés*], which at first caused some agitation.... Our primary concern is for the impression this news makes on the Negroes.... All that is done and written in the kingdom regarding the liberation of the Negroes enters the colony despite the precautions we have taken" (Pluchon 39).[45] In July 1791, two months before the slave revolt that would begin the Haitian Revolution, a procolonist paper such as the *Courrier politique et littéraire du Cap-Français* helped to spread the ideas of human rights throughout the colony, selectively reproducing the text of the 1789 Declaration, oblivious to the wider implications of their espousal of freedom of thought and the press.[46] The verbatim copying of the declaration in its heading ("The free communication of opinion is one of the most precious rights of man. Each citizen can thus speak, write, and publish freely, as long as he does so without abusing this liberty, as determined by Law") asserts to its readership the authority of objective, universal right, visually implying that it is a matter not of the opinion of a newspaper editor, but of objective Right.

On July 10, 1791, the *Courrier politique et littéraire* published a letter from a group of "négociants de Bordeaux" that renewed the call for the extension of universal rights. Might this paper have been one that a free black landowner such as Toussaint in the region of Cap Français subscribed to, and how might a free black such as himself have interpreted the logic of these "négociants de Bordeaux"? "Today, all the French, having been granted the rights of justice and equality, wish to be governed and at the same time protected by the principles of justice and equality.... These eternal principles, pure and simple like nature herself, can no longer be bent to the will of a particular class. What Frenchman can say: this [class of men] is unworthy of obtaining the rights we claim for ourselves?"[47] Such a pure logic of absolute rights and general liberty thus circulated freely throughout Saint-Domingue in the months leading up to the August 1791 revolt, to be echoed, absorbed, and reflected upon by an entire population.

The Saint-Domingue aristocrat Baron de Wimpffen's 1790 observations of the colony, for all their paternalistic condescension, document the movement of Enlightenment ideas among a population of slaves possessing a highly developed (oral) public sphere of discussion: "One has to hear with what warmth and what volubility, and at the same time with what precision of ideas and accuracy of judgment, this creature, heavy and taciturn all day, now squatting before his fire, tells stories, talks, gesticulates, argues, passes opinions, approves or condemns both his master and everyone who surrounds him" (cited in James 18). In a similar vein, Garran's *Rapport sur les troubles de Saint-Domingue* asserted that in the years before the 1791 revolt "the word liberty was in every mouth..., the signs [of political independence] everywhere on display." In such an atmosphere, and though, Garran asserts, we will never know exactly why the revolt occurred, "It would have been quite strange for the blacks alone to have been insensible to the sound of a word ["liberté"] that promised them a life so different from that in which they suffered" (2: 194).

This word, liberty, was everywhere in the air, and like Spartacus himself, Garran continues, the slaves of Saint-Domingue naturally applied its logic to their own circumstances: "It was the spirit [*génie*] of liberty alone that animated [the slaves Spartacus and Limigantes] to break their chains. It was no doubt the same for the black slaves of our colonies. As soon as the first news of the revolution was brought to St. Domingue, they caused there an enormous fermentation among the blacks, and from that moment it was no longer possible to restrain their movements otherwise than by the multiplication of punishments" (2: 194).

## 75  The Idea of 1804

Garran further develops this assertion in the opening pages of volume 4 of his study, arguing that the radical transformation of society undertaken in 1789 made it inevitable that blacks would join the debate on liberty:

> The revolution that had brought France from monarchy to a republican state, along with the aftershocks these produced in the colony, by placing even more than in 1789 the name of liberty in every mouth; the formation of clubs or their reestablishment in the principle cities of the three provinces; the public meetings held therein, where one spoke endlessly of liberty and equality; . . . all that happened in sum seemed to bear no other object than to remind the blacks of their rights to a common liberty. . . . The white colonists themselves, in their blindness, never refrained from propagating this idea, in describing all the agents of metropolitan France as philanthropists whose secret mission was to announce general liberty. (4: 29)

The constant reassertion of the need to subdue slaves through recourse to brutal force consistently betrayed the dominant class's fear that the huge slave population in Saint-Domingue would rebel against them. A letter from the Provincial Assembly of Cap-Français from July 15, 1791, in its attack on the extension of rights to mixed-race and free blacks, makes clear to anyone who cared to read the *Courrier politique* the process of terror used to subjugate slaves:

> In the colonies there must exist a class lying between the whites and the slaves, one which would make the latter aware of an immense space separating them from the whites. It is even necessary that the slaves never conceive the hope of becoming the whites' equals, and that their only desire be for emancipation granted by their masters as a kindness or compensation for their faithfullness. Gentlemen, the feeling we must impress upon our slaves must be such that it can keep six hundred thousand slaves subservient to sixty thousand free men.[48]

Any astute reader can sense the trepidation in this assertion of a brutal logic of power, and conclude, perhaps, that the slave population is by far the strongest in the colony, maintained in submission only through fear and intimidation. In fact, the letter ends with an uncanny prediction of the course of events that the planter's apartheid logic will bring about: "The agitation that we are witnessing can lead to a general explosion the effects of which would be terrible in its effects: were that to come to pass, we could only envisage a hopeless resistance, the colony itself transformed into a vast tomb."

The rapid expansion of the plantation economy in Saint-Domingue in the years before 1789 led owners to purchase slaves—often the most rebellious—from neighboring Anglophone islands; presumably these slaves, among them Mackandal, Boukman, and Henri Christophe, brought with them stories of the successful revolution that had overthrown English rule to establish the United States of America. Julius Scott describes how a network of itinerant free black and mulatto merchants and privileged urban slaves spread news of the French Revolution and its ideals from the docks and urban centers of Saint-Domingue to its plantations (Scott 45–46).

In the neighborhood of Cap Français called *Petite Guinée* because of the large number of free blacks living there, a Freemason's lodge called "l'Amitié [Friendship]" brought together citizens of different classes in the Masonic promotion of equality (Moreau de St. Méry 427). Though Masonic lodges in the eighteenth century, including those in Saint-Domingue, were open only to those able to pay their (often elevated) membership fees, they nonetheless promoted an ideology of universalism and democracy in the middle of a society characterized by the most radical discrimination and violence. It is thus significant that, as recent scholarship has shown, Toussaint Louverture was an active and high-ranking Mason, originally sponsored by his employer Bayon de Libertat, both before 1789 and as late as 1800.[49]

An extensive network of nomadic maroons who passed freely from rural settlements and plantations to urban settings and back also spread the ideology of emancipation throughout Saint-Domingue, instituting an anarchistic organization of Antillean society. "They were to be found everywhere on the public roads, in rural areas or in cities. . . . They were revolutionaries who stole (mainly from colonists' plantations or houses) what they needed for their subsistence. In a sense, their resistance to slavery was total." One can easily imagine how these nomads, who successfully refused all social structure and domination, served as a primary vector (of both information and as an example) for the transmission of a radical understanding of the human right and possibility of freedom. The leaders of the more sedentary maroon communities—who were generally also Vodun priests—also carried a message of freedom and revolt to the slaves they addressed.[50]

For all the paucity of historical documentation of this oral public sphere, we know, as Yves Benot reminds us, that the mulatto citizen Dodo-Laplaine was found guilty in 1791 of having "read the Declaration of the Rights of Man" to a group of slaves (139). How many other times did similar acts escape the notice of authorities? In a letter of October 31, 1790, Silvain Seguy de Villevaleix wrote from the plantation Breda (where Toussaint lived as a free black) of Ogé's rebellion, attributing it to the demand for the rights of man while simultaneously recognizing that such claims would perhaps inevitably be made by the much larger slave population: "If we only have these enemies to fear [the *mulâtres*], the harm should not be so great, but do we not have to fear as well those who surround us, just as interested as Ogé in claiming the rights of man?" (156).[51]

In a speech of December 1791 to the assembly, "On the Troubles in the Colonies," a defender of the planters' interests named Dumorier described the generalized circulation of antislavery discourse in 1790: "[Writings] calling for the insurrection of the blacks and the massacre of the whites circulated in the plantation workshops and were read there in night-time assemblies by black commanders, the same who turned out to be the leaders of the great insurrection" (31).[52] In 1792 an *Inquiry into the Causes of the Insurrection of the Negroes in the Island of St. Domingo* directly attributed the first slave revolt to the contradiction between the content of the *Déclaration* and the Assembly's refusal to extend its benefits to the slaves in its colonies.[53]

We know that when Sonthonax declared the abolition of slavery on August 29, 1793, the first article of his decree stipulated that "the Déclaration des Droits de l'Homme et du Citoyen will be printed, published, and posted everywhere necessary" (Césaire 213). Though we will never know how many Afro-Haitians read these postings or had someone else read them aloud, enough testimony remains to be certain that the declaration was discussed, analyzed, critiqued, and internalized by the hundreds of thousands of members of this public sphere in the years following its publication in 1789.

No censure of revolutionary texts even *attempted* to limit their flow into Saint-Domingue until December 1789 (Benot 138). The metropolitan planter's Club Massiac had only limited success in preventing free blacks and mulattoes from traveling to Saint-Domingue, and despite futile attempts to secure the ports to the flow of printed and oral information, news of the revolution fueled wild rumors of the abolition of slavery that spread throughout the island's nervous plantocracy during the fall of 1789 (Scott 166–69).

This public debate on liberty only expanded as the 1790s continued. Joan Dayan describes a civic theater that came to exist under Toussaint Louverture by the late 1790s, a now-official public sphere "adapted . . . to the social and political transformations of the colony" (186), while Sibylle

Fischer describes the 1796 play *La Liberté Générale*—commissioned in Saint-Domingue by Sonthonax—"that places in the center of revolutionary history the issue of slavery and the colonial question" (226). To what degree did this officially sanctioned public sphere further the discussion of human rights in the years leading up to the final defeat of the French in 1802–4? Such fragmentary evidence of the existence and functioning of a public sphere that cut across all classes of society in Saint-Domingue contradicts, at the very height of the Enlightenment, the Habermasian contention that the bourgeois public sphere was limited to a literate elite. Haitian slaves forced their way into this discussion from 1789 on and thoroughly radicalized the terms of the debate.

### Toussaint Louverture and the Symbolic System of Political Action

In casting Toussaint Louverture as a "spin doctor" of the Haitian Revolution, Deborah Jenson implicitly draws our attention to the shift in the locus of power that occurred in the period of the French Revolution. Like his French counterparts, Sièyes, Mirabeau, Danton, and above all Robespierre, Toussaint demonstrated a tactical mastery over the art of communication. As François Furet first argued in *Penser la révolution française*, the 1790s witnessed a social transformation in which mastery over symbolic political capital—the rhetoric of Liberty, Equality, and Fraternity—itself became a means of political power (56). Toussaint was able to assert hegemony over the unfolding events in Saint-Domingue because he combined the strategic military genius he has always been granted with a spontaneous and virtuosic grasp of the powerful role the ideology of universal human rights had suddenly come to play in international politics since August 25, 1789.

In Furet's reading, "The Revolution placed that symbolic system [of human rights] at the center of political action, and it was that system, rather than class interest, which ... was decisive in the struggle for power" (51). In a poststructuralist reading that has significantly influenced interpretation of revolutionary action since May '68, Furet argues that the signifiers of revolutionary rhetoric were entirely hollow and formal, having no social content. "Legitimacy ... belonged to those who symbolically embodied the people's will and were able to monopolise appeal to it. [And] ... the 'people' was not a datum or a concept that reflected existing society. Rather, it was the Revolution's claim to legitimacy, its very definition, as it were; for henceforth, all power, all political endeavor revolved around that founding principle, which it was nonetheless impossible to embody" (48, 51). For Furet, the Terror, as the abstract rule of contentless ideology, divorced from social reality, was the equivalent of the revolution itself (71).

And yet, I think such a view itself falls prey to the abstraction it condemns. Toussaint indisputably manipulated the discourse of human rights to consolidate power, and rightly so. Toussaint's actions retained a social and political core only as long as they were guided by a single principle: the universal abolition of slavery and the destruction of the plantation system that enabled it. Toussaint's limitations arose precisely when he began to abandon that fidelity in the late 1790s.[54] Placing for the first time the economic viability of Saint-Domingue above the criterion of universal emancipation, Toussaint thought that he could order Haitians back to the plantations by force without admitting that the destruction of slavery necessarily implied the radical refounding of an entire social system.

In the first years of the revolution, however, Toussaint had operated a radical shift in the sociohistorical understanding of universal rights, a hegemonic displacement of this discourse away from any European monopoly. "I am Toussaint Louverture. . . . I want liberty and equality to reign in Saint Domingue." In this short statement of momentous consequence, Toussaint had given a name to an absent plenitude: "Liberté." Spoken by Toussaint to his secretary, in Kreyol or French we do not know, "liberté/libete" was, in 1793 Saint-Domingue, the most abstract of concepts. "Liberté/libete" was precisely nonexistent, an utter abstraction, in this world of enslavement. Toussaint's intervention put to lie in a single stroke the assertion (still common today) that the language of Kreyol was a mere "pidgin dialect" incapable of abstraction.[55]

Rhetorical intervention here became constitutive investment, founding at once a political subjectivity, both singular and collective, and a singular universal. Without grasping the events of 1791–1804 under this logic of universal human rights, they bear no historical singularity, but remain merely unthought violence and bloodshed. Together, the idea of universal right and its singular implementation in Saint-Domingue formed a constellation that moved from a categorical imperative to the most singular experience of slavery, and back to the universal in the world's reception of that event. The events of 1791–1804 embodied the rights that the former slaves of Saint-Domingue clearly understood as perhaps no other people in the eighteenth century, giving them a singular and original form. The experience of slavery thus revealed the universal to arise not in any average comparison of all cases, but to dwell only at the heart of the most singular experience of violent disenfranchisement.

As a radical extension of the process of enlightenment—understood as the uncoerced public use of human reason—the Haitian Revolution was both a grandiose success and a failure. While I have argued in this chapter that it enacted a globalization and reconceptualization of the concept of universal human right, its ultimate limitation lay in the historical conditions of that process.[56] Since Haitian slaves could participate in this global discursive sphere only by asserting their rights through violence, they ultimately remained trapped within the logic of the very will to power that the public use of intersubjective, communicative reason in the Enlightenment hoped to overcome. While this paradox came to haunt the revolution before it was even completed, it should not blind us to the substantive contribution of the Haitian Revolution to the progress of human enlightenment and emancipation.

The Haitian articulation of this transnational public sphere open to all rational subjects was a momentous rupture in the early-modern world-system, a rupture that obliterated the slaveholding logic of eighteenth-century global capital. Its appearance was an effect of a concrete universal articulated in a highly specific historical and existential situation; its elaboration by half a million slaves on a "peripheral" Caribbean island furthered the Radical Enlightenment in identifying immanent human potentialities that remain largely unfulfilled two centuries on. The fidelity to the universal truth of human emancipation unleashed in the events of 1791–1804 began the difficult construction of an unqualified and *universal* freedom first concretized not in Philadelphia in 1776, nor in Paris in 1789, but in the new state of Haiti on January 1, 1804.

# 3 Penser la Révolution Haïtienne

> The grand, leading principle . . . is the absolute and essential importance of human development in its richest diversity.
> —Wilhelm von Humboldt, *The Sphere and Duties of Government*

TWO HUNDRED years ago, on January 1, 1804, the African slaves of the Caribbean island of Saint-Domingue defeated the greatest, most powerful army in the world (Napoleon's) in a successful guerilla war that for the first time forcefully extended the universal human right of freedom from enslavement beyond the province of Western Europe. As the preceding chapter argued, the Haitian Revolution must be understand as a radical interjection within a global system of knowledge, a system intimately linked to the early-modern world-system of agricultural capitalism. This chapter pursues that viewpoint to consider a series of geographically dispersed elements in this Enlightenment-era knowledge-system that conceptualized the inalienable human right to freedom: European natural rights theory and the 1789 *Déclaration des droits de l'homme et du citoyen*, the Kantian and Hegelian critiques of slavery, and Toussaint Louverture's politics of universal emancipation. The aim is to describe this "border gnoseology" (Mignolo) from a systemic perspective, to account for its disruptive force that broke through the hegemonic Enlightenment understanding of human freedom to encompass the perspective of the subaltern.

The previous chapter defended the hypothesis that the primary catalyst in the development of this transnational Enlightenment thought-system was the *Déclaration des droits de l'homme et du citoyen* of August 26, 1789. Alongside the American Declaration of Independence, the French Declaration was also a founding event in the history of human rights (as distinct from natural law): If various philosophical defenses of universal human rights had been formulated prior to this date, the French Declaration remains compelling because it was the first European attempt to implement and actualize such universal rights within an existing society.[1] As a properly global event that resonated far beyond its Parisian site of enunciation, both its universal truth (general emancipation) and its parochial failure (to abolish slavery) were dramatically revealed on the other side of the planet in the putatively "peripheral" events of the Haitian Revolution.

The scandal of Haiti is to have seized in 1791 a historical moment, as Lukács argued of Lenin, in which an intervention into the structure of society could truly hope to explode an entire system.[2] While in 1804 the global economic-political system had to make extreme efforts to repress the newly emergent Haitian society that threatened its very existence, by 1848 that same system was able to absorb the elimination of slavery due to the increasing availability of exploitable transnational labor (through recourse to indentured laborers from India and China in Guadeloupe and Martinique, for example). While there were of course numerous individuals who praised the Haitian Revolution and its principal actors (the most famous of which being Wordsworth in his sonnet "To Toussaint Louverture," an encomium to "man's unconquerable mind"), sympathetic and insightful analysis of the Saint-Domingue revolution as a singular and fundamental event in human history remained nearly impossible in a world whose very foundations continued to stand upon the global expansion of capital via slave-based labor and colonialism into the twentieth century. In the face of this predominant "unthinkability" (Trouillot), this chapter draws out certain explicit, more-often hidden and implicit Western attempts in the eighteenth and early nineteenth centuries to comprehend the concept of universal emancipation and its first instantiation in the Haitian Revolution not as scandal, but as a singularly progressive event of the modern age.

## From Natural Rights to Human Rights

From the periphery of the modern world-system, the Saint-Domingue revolution reoriented the essential debate of the Age of Enlightenment over what we now call human rights. To grasp the singularity of this decentralized critique of human rights from within the modern world-system requires contextualizing it within the European-based Enlightenment debate over natural rights. Although it is beyond the scope of this study to offer anything more than a coarse outline of the history of the concept of natural law and right from ancient Greece to the present, the originality of the Haitian contribution to the development of human rights can only appear in contrast to the fundamental claims of the Western tradition from which it departs.[3]

To begin, how is "natural right" to be defined conceptually? "Nature," like the attendant concept of natural right, is no unchanging essence, but a historically situated, temporal product of the human mind. In the case of natural right, the qualifier "natural" serves to postulate the existence of certain universal elements of law and right not limited to any particular human society. Natural law therefore stands in opposition to so-called positive law: the various situated, empirical codifications of law in any given social order. Since any postulate or analysis must occur within the finite limitations of human understanding, to qualify a law or right as "natural" is always to ascribe an ideological function to that law. Through the assertion that any particular right or law has a universal basis, law becomes the tool of political power (Trigeaud 160). To invoke the natural is to refer to an order of things transcending human intervention.[4] Whatever its specific determinations, the invocation of natural law or right is always an attempt to ground and legitimize the (re)structuring and policing of society through reference to a transcendental norm or foundation. To assert the "natural" rights of man is to wield a concept ideologically in the service of power, whether that power is the constituent power of a disenfranchised multitude (the *Tiers état* in 1789, Haitian slaves in 1791), or a constituted body (the State) that lays claim to "natural" rights for ideological (in the pejorative, Marxian sense) purposes.

The political invocation of natural law has been ambiguous since the ancient Greeks first theorized the existence of a justice in conformity with "nature." On the one hand, as the example of Antigone shows, reference to natural law was for the Greeks a progressive power insofar as it introduced a self-reflexive element of critique into social existence. Leo Strauss has powerfully formulated this inherent radicality of the invocation of natural rights:

> The acceptance of any universal or abstract principles has necessarily a revolutionary, disturbing, unsettling effect as far as thought is concerned, and . . . this effect is wholly independent of whether the principles in question sanction, generally speaking, a conservative or a revolutionary course of action. For the recognition of universal principles forces man to judge the established order, or what is actual here and now, in the light of the natural or rational order; and what is actual here and now is more likely than not to fall short of the universal and unchangeable norm. The recognition of universal principles thus tends to prevent men from wholeheartedly identifying themselves with, or accepting, the social order that fate has allotted them. It tends to alienate them from their place on earth. (Strauss 13)

To reflect upon the content of natural laws/rights is necessarily to call into question the doxa, the self-evident tradition-based norms of one's society, even if eventually to reaffirm those norms in a conservative-reactionary Thermidor.

Crucially, those traditional norms can no longer remain self-evident once they are confronted with the conflicting claims of natural rights, but must suddenly justify their validity. Whether this critical reflection upon the ontological norms of one's society first arose in ancient Greece, as thinkers such as Strauss, Hannah Arendt, and Cornelius Castoriadis have claimed, or in some other faraway land and time (say, the thirteenth-century Mali of Soundiata Keïta) is irrelevant in this context. What does matter is that wherever and whenever those transcendental norms have been invoked, in the Athens of Socrates and Antigone, Roman Jerusalem, Soundiata's Mali, Jefferson's Philadelphia, Gandhi's India, the Montgomery of Rosa Park, or Havel's Prague, their effect has been to call into question a given *state* of things. Reference to a natural order of justice offers a powerful and explosive ground and legitimation for normative claims to social justice for the subaltern, insofar as this norm transcends the law of any empirical legal order.

At the same time, reference to natural law/right has historically tended toward conservatism insofar as a justice in congruity with natural law was sought—from Aristotle to Aquinas—in the establishment of a social "balance" and "order" that would follow the putative "nature" of things and avoid "disorder" and disturbances.[5] Aristotle theorized this fealty to moderation and just proportion as a respect for the "nature" of things, a nature thought to be eternally dwelling in those things themselves, rather than conceived of by human reason. His defense of slavery in the *Politics* thus stands as the classic example of an "ideological" invocation of "nature": a given, historically contingent state of things (the Greek city-state's dependence upon slave labor) is defended in abstract, universal terms through reference to the philosopher's putative insight into the "nature" of things—some humans are by "nature" free, others slaves. Aristotle's logic is perfectly circular: "All men who differ from one another by as much as the soul differs from the body or man from a wild beast (and that is the state of those who work by using their bodies, and for whom that is the best they can do)—these people are slaves *by nature*, and it is better for them to be subject to this kind of control. . . . For a man who is able to belong to another person is by nature a slave (for that is why he belongs to someone else)."[6] Though Aristotle, like Aquinas after him, saw human nature as historically shifting (Sériaux 41–44), his call for the legislator to continually restore "balance" to society eternalized a contingent state of things (in which there are "naturally" slaves and masters) and merely asked what is the proper *proportion* of slaves to masters.

For Aristotle, humans were never understood as singularities, but rather generically; human nature is an essence, universally identical.[7] Human dignity is to be found in man's becoming congruent with an external, universal norm, rather than via a universally accessible process of becoming-singular. In contrast to the fundamental and radical assertion that all human beings are capable of exercising their faculties of reason and judgment regarding the problem of social justice, Thomas Aquinas, like Aristotle before him (and Leo Strauss after), sought to restrict the exercise of judgment on questions of right to a designated class of juridical authorities, an elite of the so-called "wise" (Sériaux 50–51).

It was Spinoza who first articulated a progressive concept of natural law as the undivided potentiality for the expressive singularization of all human subjects. Spinoza reformulated the ontological conception of natural law (as *jus naturale*) with utmost clarity and simplicity: "By *jus . . . naturale*, I merely mean the rules determining the nature of each individual thing by which we conceive each being as determined naturally to exist and to act in a certain manner" (2007, 195, translation modified). Natural law, in Spinoza's undivided universe in which all beings strive maximally to express their essential being, is universally operative; no ontological priority is to be attributed to human reason or society. The singular constructions of humanity (whether in extension or thought) are simply various modes of *natura naturata,* or the forms of nature.

> For example, fish are determined by nature to swim and big fish to eat little ones . . . by sovereign natural right. . . . There exists no difference in the nature of human beings and other natural beings, nor between those human beings who are endowed with Reason and others who do not know true Reason. . . . For whatever each thing does by the laws of its nature, it does with a sovereign right, since it is acting as it was determined to by Nature and cannot act otherwise. (2007, 195–96, translation modified)[8]

The consequence of Spinoza's univocity is to understand without moralistic judgment what will subsequently be called the natural "right" of humans to freedom from servitude, to understand this right simply as the form of natural law most appropriate (because most in comformity with Reason) to humanity, though this right bears no priority, or even applicability, to the natural world taken as a whole.[9] Simply, the construction of a universally emancipated society is the only one that will allow for the fullest realization of the human possibility to live in conformity with

Reason: "The State ... has been instituted to free everyone from fear so that they may retain, to the highest possible degree, their natural right to live and act . . . , to allow their minds and bodies to develop in their own ways in security, and to enjoy the free use of Reason" (2007, 252, translation modified).

Reason is, for Spinoza, not pregiven, but an inalienable *capacity* of human beings awaiting development and expression even in the most bestialized enslavement: "The mind, as far as it can, attempts to imagine what can extend or aid the power of action of the body."[10] This desire to fully express human reason, in turn, can only be realized as a political project of universal emancipation: "It is necessary . . . to construct a society such that the greatest number manage with the greatest ease and security possible to achieve such perfection" (cited in Misrahi 59). The second proposition of the *Tractatus politicus* asserts that humans maintain an inalienable capacity, in no matter how bestialized and enslaved a state, to imagine potential, perfect states of existence: "All that is real in nature [*res naturalis*] can be conceived adequately, whether or not the mind grasps it as existent" (1958, 267, translation modified).

In the passage of political thought from the ancients (from Aristotle to Aquinas and, *tardivement*, Pufendorf) to the "moderns" (Suarez, Grotius, Rousseau, Kant), the historical transformation of "natural" into "human" rights followed a conversion in the point of origination of those rights.[11] While for the former thinkers the source of natural rights lay in a "nature" external to the human mind, but which humans are capable of comprehending and striving to conform to, the modern conception of natural rights locates their origins in the human faculty of reason itself. The former *ontological* vision sees humans as thrown into a natural world they did not construct, heteronomous subjects of a "nature" inscribed by God to include the faculty of reason that allows Man, Aquinas argued, to act in conformity with "what is good and what is evil." Man is not the *source* of this law, however. On the contrary, according to Aquinas, he has rather to comply with "a law that was given to him" (cited in Sériaux 81). This natural *law*, imposed upon human subjects from a source external to their own faculty of reason, is therefore to be distinguished from natural or human *right(s)*, whose *origin* lies in human reason. Such an ontological understanding of natural law would persist in the thought of many revolutionaries of 1789, among them La Fayette, who in his famous speech of July 11, 1789, calling for a declaration of the rights of man, spoke of "the sentiments that nature has engraved on the heart of every individual."[12]

The articles on political and natural right in Diderot's *Encyclopédie* together articulated a heterogeneous analysis of natural law, bearing both traditional and modern dimensions. In the entry on *autorité politique*, Diderot presented a theory of natural law formally identical to that of Spinoza in its derivation of right from power, though the fundamentally conservative Diderot, unlike Spinoza, was careful to relegate this right of resistance to a transcendental context prior to the legality of contractual authority.[13] "Power . . . remains in force only as long as the might [*force*] of him who commands dominates those who obey, in such a manner that if the latter become in turn the strongest and overthrow their yoke, they do so with just as much right and justice as he who had first imposed it upon them" (cited in Proust 372). Unlike Spinoza, however, who refused to separate sovereign rights from individuals, his follower Diderot showed little interest in democracy, and sought in his political philosophy instead to safeguard the integrity of a sovereign authority within a political system that, though nominally grounded in the "power that belongs by right" to the *peuple*, would effectively prevent that right from any actual exercise (Proust 399).

Diderot's entry on *liberté naturelle* succinctly presented the abstract Enlightenment critique of slavery, while maintaining the traditional derivation of natural right from a transcendental source beyond the human faculty of reason. "Natural freedom" or "Droit natural," the article tells us in neo-Aristotelian terms, is given to all men by nature. It is "the first state man acquires by nature," and it "can neither be exchanged for any other, nor sold, nor alienated." This inalienable freedom is our birthright, one the article affirms in terms that will be echoed in the American and French declarations: "Naturally, all men are born free." Slavery is categorically invalidated by the article's logic: men "are not beholden to the power of a master, and no one can bear a right to them as property."

The authors of the *Encyclopédie*, like Montesquieu, Grotius, Pufendorf, and Locke before them (and the American and French revolutionaries of 1776, 1791, and 1795), attacked slavery by means of a single abstract, universal criterion: inalienable property rights.[14] *All* humans, Diderot wrote, are characterized by their *possession* of a natural "state of freedom," and the particularity of this type of property is precisely its inalienability.[15] Following this logic, it is therefore impossible for any human to alienate this freedom to a master, for to do so would make them into an animal, a logical impossibility. For the authors of the *Encyclopédie*, all humans are inalienably human in their (theoretical) possession of freedom, defined as "the power to enjoy as they wish their actions and goods." The logic of this argument, in its abstraction and refusal to consider contingent, qualifying, and discriminatory questions of history, culture, or race (that is, whether slaves are actually ready to be free, or are racially unqualified for freedom, and so on), took the immeasurable step of universally disqualifying slavery through the advancement of reason as enlightenment.[16]

Despite such high-minded idealism, it was immediately obvious to anyone who thought about the matter that in the real world of the eighteenth century, not all humans were free to "do as they wish" and "to enjoy their actions and goods." For all its vigor, this Enlightenment argument against slavery remained vulnerable to the devastating critique Rousseau would level at the *Encyclopédie* taken as a whole. The Enlightenment critique of slavery relied upon the weak force of a purely logical argument. It may well be that slavery is a logical impossibility, but the *Encyclopédie* as a project of abstract, rational enlightenment could only proceed with the weak hope that as people read its critique, slavery would vanish from the world, and that enlightened reason would make real existing slavery disappear as it uttered the spell that would conjure its disappearance. If slavery is undoubtedly the logical impossibility Diderot claims it is, readers were still confronted with the problem of its real existence after the appearance of the *Encyclopédie*.

It was here, amid the contradiction between enlightened reason and actually existing society, that Rousseau inserted his far-reaching formulation of a historicized, existential freedom. Within the context of the French Enlightenment, the passage from heteronomous natural *law* to rationally derived natural *right* (invisible linguistically due to the concepts' subsumption under the single French term *droit*) first occurred in Rousseau's critique of the abstract universalism of the philosophes. Rousseau was the first to perceive clearly the degree to which Diderot's *Encyclopédie*, in entries such as *autorité politique, droit naturel, humaine (espèce), population, esclavage,* and *liberté naturelle,* had put forward an empty, ahistorical conception of natural law.

Rousseau pointed beyond the static, heteronomous concept of natural *law,* toward the radical historicization of human experience enacted in the French, American, and Haitian revolutions. For Diderot, humans were distinguished not by their possession of free will, but by their universal faculty of reason (Hulliung 365–66). Rousseau, on the other hand, understood every human to be eminently free, what he called in the Second Discourse an "agent libre" (cited in Hulliung 365).

Like his theoretical mentor Spinoza, however, neither God nor an eternal human nature offered Rousseau the foundation of right. Instead,

Rousseau grounded human right in the contingent historical forms of society: "Right does not arise from nature; it is therefore founded upon convention" (cited in Vernière 481).[17] Glossing Spinoza, Rousseau put forth a radically novel notion of freedom and human being: freedom is not, as Diderot and other Enlightenment philosophes had argued, a natural and eternal essence of what it means to be human, but rather a historical and contingent human *potentiality*.[18] Human freedom and perfectibility are indeed inalienable, says Rousseau, but only as universally immanent possibilities awaiting their historical development in a just society (see Hulliung 67–68).

Humans are quite visibly and everywhere enchained and unfree in the actually existing world, Rousseau observed, and in contrast to the slavish alienation of modern society, a natural existence might well be preferable. But Rousseau was no defender of a return to nature; he repeatedly pointed out its impossibility and futility. Instead, writing in 1762, a generation before the French and Haitian revolutions, Rousseau observed the antinomy between the unfreedom he saw everywhere around him and the human freedom of which he could conceive, and his sweeping intervention was to imagine a social structure, a state and rule of law in which the latent and universal potential of human freedom could become actualized.[19]

The *Contrat social* presented humans as radically historical, "perfectible" beings, beings whose existence precedes their essence, beings who universally possessed the potential to become free in a social world that would develop this capacity. Recall Rousseau's famous words: "This passage from the state of nature to that of civil society produces in man a most remarkable change, substituting in his conduct justice for instinct. . . . Though he deprives himself in this state of numerous advantages that he receives from nature, he garners in exchange others so great, he exercises and develops his faculties, his ideas extend themselves, his feelings are ennobled, . . . to such a point [that] . . . he should forever bless the happy moment that tore him forever from that earlier state, and which turned him from a stupid and obtuse animal into an intelligent being and a man" (261). Following Spinoza, Rousseau argued that it was only in society that human beings could achieve the fullest development ("perfection") of their inherent possibilities.[20] Seen in this light, the development of the Haitian Revolution as a fulfillment of the Radical Enlightenment stands in contrast to the politics of the isolated, heroic "maroon" of the West Indian plantations, a fragile being constantly at the mercy of nature.[21] Human autonomy can only realize itself within universally just social relations.[22]

Rousseau's Spinozian view of human nature as a mutable, historical construct, and not some unchanging essence, would come to characterize the thought of many Jacobin revolutionaries. It received its most memorable formulation in Robespierre's project for a declaration of the rights of man and citizen submitted to the Convention on April 24, 1793. There, Robespierre sought to ground all social structures upon the inalienable human right to freedom. The latter he understood, in Rousseauian fashion, not as a static, unchanging absolute, but as the historical possibility of "the development of all his faculties" (cited in Gauthier 82). Grégoire spoke in similar terms of the historical possibility to "reconstitute human nature," while the Girondin Jacobin La Révellière-Lépeaux wrote that one might "modify the substance of man" (cited in Higonnet 137).

To become fully human, that is to say, to become free, was for Rousseau and his Jacobin followers a project, not a preestablished essence, one in which humans abandon a violent natural existence for an autonomy realizable only in a free society. Rousseau's was an exchange "of natural independence for freedom" (73). While his famous assertion that reticent subjects must be "forced to be free"—like the *Contrat social* itself—has been interpreted in many ways, to view it as extolling the terroristic obliteration of all difference and particularity under the abstraction of the General Will utterly mistakes its object.[23] Rousseau did not argue against the expression of "private passions" and "personal appetite,"[24] but rather spoke only of the "substituting" of "justice for instinct." *Private* passions and *personal* appetite are functions of *social* life. These only occur and develop (and, for Rousseau, overdevelop) *within* a society existing under some form of social contract.

Rousseau's political thought was instead concerned with the instinctual life of "nature," which he opposed to "justice." Thus, his critique was not directed to the whims and caprices of individual passion and appetite (which he of course critiqued elsewhere), but rather to the passage from the state of nature to that of society, a far more fundamental distinction prior to any decadence of the salons and philosophes. The instinctual, natural life that Rousseau wished to destroy was the opposite of justice, that is to say, a natural life characterized by the absence of the rule of rational Law. Rousseau condemned the violent destruction and domination of man over man in the state of nature, the enslavement of one human by another, and a state of universal war and terror. He called instead for the rule of law and for justice, rather than the exercise of raw power and might, whether in the form of arbitrary imprisonment in the Bastille or, proleptically, the threat that one be taken away at night and summarily executed as a "counterrevolutionary" by Robespierre and Saint-Just's Committee for Public Safety, by Toussaint (the summary execution of his nephew Moïse) or in twentieth-century Haiti by Duvalier's Tonton Macoutes.

In the world-systemic articulation, transmission, critique, and rearticulation of the concept of natural rights in the Radical Enlightenment, one could say that Toussaint Louverture stands in relation to the French Revolution as Rousseau had to the Enlightenment abstraction of the *Encyclopédie*. As Aimé Césaire observed in his 1959 biography, Toussaint carried forward an abstract idea into concrete reality (343).[25] Toussaint's understanding of human rights, arising as it did from the lived experience of actual—rather than metaphorical—slavery, reached beyond the insights available to Rousseau in one crucial dimension. Rousseau's conception of human rights remained limited by the unequivocal defense of property rights, a contradiction that would in fact remain unresolved in global modernity until its theoretical critique by Robespierre in 1793 and its practical subordination to human rights in Toussaint's 1801 Constitution. For while Rousseau steadfastly defended human rights as inalienable, since private property was counted by him among these inalienable human rights, a concrete critique of really-existing slavery remained unthinkable for the apostle of the social contract (Bloch 63; Sala-Molins). Only when the right to property became qualified (as explicitly not extending to *human* property) and subsidiary to the human right to freedom could human rights achieve truly universal extension.

Diderot's anonymous contributions to the 1781 edition of Raynal's *Histoire philosophique et politique des deux Indes* stand in marked contrast to the earlier idealism of the *Encyclopédie*'s logical critique of slavery. These later articles, with which Toussaint was intimately familiar, constitute instead a radical affirmation of Rousseau's call for social relations derived from the human capacity to construct society in consonance with a rational program of immanent justice. While the earliest two editions (1770 and 1772) of this canonical text of the Enlightenment public sphere had sold upwards of 25,000 copies, the 1781 edition created a true *succès de scandale* when it was banned thanks to Diderot's inflammatory (unsigned) contributions condemning tyranny and supporting the right to revolution.[26] Between its appearance in 1772 and 1789, the *History* was reedited thirty times. Nearly alone among Enlightenment thinkers, the Diderot of the *Histoire des deux Indes* stood willing (if anonymously, hidden behind the name of Raynal) not only to condemn slavery with fine logic but also to call for the violent overthrow of this system of human debasement: "I [the slave]," he wrote, "hold from nature the right to defend myself.... If you think yourself authorized to oppress me, because you are stronger and more adroit than I, do not complain therefore, when my vigorous arm shall open your breast to find your heart within" (193).[27]

In this new edition the book sold quickly, becoming one of the founding texts of the French Revolution, and the conservative, scandal-mongering Raynal (who, though forced into exile following the publication of his history of colonialism, had himself profited from the slave trade) came to be hailed as the putative "Father of the Revolution" ("Avertissement," in Raynal 7, 12). While chapter 23 of book 11 (attributed by Yves Bénot to Pechmeja) offered a weak and compromised call merely to "make the state of slaves more bearable" (178), the following section attributable to Diderot presented the famous forecast and justification of a violent slave revolution in the Americas that would "break the sacrilegious yoke that oppresses them" and the consequent call for a "great man ... [who] will raise the sacred flag of liberty" that inspired Toussaint Louverture (202).[28]

Diderot's intervention progressed beyond Pechmeja's compromised gradualism, moving somewhat confusingly between a Lockean view of freedom as property rights (to one's own person) and a purely rational condemnation of slavery based on "truths important for humanity" (184). Following Locke, Diderot defined slavery in terms of the human being as property; it is "the state of a man who ... has lost the property of his person and of which a master can dispose as if of a thing."[29] Diderot defined freedom as "the property of one's self [*la propriété de soi*]" (191). Of the three forms of freedom he identified (natural, civil, and political), the first was for Diderot the primary and distinguishing characteristic of humanity, since it is characterized by free will ("natural freedom is the right that nature has given to every man to dispose of his self as he wishes [*à sa volonté*]").

Freedom of the will had thus come by the time of his contributions to Raynal's *Histoire* to determine for Diderot the natural right of all humans against enslavement, insofar as this nature could never be alienated: "If there exists no power under the sun that can change my [bodily] organisation and bestialize me, there is likewise none that can dispose of my freedom" (192). For Diderot these human rights to freedom and the property of one's self are timeless and absolute, "eternal and unchanging." Finally, in this brief accumulation of arguments whose guiding principle is more rhetorical force than logical clarity, Diderot explicitly refused empirical arguments in favor of slavery (its historical and social predominance in human societies), to ask his reader instead, "Should one question in such matters social custom or one's conscience?" (193).

The Saint-Domingue revolution progressed beyond the European Enlightenment conception of human rights precisely at the point at which, in Diderot, and even more clearly for Kant and Fichte, rights were understood as a product of the legislative faculty of pure practical reason, independent of empirical circumstances (Bloch 67, 71). With Grotius's agnostic refusal to locate the source of laws in God, human reason had become (potentially) the origin of natural right. The genius of Kant was to have mediated these two extremes of an ontological natural *law* that each subject receives heteronomously and the universal faculty of constitutive reason. Yes, every moral subject finds herself subject to immanent laws of practical reason, just as each subject finds herself the bearer of the categories of pure reason, but the inherent, universal logic of these laws is that the subject must herself legislate the practical imperatives of her own freedom (insofar as they can conform with the test of universalization). "Act as though," Kant famously wrote, "the maxim of your action should be constituted by your will as a universal law of nature" (cited in Sériaux 84). In the passage from natural law to human rights, Kant moved beyond the ontological priority of law as a primary or first nature for what Hegel called "a second nature[,] . . . the system of right [as] the realm of actualized freedom" (1991, 35). At the same time, Kant explicitly sought to ban the violent overthrow of unjust societies, a complex problem to which I will return below.

In Saint-Domingue, however, the universal human faculty of judgment, which Kant wished to separate categorically from practical reason and limit to the domain of aesthetics, suddenly and startlingly (for the North Atlantic slaveholding powers) operated synthetically to unite the lived experience of human suffering ("Au compas de la souffrance," as Césaire described the moral logic of Negritude) with the pure categorical imperative of human emancipation.

This synthesis allowed Toussaint, for example, to write to Paris in 1797, when the reimposition of slavery began to menace the colony, of "the oath that we renew to you to bury ourselves beneath the ruins of a land reanimated by Liberty, rather than suffering the return of slavery." It allowed Toussaint to grasp the radical transformation of "Enlightenment thought" that had occurred in this peripheral colony in the 1790s: the slaves of Saint-Domingue spontaneously and autonomously understood a text, a phrase, a word they chanced upon in their daily existence ("Men are born and remain free and equal in rights" [*Les hommes naissent et demeurent libres et égaux en droits*]); they brought to bear upon it their universal faculty of reason, and this without *any instruction* from the so-called enlightened elite. "Can only civilized people distinguish between good and evil or have just notions about benevolence and justice?" Toussaint asked the Parisian Directors in another letter of 1797. "The men of Saint Domingue have been deprived of education; but precisely because of that they have remained closer to nature, and they do not deserve to be put in a separate class from the rest of humanity, and to be confused with animals."[30]

This practical application of universal reason was itself an act of emancipation, manifest not only in Toussaint's eloquent address but on the part of all in Saint-Domingue who analyzed and interpreted the words and phrases of 1789 for themselves, ideas that had circulated clandestinely for many years and had been posted publicly throughout the island in 1793. These enlightened subjects knew to ignore any doctoral exposition by the Parisian and plantocratic *maîtres* who repeatedly explained, in word or deed, that these were really only the rights of white, male, propertied classes; these slaves knew what the words they encountered meant. They needed no "enlightenment" from on high, but had only to invoke their (universal) faculty of reason and judgment. They consequently saw only what these words said, their pure logic: they were a call for the destruction of a world divided between the anointed who claim to know how society is to be organized and those who "naturally," as Aristotle put his defense of the institution of slavery, are destined to labor.

A text (the 1789 Declaration) placed between two intelligences, without the intercession of any enlightened *maître penseur* (à la Condorcet) to (mis)*interpret* it, suddenly opened onto the immanent utopia of a universal, undivided community of intelligences (see Rancière 1987, 66). This peripheral community fully demonstrated one of the principle claims of the Radical Enlightenment, that any and all humans are immediately capable of forming what Spinoza called "common notions," and that these ideas arise not from opinion, imagination, sensation, or even experiment. Such ideas, Spinoza argued, are proved not by the coherence of subject and object but from pure induction. They are formed by the creative power of the intelligence out of the pure collision of ideas, bypassing all doctoral interpreters with their certificates of analytical mastery. Such common ideas invert the traditional order of truth, not deriving it from empirical conditions, but rather starting from a truly adequate idea (one capable of universalization in the face of plantocratic totalitarianism) to then figure the empirical conditions for its implementation.

## Kant and Haiti

The philosophy of Immanuel Kant may seem a less than ideal apparatus for interpreting the Haitian Revolution. After all, though Kant defended the idea of the French Revolution in his writings of the 1790s such as "The Contest of the Faculties," he never wrote about the events in Saint-Domingue. Moreover, Kant explicitly and repeatedly denied the right of individuals to overthrow an unjust society by revolution. For Kant the French Revolution could serve only as a regulative moral ideal that would lead to "gradual reform in accordance with firm principles" (1996, 492). Repeatedly, in texts from the 1790s such as "On the common saying: That may be true in theory, but it is of no use in practice" (1793) and the *Metaphysics of Morals* (1797), Kant explicitly rejected the violent overthrow of the rule of law, no matter how unjust the latter may be:

> Any resistance to the supreme legislative power, any incitement to have the subjects' dissatisfaction become active, any insurrection that breaks out in rebellion, is the highest and most punishable crime within a commonwealth, because it destroys its foundation. And this prohibition is *unconditional,* so that even if that power or its agent, the head of state, has gone so far as to violate the original contract and has thereby, according to the subjects' concept, forfeited the right to be a legislator inasmuch as he has empowered the government to proceed quite violently (tyrannically), a subject is still not permitted any resistance by way of counteracting force. (1996, 298)

While Kant did condemn slavery unconditionally, he did so merely in formal terms essentially identical to earlier Enlightenment thinkers such as Diderot, terms that appear to leave the actual social institution of slavery untouched. "A contract by which one party would renounce its freedom for the other's advantage," he writes in the *Metaphysics of Morals*, "would be self-contradictory" (1996, 431). Because all humans are free by virtue of their autonomous reason—and Kant explicitly and repeatedly included as free *all* reasoning beings, regardless of genus, race, social practices and forms, or geographic origin (see also 417, 490)—slavery is for him categorically and a priori immoral in its attempt to deny the free nature of humans: "As with the Negroes on the Sugar Islands, . . . [a slave] will in fact have given himself away, as property, to his master, which is impossible" (472).[31] Clearly, Kant was aware of the existence of slavery in the Caribbean and the extent of its injustices, yet in his final statement on morality, *The Metaphysics of Morals,* he remained silent on what was to be done about it, content, like the *Encyclopédie* before him, to demonstrate its mere (logical) "impossibility."

Like so many moderate Enlightenment thinkers before him, Kant tried to avoid bringing the often highly subversive logical implications of his theoretical philosophy fully to bear upon the political sphere. Whether in good or bad faith, consciously or unconsciously, the authoritarian social habitus of eighteenth-century philosophers encouraged, if not outright pandering and submission to authority (Leibniz, Locke), at least the creation of a sense of uncertainty in the public sphere regarding the true radicality of one's ideas (Bayle, Fontenelle, Diderot and the *Encyclopédie*). The violent response visited upon thinkers suspected in the slightest of espousing "Spinozian" ideas made the public pursuit of critical philosophy a dangerous and complicated affair.[32] In response, moderate Enlightenment thinkers from Fontenelle, Newton, and Leibniz to Locke and Wolff, for all their differences, each sought to construct strictly binary conceptions of the universe, distinguishing in their various ways between an immanent realm subject to the mathematical predictability of natural laws, and a transcendent realm of divine intervention and the miraculous.

This binary ontology was more than a logical distinction: a clear parallel existed between the divine right of God to enact miracles and the divine right of kings (and the Pope) to make sovereign decisions in the name of the nation they represented. The appeal of Newtonianism in particular lay in its ability to integrate a unified mathematical model of the natural world with the theological imperative of a God unlimited by Spinozian necessity, a divinity acting freely upon matter but unhindered by its laws. In turn Jonathan Israel has argued, "Newton's overarching 'dominion of God' and notion of the constantly regulated, divinely supervised orderliness of the world, inevitably imparted a degree of legitimacy to the existing order of things as encountered in society and politics too.... In politics, Newtonianism encouraged, at the very least, a passive attitude, if not one of active veneration, for existing structures of authority and institutions" (Israel 518–20).

In contrast to such subservience, a diverse group of Radical Enlightenment thinkers such as Diderot followed Spinoza's assertion of a single, universal substance, the adherence of motion within matter itself, and the political corollary of these axioms that, as Spinoza stated, one must "preserve natural right in its entirety" rather than alienating it to a representative authority. These thinkers could publicly articulate such threatening and subversive views only with a good dose of subterfuge and obscurity, ranging from the anonymous publication of books with false dates, places of origin, and nonexistent publishers, to the famous system of *renvois* in the *Encyclopédie* and its smokescreen celebration of Newtonianism, the better to hide its more radical undercurrent of ideas.[33]

Insofar as he maintained a basic distinction between the noumenal and phenomenal, Kant was certainly no radical; his system was in this sense the true culmination of the moderate line of Enlightenment thought.[34] His practical philosophy, however, holds certain logical consequences that Kant's many public statements in deference to established authority can only partially paper over. The least that can be said is that Kant failed in the case of slavery and the global system enabling it to pursue the full implications of his own moral theory. His defense of the rule of law, of *any* rule of law, bowed down in servility before "the monarch"—the latter understood by Kant not as a human bearing rights equal to those of any other rational being, but as the (auratic) incarnation of the law itself: "Everything the monarch did, in his capacity as head of state, must be regarded as having been done in external conformity with rights, and he himself, as the source of the law, can do no wrong" (464).[35]

In deference to the law, any law, Kant disregarded the defense of the upright "dignity" of all humans that was the very foundation of his moral theory. An individual, he wrote elsewhere in the same work,

> must regard himself not only as a [biological] person generally but also as a human being, that is, as a person who has duties his own reason lays upon him, his insignificance as a human animal may not infringe upon his consciousness of his dignity as a rational human being. . . . He should pursue this end, which is in itself a duty, not abjectly, not in a servile spirit (*animo servile*) as if he were seeking a favor, not disavowing his dignity, but always with consciousness of his sublime moral predisposition. (557–58)

Though Kant's categorical refusal of the right to revolution seems straightforward enough, I want to argue that its enunciation stands in contradiction with other, perhaps more basic elements of his moral philosophy, and that we must therefore push on and read Kant against himself on the matter of slavery, applying Kantian moral philosophy to critique Kant's own personal political moderation and quietism. To begin to do so, we can look beyond both Kant's limitation of protest to the public sphere of verbal debate as well as his explicit rejection of the right to violent revolt, to ask instead whether these empirical prescriptions are in fact tenable within a properly Kantian moral philosophy.

To begin with, Kant's ban on the violent assertion of right directly contradicts one of the fundamental tenets of *The Metaphysics of Morals*: that "right is connected with an authorization to use coercion" (388). Under this chapter heading, Kant points out that freedom can only rightly express itself if it furthers freedom universally, in all others as well: "Whatever is wrong is a hindrance to freedom in accordance with universal laws. But coercion is a hindrance or resistance to freedom. Therefore, if a certain use of freedom is itself a hindrance to freedom in accordance with universal laws (i.e., wrong), coercion that is opposed to this (as a *hindering of a hindrance to freedom*) is consistent with freedom in accordance with universal laws, that is, it is right" (388).

In essence, Kant's abstruse formulation hides a radical defense of revolutionary violence; as we routinely decode the historical content of Hegel's *Phenomenology*, this statement should be read as a defense, conscious or not, of Robespierre and Saint-Just's Terror. For, no matter what his intent, Kant's logic tells us that the coercion of a master who dominates a slave and limits her human freedom would indeed be an expression of the former's freedom, but insofar as that expression of freedom is a "hindrance" of the freedom of the slave, it does not further the universal freedom of all humans, but only that of a single individual. In such a case, a "coercion that is opposed to this" primary coercion, say, the slave's revolt against the master to overthrow the slaveholding system that would deny her human freedom, "is consistent with freedom in accordance with universal laws." This Kantian logic should thus be read as a radical defense of emancipatory, revolutionary violence (see also Žižek 2008). Though Kant himself never explicitly argued for—or against—the right of slaves to revolt, the overthrow of slavery, in this view, "is right" insofar as it furthers the universal freedom of all humans as reasoning beings possessed of free will. This stands in contrast to the expression of the limited freedom of a single individual or group (the slaveholder or the class of slaveholders) who expresses his freedom only as an individual through the negation of an Other's freedom.

While this conclusion appears to fly in the face of Kant's rejection of the right to revolt, it might nonetheless belong "in" the Kantian system as a situation that is "outside" the moral compass of human society. In other words, slavery, as an inhuman relationship, does not occur within the basic social unit of a human "commonwealth"; the situation of slavery lies *before any possible social contract* in a state nature. In this, Kant echoes Diderot, who had proscribed popular revolt against the despot who acts against the General Will, but who, elsewhere (and anonymously) in Raynal, explicitly called for the violent overthrow of slaveholding society.

Similarly, Robespierre called for the death of Louis XVI while simultaneously and repeatedly arguing against the death penalty as a legal institution. This was no contradiction; rather, the king's flight to Varennes had in Robespierre's estimation returned France to a state of nature prior to any social contract. The mere continued existence of Louis, he claimed, made the foundation of a new, democratic state impossible and justified the "devoir d'insurrection" that he, unlike Kant, called for and repeatedly defended (2000, 195).

The question of slavery, as an institution occurring outside the bounds of rational, contractual society, proved for a whole range of Enlightenment thinkers from Diderot to Hegel to be the exception to their general proscription of popular revolution. In Kant's case, quite simply, the institution of slavery *as he understood it* (as "impossible" within any human society) is thus not admissible within his own prohibition of revolt. Kant's ban of revolution in favor of gradual reform depended crucially on the argument that one should never overthrow the rule of law by means that would regress to a state of violence (464). In Kant's understanding of the social contract, however, the rule of law depends on the (possible, rather than historical) accord of freely reasoning parties; in other words, the social contract can come to pass only as the (reasonable, though hypothetical) decision of human beings to live in society and not the state of nature. There can be no social contract, in Kant's formulation, between a freely reasoning human and an unfree natural being—a stone, say, or an animal subject only to the will of its natural instinct (1996, 296).

In this view, pitting Kantian moral philosophy against Kant's own empirical social analysis, the case of slavery would not be subject to the ban on revolt, because *there can be no rule of law when that law is premised on the bestialization of one of the "contracting" parties.*[36] Insofar as slavery as a "rule of law" (as in the French *Code Noir*) reduced slaves to the unfree property of a master, there can exist in the plantocratic state no conscious contract, since "a contract by which one party would renounce its freedom for the other's advantage would be self-contradictory" (1996, 431).

## Kantian Singularization and the Anthropology of Human Freedom

Though Kant never explicitly addressed the question of slavery in such practical terms (that is, as an actually existing human institution), his philosophy of human freedom sheds light on the radicalization of the revolution in Saint-Domingue insofar as he unambiguously condemned not only slavery but also imperialism itself in its denial of the autonomous self-determination of certain groups of human individuals. As Sankar Muthu has shown, the received understanding of a Kant who promoted an abstract notion of reason based on European social norms is mistaken. Kant explicitly condemned Western imperialism and colonialism based upon the universal grounds of his moral system as "a veil of injustice . . . to be repudiated" (Kant 1996, 417; see also 420, 490). Moreover, while Kant's notion of human freedom is universalist in form, it can only ever instantiate itself in the world through the expression of *difference,* through the free articulation of human singularity, in which humans spread across time and space express their freedom in the infinite variations that differentiate human societies from instinctual nature (Muthu 130). Such a reading of Kant puts in question the often-repeated critical commonplace that, as Seyla Benhabib has claimed, "Kantian ethics is *monological,* for it proceeds from the standpoint of the rational person, defined in such a way that differences among concrete selves become quite irrelevant" (1986, 300).

In contrast to such a view, Kant's "Anthropology" offers an empirical study of humans in the fullness of their differentiation, the free creators of their social existence; it is the study of "what the human being as a being of *free activity* makes, or can and ought to make, of himself" (*was er als freihandelndes Wesen aus sich selber macht, oder machen kann und soll*) (1968, 119; my emphasis). Kant recognized no hierarchy within the various empirical instantiations of human diversity save one: the degree of autonomy of any individual or community.[37] "The most important revolution within man," he concluded in the *Anthropology,* "is 'his leaving the tutelage for which he himself is responsible'" (1974, 97). In light of this single overarching criterion of enlightenment, one that recognizes neither racial, nor political, nor historical criteria by which to judge the various civilizations of planet earth, Kant explicitly celebrated the "infinite variety" of the "great diversity of men" (96).

Though, as Kant repeatedly argued, we cannot *prove* the freedom of our empirical actions, such freedom nonetheless constituted the fundamental and universal *presupposition* of his investigation of creative, human action (44). Kant did not celebrate pure difference as difference in itself, "anthropology" as a purely relativistic investigation of what he derisively called "local" practices. Instead, he drew attention to the ontological foundation of all human singularization, a process he called the development of "character" (*der Charakter der Person*), a "higher faculty to make use of the faculties and capacities" for human differentiation and specification (cited in Stark 28).

Human beings are typified for Kantian anthropology not by their universal rationality, but rather by their contingent "capacity for reason," what Kant (like Rousseau and Condorcet) called the capacity of human "perfectibility."[38] Kant's affirmation of the *impossibility* of defining the essence of human nature should itself be understood to constitute the ontological nature of human (or any reasoning) beings: their radical and universal openness to constant self-redefinition and cultural creativity. We will never be able to totalize our knowledge of human psychology and behavior to the point where we could predict human actions as we can predict "eclipses of the sun and the moon," but this impossibility is itself testimony to a universal empirical freedom for rational self-redefinition (cited in Alan Wood 2003, 45).

Rather than the abstract (European) universal it is often taken for, Kantian universalism is precisely the apperception of a universal freedom possessed by every individual and community to define themselves in their differential singularity.[39] This Kantian universalism is linked in turn to a descriptive anthropology of human difference and multiplicity, one that explicitly rejects the contingent empirical injustice of imperialism. Furthermore, Kant enunciates a prescriptive universal moral imperative for the singularization of every individual as an end in herself. A Kantian anthropology of universal human creativity would point not only to the rare, revolutionary moments that reconfigure human history,[40] but to the often indiscernible micro-Events that occur each day throughout human societies, moments in which the transcendental spontaneity of human imagination breaks free from the dominant state of things.

Kantian humanity is characterized by its capacity for self-transformation, for "enlarging our talents," which Kant, following Rousseau, called the cultivation of "perfection" (56, 518). Kant defined humanity through three characteristics. While *animality* refers to a human being's existence as a biological fact of nature, and *humanity* is the capacity of humans to freely produce their cultural existence (what one could call, following Cassirer, the production of symbolic forms), *personality* refers to the human being as "an end in itself," a being that can have no "price" (557).[41] It is worth quoting Kant's distinction at length:

> In the system of nature, a human being (*homo phaenomenon, animal rationalis*) is a being of slight importance and shares with the rest of the animals, as offspring

of the earth, an ordinary value (*pretium vulgare*). Although the human being has, in his understanding, something more than they and can set himself ends, even this gives him only an *extrinsic* value for his usefulness (*pretium usus*); that is to say, it give one man a higher value than another, that is, a *price* as of a commodity in exchange with these animals as things. . . .

But a human being regarded as a *person*, that is, as the subject of a morally practical reason, is exalted above any price; for as a person (*homo noumenon*) he is not to be valued merely as a means to the ends of others or even to his own ends, but as an end in itself, that is, he possesses a *dignity* (an absolute inner worth) by which he exacts *respect* for himself from all other rational beings in the world. He can measure himself with every other being of this kind and value himself on a footing of equality with them. (1996, 557)

For Kant, Personality thus refers to the "dignity" of every human being, to "humanity insofar as it is capable of morality"; a human being, understood as personality, can have no value as a commodity (as a slave to be bought and sold in the marketplace), nor can his labor (his "skill and diligence") be a mere object of instrumental use (say, to produce more cotton or sugar). "Personality" stands opposed to animality insofar as the former is for Kant "freedom and independence from the mechanism of the whole of nature"; and yet the human as personality is nonetheless "subject to special laws—namely pure practical laws given by his own reason" (Kant 1996, 210).[42] As a result, while humans as animal beings are universally subject to the same natural laws (of nutrition, procreation, sickness and mortality), "a person belonging to the sensible world is [nonetheless] subject to his own personality insofar as he also belongs to the intelligible world" (cited in Muthu 139).

Humanity as personality, what Kant called *Homo noumenon*, humanity as a *ding an sich*, can never be a mere means, but must always be an end in itself. As such, Kant necessarily implies that all three dimensions of human existence (animality, humanity, and personality) must be protected and cultivated—and in all three dimensions, the case of slavery fails this Kantian test. The human as biological animal must obviously be preserved as a mere existence out of which humanity and personality may arise. Humanity, the capacity for autonomous self-definition of every human individual and community, must not be eliminated (as in the erasure of African cultures in the Middle Passage) or used as mere heteronomous means of production. Finally, personality as universal moral reason must be cultivated so that "as a person (*homo noumenon*) [a human being] is not to be valued merely as a means to the ends of others or even to his own ends, but as an end in itself"—because the instantiation of this norm is the measure of autonomy itself. Freely giving oneself a norm that passes the test of universalization (I wish not only my own freedom to determine my existence, but that of every other rational being to do the same) must be the measure of a truly moral action.

It is crucial to avoid construing Kantian *personality* as a form of humanism, for if practical moral reason were merely the capacity of a certain empirical species, all those not included in that taxonomic category at a given historical moment (such as putatively "subhuman" African slaves) would be excluded on empirico-historical (racist) rather than logical-moral grounds.[43] Instead, Kant repeatedly construed his conception of universal moral reason as applicable to *all* reasoning beings, human or otherwise (though Kant himself knew only of reasoning *humans*): "because moral laws are to hold for every rational being as such, [they must be derived] from the universal concept of a rational being as such" (1996, 65).[44] In an age when Europeans increasingly came to define Africans as bestial Others, Kant reversed this order of attribution. Since Kant sought to prove freedom "as a property of all rational beings," it could not be derived "from certain supposed [empirical] experiences of human nature," for to do so would have rendered it dependent and secondary, a clear contradiction of the concept of autonomy.[45] For Kant, it was not an empirical classificatory scheme (as for Moreau de St. Méry or Gobineau) that determined an individual's humanity, but rather a universal norm and a priori principle.

Following Jacob Rogozinski, I would argue that the Kantian *person* cannot be understood as the autonomous human subject who would produce his freedom through a (quasi-Sartrian) *project* (171). Opposed to the inward narcissism of the subject is the universal moral Law itself: not someone's law (the empirical law of the Master), but moral reason itself, to be determined in every singular case by the test of its own capacity for universalization. Kantian personality is the systematic practice of despecification from prescriptions of social identity and normativity. The Law can be derived neither from an empirical order (code) nor from a constituted Subject. Personality, as the participation of every singular being in (potentially) universal reason, is always already beyond the individual. Personality is a common characteristic, a feature of every reasoning being, yet it is achievable only as a universal singularization of freely reasoning beings. Kantian personality can no more be directly derived from the self (as for Sartre), than from the Other (Ricoeur, Lévinas) (177). Personality cannot be a fully embodied positive characteristic of humanity (a normative phenotype); not only would this render moral reason a secondary derivative of a contingent empirical given (that is, heteronomous), but it would erase the singularity of every free being beneath a homogenized identity. Kantian universality explicitly rejects such a homogenization, considering universality to arise only as universal singularization.

Among the fundamental theoretical claims of this book to be derived from an examination of the Haitian Revolution is that *personality as singularization is a transcendental condition of autonomous experience.* This ground is a condition of experience that precedes any historical, cultural, or even biological distinction between the self and an other. The Law is not to be understood as the law of an Other (the Master) or even of the Self, but as the transcendental a priori condition *allowing* for autonomous singularization and despecification. This Kantian Law is virtual, in the Deleuzian sense. It does not say what one will become (the Human is not a predefined essence), and certainly not that one can simply become anything one wishes in defiance of one's situated historical constructedness, but rather consists in the potentiality for autonomous self-definition within the parameters of any given situation. In the case of Saint-Domingue, the law of universal human perfectability did not predefine what specific form freedom would take, but rather offered the possibility for reasoning beings to define and instantiate their singularity (through, say, a universal ban on slavery in a novel political structure).

Does Kantian "personality," understood in this way as a transcendental condition of human freedom, remain within the limits of a philosophy of immanence? Attention to Kant's argument in the *Groundwork* supports such a reading. After putting forward his fundamental claim that moral action cannot be based on any empirical results, on its "usefulness", but rather on its a priori universality, Kant comes to speak of a "respect" for the law (*Achtung furs Gesetz*). Under this law, the human being "is subject *only to laws given by himself but still universal*" (82; Kant's emphasis). This respect, if it is not owed to any *being* outside of ourselves (whether god or man), can only be understood as virtual, as an ontological ground preceding and allowing the historical, contingent specification of any ontically singular human being, the science of which specification Kant calls "anthropology." In the introduction to the "Doctrine of Right" in the *Metaphysics of Morals*, Kant defines moral law precisely as the general, preexisting ontological *conditions* that allow for free human action and self-determination: law is "the sum of the conditions under which the choice of one can be united with the choice of another in accordance with a universal law of freedom" (cited in Balibar 118).

To read Kant in Heideggerian terms, we find ourselves thrown into the world, cast into a space in which we find that we have a certain (ontological) capability freely to specify and develop ourselves as human singularities.[46] "Human freedom," Heidegger says in speaking of Kant, "is the freedom that breaks through in man and takes him up into itself, thus making man possible" (2002, 93). Kant's lengthy footnote in the first pages of the *Groundwork* is crucial: "What I cognize immediately as a law for me I cognize as respect, which signifies merely consciousness of the *subjection* of my will to a law without any mediation" (56; Kant's emphasis, translation modified). Though we can redefine and shape the modalities of our existence, we cannot choose to have the *possibility* to do so. This most human faculty must remain a noumenal mystery. "Even as to himself, the human being cannot claim to cognize what he is in himself" (98). What Kant calls respect, therefore, is ultimately to be accorded not to any human or divine master (though in practice, Kant did not always respect this injunction), but to the existence of this open-ended possibility of self-determination. This potentiality is that of "the development of all natural capacities" and of what he calls our capacity for the "enlarging of our talents" in unforeseeable directions through the exercise of reason (cited in Balibar 123).

How might we figure this ontological ground of a human opening toward freedom? Kant explicitly refuses to offer any positive content in his assertion of the immanent reality of human freedom. This, I think, is the true importance and value of his unapologetic defense of "formalism": we must remain "without the least pretense to think of it [free will] further than in terms merely of its *formal* condition" (1996, 104). We cannot attribute to freedom any a priori content or empirical being, for that would contradict its open-endedness; instead, this limitation of freedom "is only a negative thought with respect to the world of sense: it gives reason no laws for determining the will and is positive only in this single [ontological] point: that freedom as a negative determination is combined with a (positive) capacity as well . . . , a capacity so to act that the principle of actions conforms with the essential constitution of a rational cause, that is, with the condition of universal validity of a maxim as a law" (104). Any action can be considered moral only if it demonstrates the universal capacity of humans for their own self-definition.

Kantian freedom, this ontological ground of human singularization, is properly *virtual*. Deleuze's distinction between the virtual and the possible allows us to characterize more precisely this immanent ontological clearing in which human freedom can appear. In *Différence et répétition*,

Deleuze writes that "structure is the reality of the virtual" (270). The virtual "does not oppose the real" because it is simply another *mode* of the real, that is to say, the world's reality as structure (see May 71).[47] If we were to understand the difference between the virtual and the possible not as that of, respectively, true and false concepts (as Deleuze often implies), but rather as two different modes of understanding the world in a philosophy of immanence, an unexpected twist occurs. The virtual would constitute the immanent, historically evolving *ontological* ground that enables any ontic becoming-singular, comparable to an open-source computer system code, or to the development through natural selection of the genetic code that enables and determines the becoming-singular of any biological being. The possible, in such a philosophy of immanence, would then occur not in some transcendent Beyond or as the mere illusion of representation, but rather would appear, in time, as the multiple, unpredictable, and contingent *ontic* instantiations of singularity that may come to be in any being.

Such a reading of human freedom itself lies virtually encoded within Kant's practical philosophy. This immanent universality of freedom as a virtual possibility for autonomous self-definition is at once historical (as a fact of human evolution), contingent (there are some humans who are not born with such a capacity, nor are all, through circumstances or personality, able or willing to develop their innate capacities), and immanent (as the biological capacity of human animals to reason and act in ways not predictable from the state of any situation). No humanism, it instead follows Foucault in "plac[ing] within a process of development everything considered immortal in man" (1977, 153). The *capacity* for autonomous singularization, while forming the ontological, transcendental ground to any ontic becoming-singular, is nonetheless frail and furtive, bound to time, history, and its own mortality in the moment it is thwarted or extinguished in the violence done to any individual, community, or species. But can we agree with Foucault's conclusion that "nothing in man—not even his body—is sufficiently stable to serve as the basis for self-recognition or for understanding other men" (153)? Can we recognize in all others, not a phenotype (as for Fichte), but the (historical, contingent) *capacity* to distinguish and singularize themselves?

Singularization must, in the end, be understood as a process transcending mere human reason, and indeed transcending reason itself, as Kant understood it. As Kant hinted at in his "universal concept of a rational being," the localized expression of reason on planet earth as the capacity of humans to freely determine the parameters of their existence is merely one possible mode of singularization. No friend of Kant, Nietzsche nonetheless pointed out "the humor in the fact that man regards himself as the goal of the existence of the world and that humanity, quite seriously, is only satisfied with the perspective of a universal mission. If a god created the world, he created man as the *ape of God*, as a source of perpetual amusement in his overlong eternity.... This drop of *life* is without importance in the general character of the immense ocean of becoming and perishing" (227–28). Freedom as singularization is closest to what Deleuze called "*différanciation*": "the actualization of a virtuality," of "all the individuating differences or intrinsic modalities" of Being (1967, 267, 53). From birds to bees, plants to planets, singularization is the actual, unpredictable instantiation of the infinite possible modes of Being.

In the final pages of the *Anthropology*, Kant conceded that "the problem of indicating the nature of the human species is quite insoluble" (1974, 183). In light of the impossibility of comparing our species with any other possessing the faculty of reason, Kant reiterated the criterion of "perfectibility" that he took from Rousseau: "All we have left, then, for assigning man his class in the system of animate nature and so characterizing him is this: that he has a character that he himself creates, insofar as he is capable of perfecting himself according to the ends that he himself adopts" (183).

Kant's defense of human dignity as an unhindered potential for singularization allows one to perceive the radical reformulation of universalism at work in the Saint-Domingue revolution. Did any being or group (including the slaves of Saint-Domingue)—regardless of phenotype or geographic origins, be they man, ape, or extraterrestrial—"so act that [they] use humanity [not here the empirical species, but all beings capable of reason] always at the same time as an end, never as a means" (80)? The humanity of the revolutionary slaves of Saint-Domingue was not to be attributed—or denied—externally by others, but instead concretized through their own actions as autonomous beings proceeding in accord with a universal norm of human autonomy: all humans must be free. The attribution of humanity in Saint-Domingue was not to be granted by others, but instead *demonstrated,* through the singular act of autonomous self-definition that was the Haitian Revolution and declaration of Haitian independence of January 1, 1804.

The Imperial Constitution of Haiti promulgated by Dessalines in 1804 clearly articulated, as Sybille Fischer has shown, the interdependency of Enlightenment universalism with the cultivation of singularity that I am arguing grounds a Kantian interpretation of the Haitian Revolution.

Fischer's *Modernity Disavowed: Haiti and the Cultures of Slavery in the Age of Revolution* addresses the Haitian Revolution from both the transnational perspective first investigated in David Geggus's *The Impact of the Haitian Revolution in the Atlantic World* and via the specificity of the Haitian negotiation of the competing claims of universality and particularism implicit in the events in Haiti itself. Her analysis charts the archival and literary traces of the impact of the Haitian Revolution in nineteenth-century Cuba and Santo Domingo. There, the threat that the victorious Haitian Revolution might spread to those slaveholding lands manifested itself in explicit denunciations of the Haitian revolutionary sequence and in racist invective against dark-skinned Haitians in both literature and political tracts.

Fischer marshals a complex psychoanalytic typology of trauma and its discursive delays, repetitions, and suppressions to show how the events in Haiti were paradoxically figured as "the unspeakable, as trauma, utopia, and elusive dream" (2). She demonstrates that the Haitian Revolution and its radical politics of antislavery have been repressed in predominant accounts of Western modernity, while arguing that an awareness of their singular contributions to modernity transforms our understanding of the centrality of race and politics in the West. "Approaching Haiti," she writes, "through the records that have informed Western narratives—the records of Haiti's most immediate neighbors, Cuba and the Dominican Republic, but also the records in the European metropolises—allows for the kind of reflection on the operations of suppression and denial that purely structural or empiricist accounts would most likely preclude. It is in light of the intellectual, political, and cultural efforts that were necessary to make the slave revolution of 1791 to 1804 vanish from respectable modernity that we can come to recognize what was really at stake" (273).

The most original contribution of *Modernity Disavowed* to our understanding of the Haitian Revolution is its analysis of the various constitutions promulgated in the period, beginning with that of Toussaint Louverture (1801). Taken as a whole, these constitutions legally instituted the unqualified abolition of slavery while doing so within the transnational context of continuing slaveholding regimes throughout the West that actively attempted to limit their practical extension. As such, Fischer argues,

> We should not discard these constitutional texts as irrelevant chimeras of elite ideology, but rather read them as fantasies of statehood or foundational fictions ... that need to be scrutinized with careful attention to tone and implication. That they are ideological conceits does not mean they were not constitutive

of reality. . . . Viewed from this perspective, the early Haitian constitutions function more like declarations of independence than legal codes; they are expressions of aspirations and desires that went beyond any given political and social reality. (229)

"All mortals are equal," the preamble to Toussaint's 1801 Constitution states. This equality, however, is manifested not by the *erasure* of particularity, but by its flourishing: the "Supreme Being . . . has scattered so many kinds of different beings over the surface of the globe for the sole purpose of manifesting his glory." "The preamble," Fischer observes, "sketches a conceptual frame in which equality and difference, universalism and identity-based or historical claims, show themselves as intimately linked and indeed inseparable. Universalism and particularism continuously refer back to each other—racial equality cannot be achieved without particularistic claims, and particularism is ultimately justified by a claim of universal racial equality" (231–32).

Fischer's analysis of the Haitian constitution's invocation of a singular, differential understanding of universalism portends a Kantian analysis of the Haitian Revolution. Kant's ethics of universal singularization affirms that no individual is automatically to be presumed to be human; each must cultivate the capacity for humanity latent in every reasoning being and community, the capacity to become a freely self-determining entity. In turn, this freedom is no mere culinary inwardness of the self-same subject (as individual or nation); the recognition of one's freedom can arise only through the cultivation of a universal moral process: the autonomous singularization of every reasoning being (individual or community) as the only possible grounds for the existence of humanity.

It is essential to note certain limitations of Kantian moral philosophy in the context of the defense I have constructed here. Most obviously, as stated above, this defense is only "virtual," operating through a concatenation of disparate elements of Kantian philosophy—moral, political, historical, anthropological—that Kant himself leaves isolated from one another. More significant, one might argue that this compartmentalization is not merely contingent; that is, that had Kant had a few more years in his long productive life, he would have brought these strands together in something like the fashion I have done here. Rather, in its formalism that seeks to disqualify all empirical considerations from moral judgment in a pure ethics of conviction (*Gessinnungsethik*), Kant allowed questions of human rights and dignity to encompass only humanity in its abstract identity, limited to the domains justice and abstract right.

Though I have argued that this dignity can be understood only as the flourishing of autonomous singularization, Kant himself relegated this process to his "anthropological" lecture classes (and only hastily wrote up his scattered reflections on the subject at the very end of his career). This focus on what Carol Gilligan and Seyla Benhabib have called the public, juridical rights of the "generalized other" are the subject of what a recent volume groups as his "practical philosophy." Though these texts may well admit that humanity is constituted of singular individuals, they nonetheless systematically restrict these "anthropological" differences to the private realm of friendship, caring and solidarity (Benhabib 1986, 341). Kant maintained and reinforced the Hobbesian distinction between public rights and civic and domestic intersubjective responsibilities, limiting, in this view, the scope of moral and political autonomy to the abstract universal subject, sidelining to the private domain, if not silencing altogether, the particular claims of singular individuals. The claims of women and minorities were in this way depoliticized and actively suppressed by Kant, who codified and formally justified in this way white, male hegemony.[48]

Similarly, Kantian moral philosophy inaugurated and codified a philosophy of productive subjectivity, in which the subject was understood as the autonomous producer of its universalizable maxims. Incontestably, the dimension of intersubjectivity exists in Kant's writings, but it as well remains bracketed: discussion of the concept of publicity and the public sphere is itself deprived of the nobility of a "Critique of Public Reason," and is instead relegated to Kant's epiphenomenal, journalistic texts. Autonomous practical reason is for Kant a productive faculty that cannot be subservient to opinion and discussion; for all Kant's vigorous defenses of publicity, the public sphere remained for him a realm of empirical experience, not pure practical reason. As has been endlessly documented from Hegel to Habermas, Kantian philosophy cannot account for the public nature of all moral claims, for their status as products of symbolic exchange in which all practical reason is always already mediated, and in which all public language acts enter as well into the intersubjective process of interpretation and implementation that is the struggle for ideological hegemony (see Benhabib 1986). Kant cannot account, in other words, for the radical productivity of public reason, in which participation in the public realm itself allows for the self-constitution of new, unheralded subjects of universal right.[49]

Kantian practical philosophy cannot account for the fundamentally historical nature of moral reason; in other words, the fact that moral reason as Kant himself understood it depends upon the historical appearance of the autonomous (bourgeois) subject. The putatively autonomous activity of moral reason bears—and must bear—an indissolvable element of heteronomy and subjection to the "empirical." Quite simply, if any action following the categorical imperative were not to some degree predetermined by the empirical qualities of the object of that action (its suffering, its inherent potentials), the categorical imperative could never be more than the same exploitation and manipulation of others it hopes to overcome: the self-serving aestheticism of Hegel's "beautiful soul." A pure moral action resulting only from rational considerations would violate the categorical imperative to treat others as ends in themselves, not as the mere means for completing one's own universalizable moral actions.[50]

While such well-rehearsed and familiar critiques of Kantian moral philosophy must certainly be acknowledged, my argument has been that to consider Kantian philosophy as inapplicable to the Haitian case is precisely to ignore the lesson of the Haitian Revolution itself. Kant may well have relegated discussion of the public sphere to his secondary texts and strictly separated issues of political and juridical right from those of putatively private domesticity. He may never have accounted for the public, intersubjective nature of moral reason nor its dependence upon particular historical conditions. Nonetheless, this cannot change the fact that in the closing years of the eighteenth century, it was his philosophy (building upon that of the Enlightenment) that provided the means to conceptualize the historical processes—demands for universal emancipation and undivided *égaliberté*, the invention and globalization of the public sphere—that occurred throughout colonial modernity in the wake of 1776 and 1789. The slaves of Saint-Domingue were not "qualified" to participate in the public sphere as Kant understood it; yet it is a fact that they participated. They were not "theorized" as thinking beings by Enlightenment philosophy, and yet they thought and acted upon the conclusions they drew. The empirical experience of slavery, of the whip across one's back, should in a purely Kantian view have remained bracketed from the exercise of pure practical reason; yet it did not. Only if we mediate the philosophy of Enlightenment with the historical events of the period can its truth content continue to unfold.

My claim here is twofold: on the one hand, historical processes such as the Haitian Revolution and Olympe de Gouge's struggle for women's rights do not invalidate, but on the contrary, actually *fulfill* Kantian philosophy. They bring it out of the realm of abstract speculation, the biographical realm of Kant the obsessive of Königsberg, to draw it into a process of historicization that instantiates and gives determination to its abstract claims of universality. Only through this mediation with its extreme negations does a philosophy of universal rights progress; only via such mediation, moreover, does it become apparent that such oppositions are in fact illusory.

Furthermore, it is only when we bring the events of the Haitian Revolution out of their locality, into the horizon of such contemporary philosophical reflection, that their radicality can be fully articulated. By no means need this theoretical material be white, male, European philosophy. If the actors in the Haitian Revolution—from Parham's anonymous slave to Toussaint himself—were perhaps less familiar with the philosophical cosmology of Kongo civilization than they were with Raynal and the Declaration of the Rights of Man and Citizen, John Thornton is nonetheless correct to reconfigure our understanding of the philosophical richness and depth of this revolution when he underscores its status as a transcultural theoretical event extending far beyond the confines of a colony to encompass the complex weave of global, Black Atlantic modernity. The falsity of Kantian parochialism, racism, and schematism is itself transfigured in the light of the pure practical truth of the Haitian Revolution.

A properly Kantian political philosophy, something the conservative Kant himself never undertook, would seek to describe the sociohistorical forms in which human communities might organize themselves in order to maximize the autonomy of every member. The reactionary nature of Kant's political prescriptions—his ban on violent revolution, his defense of the state as the sole locus of sovereignty and reform, and his identification of the authority of law with a transcendental God—all of these need not blind us to the fact that Kant's moral philosophy is an unwilling, subterranean prolegomenon to modern philosophy of anarchist despecification. From Marx's analysis of society as the autonomous production of social forms by individuals themselves in the *German Ideology* (Bourgeois 120–21), to Cornelius Castoriadis's call for a *société autonome*, "the permanent and explicit self-construction of society" (60), despecifying thought understood as the maximization of human singularization can indeed be referred to as Kantian anarchism.

The limitation of Kant's political philosophy, if the latter can be said to have existed at all, is never to have asked what consequences follow from his *moral* philosophy for the sociopolitical organization of human beings. But those political thinkers coming after Kant—from Toussaint Louverture, Robespierre, Bakunin, and the young Marx to Chomsky, Castoriadis, and even Hardt and Negri—are all, I would argue, properly

Kantian in this, and perhaps only this, precise sense. They are thinkers who base their philosophy of society, more or less explicitly, upon a formalist understanding of human nature as the universal, indeterminate possibility for historical singularization, and who furthermore offer a formalist political philosophy of the abstract social structures that would allow singularity to flourish. And they are Kantian as Kant himself never was.[51]

## Hegel and Haiti Reconsidered

In the years following the independence of Haiti in 1804, the triumph of the world's first postslave republic remained a scandal; Haiti was quarantined by the Western powers, and the southern United States in particular feared the spread of this rebellion to its territory (Geggus 2001). The astounding events of the Haitian Revolution were a topic of passionate discussion throughout Europe and the Americas (Buck-Morss, Scott). And yet, few true analyses of the revolution—rather than mere expressions of support—would appear until the founding studies of Thomas Madiou (*Histoire de Haïti*, 1847–48) and Beaubrun Ardouin (*Études sur l'histoire d'Haïti*, 1853–60).

Not until the abolition of slavery by France in 1848—and really not until Victor Schoelcher's 1889 *Vie de Toussaint Louverture* and C. L. R. James's 1938 *The Black Jacobins*—did works appear outside Haiti that began to analyze the remarkable events of the 1804 Revolution in all their singularity.[52] In 1820, however, a brief philosophical analysis of the Haitian Revolution was published in Prussia that, like that of Diderot in *Les deux Indes,* took the risk of defending in the strongest terms the absolute right of slaves to overthrow a slaveholding society. What is more, and in contrast to Diderot's somewhat muddled, heteroclite argument, it offered an analysis of this historical conquering of freedom that remains, for all its brevity, among the most penetrating theorizations of the revolution in Saint-Domingue. This short analysis, consisting of a mere three pages in a nearly 400-page volume, seems never to have been noticed in the literature on Haiti. And yet it appears in what is perhaps (with Marx's *Das Kapital*) the single most influential and widely read work of social and political theory of the nineteenth century.

And yet this obscurity is not at all surprising, and not only because Hegel never actually refers to Haiti by name in the *Philosophy of Right*.[53] The long-standing reputation of the *Grundlinien der Philosophie des Rechts* as a reactionary defense of the Prussian monarchy, to say nothing of Hegel's infamous comments on Africa in his various (posthumously published) lectures on the *Philosophy of History,* have perhaps kept commentators from noticing this explication and justification of the right of slaves to revolt. Regarding the *Philosophy of History,* nothing is to be said in Hegel's defense. This philosophical genius was willing here merely to repeat unthinkingly the racist views on Africans that he had absorbed from the travel literature of his time (though he did at least bother to read every narrative he could get his hands on for these lecture notes). Susan Buck-Morss puts the matter bluntly: "In an effort to become more erudite in African studies during the 1820s, Hegel was in fact becoming dumber . . . [even as he was] adding empirical material from his reading of the European experts on world history" (863–64).

The passages from the *Philosophy of History* are well known and the staple of offhand rejections of Hegel's importance for postcolonial thought:

> [Africa] has no historical interest of its own, for we find its inhabitants living in barbarism and savagery in a land which has not furnished them with any integral ingredient of culture. . . . [It is] the land of childhood, removed from the light of self-conscious history and wrapped in the dark mantle of night. . . . The characteristic feature of the negroes is that their consciousness has not yet reached an awareness of any substantial objectivity—for example of God or the law—in which the will of man could participate and in which he could become aware of his own being. The African, in his undifferentiated and concentrated unity, has not yet succeeded in making this distinction between himself as an individual and his essential universality. (1975, 174, 177)

Ignoring for the moment the fact that the Haitian Revolution—whose events he knew of[54]—and Toussaint's 1801 constitution demonstrate the sheer falsity and absurdity of this last statement, the astounding partiality and ignorance of his comments stand as a negative confirmation of the Hegelian methodology he would have done well to hold to. Rather than "immersing" himself in the "content" of African experience, as the preface to the *Phenomenology* had encouraged—by actually encountering and attempting to understand Afro-Atlantic culture, that is—he remained content merely to base his analysis on abstract, secondhand opinion. Were there sources available to him in Berlin in 1820 that would have revealed even an inkling of the millennial traditions of the various African religions and social structures? Perhaps not. In any case, he felt confident enough to pontificate from his Berlin chair on the "barbarism and savagery" of Africans he had never encountered.[55]

In an influential article entitled "Hegel and Haiti," Susan Buck-Morss marshaled conclusive evidence to argue that the *Herr* and *Knecht* that

Hegel speaks of in the *Phenomenology* are in fact "real slaves revolting against real masters . . . within the contemporary context" of 1791–1804 Saint-Domingue (52). Buck-Morss, following Sala-Molins, extensively reviews the contradictions of Enlightenment thinkers who criticized so-called economic and political slavery while largely ignoring the actual enslavement of Africans in the New World. It was this exploitation, she reminds us, which underwrote the expansion and consolidation of North Atlantic economic and political hegemony in the Enlightenment-era world-system. Buck-Morss then goes on to show how *Minerva*, the most important political newspaper of its day in the German-speaking world—a paper that Hegel read daily in the period he composed the *Phenomenology*—for more than a year (1804–5) extensively analyzed and documented the events of the Haitian Revolution in over a hundred of its pages, "including source documents, news summaries, and eyewitness accounts" (50).

Buck-Morss concludes from her reading of the master-slave dialectic that, though it never explicitly refers to the events in Saint-Domingue, "given the historical context that provided the context for the *Phenomenology of Mind*, the inference is clear. Those who once acquiesced to slavery demonstrate their humanity when they are willing to risk death rather than remain subjugated" (53). And Buck-Morss concludes from her analysis: "Beyond a doubt Hegel knew about real slaves and their revolutionary struggles. In perhaps the most political expression of his career, he used the sensational events of Haiti as the linchpin in his argument in the *Phenomenology of Spirit*" (54). In fact, however (and though she conclusively proves that the *Knechten* of the *Phenomenology* refer—in part, if not exclusively—to the slaves of Saint-Domingue), Hegel's argument in the *Phenomenology* is more ambiguous than Buck-Morss's account allows.

Since at least Jean Hyppolite's analysis, it has been well recognized that the master-slave dialectic leads not to revolt, but instead to the *establishment* of the very social relation the actual slaves of Saint-Domingue overthrew.[56] The slave's life-and-death struggle in fact leads dialectically to the *creation* and *institution* of the lord-bondsman relationship. For Hegel, the life and death struggle is *antecedent* to the institution of slavery, not its result. The master-slave relation is explicitly *not* undone by the autonomous activity of a revolution such as the one occurring contemporaneously in Saint-Domingue, but by the inactivity or passivity of the lord.

Rather than revolution, the path out of slavery that Hegel proposes in the *Phenomenology* is explicitly (and dialectically) gradualist: labor on the part of the bondsman (*Knecht*) within the slaveholding system itself, which leads (diagetically and dialectically) in turn to "Self-Consciousness."[57] Hegel even explicitly draws such a conclusion in the *Philosophy of History*: "It was not so much from servitude [*aus der Knechtschaft*] as through servitude [*durch der Knechtschaft*] that humanity was emancipated" (cited in Durst 9). This point leads Hyppolite to draw the obvious conclusion from the *Phenomenology*'s dialectic of *Herrschaft* and *Knechtschaft*: "Hegel thinks that the discipline of service and obedience is essential to self-consciousness." Consequently, Hyppolite concludes that in the *Phenomenology*, "'imperialism' and 'colonialism' at certain stages of development are given a justification" (cited in Durst 13). Through labor, Hegel famously writes, "the bondsman realizes that it is precisely in his work wherein he seemed only to have an alienated existence that he acquires a mind of his own. . . . Without the discipline of service and obedience, fear remains at the formal stage, and does not extend to the known real world of existence" (Hegel 1977, 119).

Though this evidence may lead one to question Buck-Morss's conclusion that the *Phenomenology* represents the "most political expression of [Hegel's] career," her scholarship is compelling, and should lead readers to pursue the investigation she broke off before examining Hegel's truly authoritative statement of political right.[58] The next clue to the mystery of Hegel and Haiti is already contained in Hegel's linguistic shift in his later text from the archaic *Knecht* to the more modern *Sklaven*.[59]

The argument of the *Philosophy of Right* regarding the overthrow of slavery is quite different from that of the *Phemenology*. If the *Phenomenology* had defended slavery as the dialectical means of the slave's coming-to-self-consciousness, the *Philosophy of Right* takes the further and crucial step of concluding that the necessary consequence of this enlightenment should be the overthrow of the slaveholding *system* by those now self-conscious slaves. Since the 1950s, commentators such as Eric Weil and Joachim Ritter have critiqued received scholarly wisdom, to the point that "there is now a virtual consensus among knowledgeable scholars that the earlier images of Hegel, as philosopher of the reactionary Prussian restoration and forerunner of modern totalitarianism, are simply wrong."[60] To be sure, Ernst Bloch is certainly right to disparage Hegel's bureaucratic, representation-based, rabble-despising vision of the concrete instantiation of human freedom that concludes the *Philosophy of Right*. In Hegel's normative analysis, the freedom of the totality (as *Sittlichkeit*) "has supreme right against the individual, whose supreme duty is to be a member of the state," war is cynically defended as "the yeast of the public," and the death penalty described as "the greatest happiness of freedom."[61]

The *Philosophy of Right* is a highly contradictory text, however, insofar as its defense of constitutional monarchy and the bureaucratic class stand opposed to its own most fundamental principles. Hegel quite clearly abandons his own emancipatory logic in the final sections of the *Philosophy of Right*. If, on the one hand, it is true that "concrete freedom requires that personal individuality and its particular interests should reach their full development" in the state (282), Hegel utterly fails to attend to this claim when he comes to describe the actual modern state he envisages. Firstly, he allows for no existence of the truly singular or unassimilable difference, but instead maintains that "the universal cause must become [the individual's] cause. . . . Particular interests . . . should be harmonized with the universal" (284–85). All difference must be transculturated difference, bowing in subservient agreement and harmony to the path of the "universal."[62]

What is more, for Hegel, freedom is *only* realizable through the individual's subjection/becoming subject to a transcendental state apparatus: "The determinations of the will of the individual acquire an objective existence through the state, and it is *only* through the state that they attain their truth and actualization" (285; my emphasis). Freedom is for Hegel only the freedom of individuals to position themselves within the hierarchical, normative structure of the universal state; that a multitude such as the slaves of Saint-Domingue could refuse such subsumption while actually possessing what Laclau has called "populist reason" is explicitly denied by Hegel: "Without its monarch, . . . the people is a formless mass. . . . The term 'the people' . . . refers to that category of citizens *who do not know their own will.* . . . [Direct democracy is] devoid of rational form" (1991, 340, 347; emphasis in original).[63] Instead, Hegel maintains that the "highest officials within the state necessarily have a more profound and comprehensive insight into the nature of the state's institutions and needs" (340). If the slaves of Saint-Domingue had lived by such precepts, passively witnessing the Parisian Assembly's defense of slavery, the Haitian Revolution would never have occurred. By this late point in the *Philosophy of Right*, Hegel's initial critique of servitude is long forgotten, however, and the unreasoning masses are advised to submit passively to the all-knowing intelligence of the monarch and his faithful bureaucrats.

Hegel's actual critique of slavery in section 1 of the *Philosophy of Right*, however, remains uninfected by such elitist paternalism. Attention to this critique reveals a far different political philosophy, one that, for all its brevity, is among the most theoretically rigorous critiques of slavery of the Radical Enlightenment. *The Philosophy of Right* is in its fundamental theoretical claims a distinctly progressive work, as Allen Wood has shown. It is a work that in its defense of human freedom, as well as its specific call for a republican (albeit monarchical) state, stands in contrast to the turn to conservative authoritarianism of 1820s Prussia.[64] In contrast to Hegel's disparagement of the possibility of a true expression of populist reason by the multitude, Joachim Ritter describes another Hegel, for whom the French Revolution remained the defining historical event of modern times, one he celebrated with friends every year of his life with a toast to the fall of the Bastille: "For Hegel, the French Revolution is that event around which all the determinations of philosophy in relation to its time are clustered, with philosophy marking out the problem through attacks on and defenses of the Revolution. Conversely, there is no other philosophy that is a philosophy of revolution to such a degree and so profoundly, in its innermost drive, as that of Hegel" (43).

Hegel's racist and ignorant dismissal of Africa in the *Philosophy of History* is of no more than passing interest; a mere moment of senile crankiness, it blinds us to the fundamental dimension of Hegel's entire thought that makes his one of the most important philosophical doctrines for postcolonial thought, as figures such as Césaire and Fanon clearly recognized: Hegel's is a philosophy of freedom and, in the *Philosophy of Right,* "Hegel takes up the idea of freedom and makes it the 'basic element' and 'sole matter' of his philosophy" (Ritter 47–48). Similarly, Eric Weil points to the unresolved issue confronting those who would dismiss Hegel's (or Kant's) work because of its random moments of racist ignorance: the *Philosophy of Right* undertakes "the science of the historical realization of freedom" (36) and as such is of interest to all those who see freedom not merely as a problem of one specific group, but of all humanity. Hegel's concern is precisely freedom as a *universal* problem confronting humans.

In attempting philosophically to understand human freedom not as a mere concept, but as an unfolding historical reality in the world (*Wirklichkeit*), Hegel's thought offered a philosophical foundation for the elaboration of postcolonial theory. Even more than 1789, the Haitian Revolution in its uncompromising and absolute struggle for freedom, decolonization, and the destruction of the society that enabled these processes operated according to Ritter's formulation: "In Hegel's view, the essence of modern political revolution, which differentiates it from all other forms of upheaval, uprising, rebellion, and putsch, lies not so much in the particular political form which the violence takes, but rather in the social emancipation underlying it and in the establishment of an order that according to its own principle is presuppositionless, excluding everything preexisting, historical, and traditional, like a radical new beginning that nothing should precede" (76).

In a process analogous to Rousseau's critique of the philosophes, the *Philosophy of Right* strives to overcome the formalism of Kantian morality to argue that freedom can only exist as a substantial ethical community (*Sittlichkeit*). Moving beyond Kant's *Metaphysics of Morals,* Hegel's *Philosophy of Right* proceeds to examine the unfolding of human freedom as inseparable from its social institution, tracing it through the development of property, morality, family, civil society, and, finally, the (true) state. Hegel understands the latter not as its various historical instances of alienating domination over individuals (of which he was of course aware, and which he unambiguously condemned), but rather in its true (as yet unfulfilled) potentiality to realize the freedom of determinate, heterogeneous individuals in a universal ethical state: "Concrete freedom requires that personal individuality [*Einzelheit*] and its particular interests should reach their full development and gain recognition of their right for itself. . . . Thus, the universal must be activated, but subjectivity on the other hand must be developed as a living whole" (1991, 282–83).[65] Early on in this analysis, in §57 of his discussion of the abstract right of property as "Taking Possession," Hegel addresses the human being's capacity to "take possession of himself," that is, to realize his autonomy.

The first paragraph of Hegel's published text remains abstract, not yet explicitly mentioning slavery until the commentary that follows. "The human being," Hegel begins, "in his immediate existence in himself, is a natural entity, external to his concept; it is only through the development of his own body and spirit, *essentially* by means of *his self-consciousness comprehending itself as free,* that he takes possession of himself and becomes his own property as distinct from that of others" (all italics in original). This sentence recapitulates the process first described in the *Phenomenology* of a production-based subjectivity in which the slave comprehends and substantiates his freedom through labor (Nesbitt 2003, 21–33). Hegel rejects Locke's influential critique of slavery—the view that "every Man has [an inalienable] *property* in his own Person" (Locke 328)—as a view that reduces humans to the level of sheer animality (as mere natural, physical property).[66] Instead, Hegel's idealism seeks to found its critique of slavery on the uniquely human (claims Hegel) faculty of reason, a faculty that differentiates humans, through their free will, from mere nature.[67]

When the physically unfree slave knowingly and freely produces an object he has conceived of, he suddenly attains the humanity—defined by Hegel as the capacity to knowingly transform and set oneself in opposition to nature—that had been merely an implicit *possibility* in the natural world of which humans are also a part. He realizes that he is free to transform the world, while the master is in fact unfree, the latter dependent upon the slave's labor for his very existence as master. "By this means, what one is in concept [that is, a free being] is posited as one's own, and also as an object distinct from simple self-consciousness, and it thereby becomes capable of taking on the *form of the thing*." Many interpretations of this abstract passage are possible; Hegel habitually leaves it up to his readers to fill in the content of his logical analyses. Hegel goes on, however, to interpret this passage explicitly as a critique of contemporary, modern slavery, and to defend the need for its revolutionary overthrow.

While much has been made of the fact that the *Phenomenology*'s analysis of the master-slave dialectic uses the archaic term *Knecht*[68] (translated by A. V. Miller as "bondsman"), strangely, no commentators seem to have noticed that the *Philosophy of Right* no longer speaks of *Knechten* and *Knechtschaft*.[69] Instead, Hegel's published commentary begins: "The alleged justification of *slavery* [*Sklaverai*] . . . depend[s] on regarding the human being simply as a *natural being* whose *existence* . . . is not in conformity with his concept." Hegel thus begins his analysis in explicit reference to the institution of slavery, rather than feudal relations of indentured servitude.[70]

Hegel's analysis begins by contrasting the two traditional stances regarding slavery that held prior to the Haitian Revolution. Those who would defend slavery, he argues, point to the subhuman state of Africans (absence of reason, religious spirituality, and the like, just those characteristics that Hegel himself would ignorantly refuse Africans later, in the 1820s), to a debased, instinctive, merely animalistic existence, a *Naturwesen* or natural essence. Slaves are not human, in this view, because they do not meet the criteria for humanity that their enslavers have defined (the "concept" of the human).

In contrast, for those who would critique slavery based upon "absolute" natural rights (as in the Enlightenment standpoint of the *Encyclopédie*), "the claim that slavery [*Sklaverei*] is absolutely contrary to right" is no less partial in its absoluteness and abstraction; it is "firmly tied to the *concept* of the human being as spirit, as something free *in itself,*" and in this, it is a mere abstraction, not actual freedom, "one-sided inasmuch as it regards the human being as *by nature* free." Should there be any remaining doubt that Hegel is here talking not about feudalism but about the contemporary institution of Atlantic slave labor, in his 1818–19 Berlin lectures on the *Rechtsphilosophie,* he explicitly refers his listeners at this point to the absolute universal he has in mind in his critique of slavery: the 1789 Déclaration des droits de l'homme, using both the French "Droits de l'homme" and German "Menschenrechte" (*Naturrecht und Staatswissenschaft*: 264).

In contrast to modern human rights, the abstraction of *natural* rights, Hegel says, is a mere "antinomy . . . based on formal thinking, . . . so that both [the slaveholder's and the Enlightenment concepts] are lacking in truth and do not conform to the Idea."[71] These, then, were the views held in the debate on slavery up to the radical intervention of the Haitian Revolution. As such they were indeed mere debate, in which the two sides remained in abstract separation, a text like Condorcet's 1781 *Réflexions sur l'esclavage des Nègres* no more than mere "reflections" devoid of real historical effect.

It is here that Hegel inserts his far-reaching estimation of the importance of the Haitian Revolution. Hegel, in 1820, offers exactly the analysis that Aimé Césaire would arrive at in 1960, an analysis that, in Hegel's case, derives directly from the Spinozian maxim that right is not an eternal fact of nature, nor an inward state of mind, but the historical manifestation of the power to express oneself freely. Whether one is free is determined only by whether one's mind and body (as a complex, composite whole) are constrained or instead express themselves freely: "The free spirit," Hegel writes of the emancipated and autonomous former slave, "consists precisely in not having its being as mere concept . . . but in overcoming [*aufheben*] this formal phase of its being [as merely *naturally* free, "born free," yet still and nonetheless a slave in the actually existing world] and hence also its immediate natural existence [as unfree, bestialized slave], and gives itself [autonomously, without the paternalism of a Condorcet or Grégoire], an existence which is purely its own and free."[72]

While it may appear, Hegel continues, that the brutality of the slaveholding system has the upper hand against the mere logical arguments of Enlightenment, this is an illusory appearance of nature (*Naturwesen*), what we would today call the racist ideology that describes Africans as *essentially* and *naturally* inferior or subhuman. In fact, as it had in the earlier logic of lordship and "servitude"—here Hegel explicitly refers his listeners to the *Phenomenology* and tellingly reverts to his earlier terminology of *Knechtschaft*—this mere appearance of a natural "essence" is overthrown by the slave himself, because his perception of his freedom (achieved through labor) "contains the absolute *starting point*" for the realization of the Idea of a historically actualized freedom (as opposed to its mere logical concept).[73]

But if the *Phenomenology* had presented this process as an abstraction, "merely in its subjective content," says Hegel in a moment of autocritique, the enormous step of the *Philosophy of Right* is to defend the idea of an autonomous revolution against slavery. The Haitian Revolution was, according to Hegel, a struggle for the realization of the Idea of freedom neither as mere empty concept (abstract, ahistorical natural right), nor as a limited, local event devoid of relation to the universal (rebellion). Hegel's Spinozian argument is unambiguous and of momentous radicality, a culminating theoretical moment of the Radical Enlightenment: "The ineligibility of the human being in and for himself for slavery should no longer be apprehended merely as something which *ought* to be," as for the philosophes or Brissot's *Amis des noirs* arguing inconsequentially to deaf ears that slavery *should* be abolished, someday. Instead, it must be instantiated immanently, as a real historical and political fact, and this, Hegel concludes, "is an insight which comes only when we recognize that the Idea of freedom is truly present only as *the state.*"

Here, in abstraction, is precisely the interpretation of the Haitian Revolution that Césaire and later Eugene Genovese would put forward in a more concrete and historically explicit fashion: freedom as a universal Idea is not attained through mere local *revolt* against the harshness of slavery, lessening punishments or ameliorating working conditions, opening the way for a few maroons to return into a state of nature. Freedom as a concrete and actual universal Idea is to be attained only through the institution of a (potentially universal) state, that is to say, through the total overthrow and destruction of the social system (colonialism) that instituted the slave's debasement to a mere natural, animalistic being. Precisely what Toussaint Louverture first accomplished with his Constitution of 1801 declaring the unconditional abolition of slavery and de facto independence of Saint-Domingue, processes that the former slaves with Dessalines at their head then brought to fruition on January 1, 1804.

In the face of this radical and explicit defense of slave revolution, Hegel's concluding oral commentary (preserved as H. G. Hotho's student notes from the 1822–23 semester) threatens to throw us back into confusion regarding his standpoint:

If we hold firmly to the view that the human being in and for himself is free, we thereby condemn slavery [*Sklaverei*]. But if someone is a slave, his own will is responsible, just as the responsibility lies with the will of a people if that people is subjugated. Thus the wrong of slavery is the fault not only of those who enslave or subjugate people, but of the slaves and the subjugated themselves. Slavery . . . occurs in a world where a wrong is still a right. Here the wrong *is valid*, so that the position it occupies is a necessary one.

Slavery is "the fault of the slaves" and a "necessary" wrong!? Though one might see this as a foreshadowing of the conservative racism of the *Philosophy of History*, close reading reveals that it is in fact consonant with the previous passage's call for slave revolution. Slavery is an absolute wrong; Hegel does not waver on this point and repeats it unambiguously here. But slavery exists, and freedom can be achieved no more by simply having it bestowed upon slaves by benevolent masters than through the expression of pious sentiments or abstract logic. Following Spinoza, Hegel argues that servitude must be conquered and actualized autonomously, and until slaves actually take that step, they share the responsibility for its continued existence.

In this call for slave revolt, Hegel subscribed to the radicalism of Spinoza and Diderot. It was Spinoza who first maintained—in strict accord with his derivation of rights from the immanent degree of power of any natural being—that as long as the slave cannot free himself, he has no "right" to do so; as soon as he can, however, he has every right to, and must, in fact, do so (Lazzeri 146, 220).[74]

For Spinoza, like Hegel after him, the question of slave revolt was above all an *ethical* (existential or historical) and not an ontological or logical problem (as it was for the French philosophes). To misread Spinoza's chef d'oeuvre as an ontological study of the being of the universe, and not as the "Ethics" he intended it to be, would logically lead one to wonder in the face of actually existing slavery whether it is the "essence" of any being who (contingently) finds herself a slave, in fact to *be* a slave? Like Hegel's philosophy of Spirit, Spinoza's *Ethics* offers the reader no "scientific" criteria that would allow an observer to determine the timeless essence of any object.

In a Spinozian ethics, the essence of any singular subject cannot be determined from observation of an actual state of affairs. Spinoza, like Hegel after him, can only locate an answer to the problem of slavery (like that of "essence" in general) in the expressive potential of an enslaved being (*"De la servitude humaine"*).[75] Does a being have the power to express freely all that its being is capable of? Spinoza's *Ethics* refuses—as does the analysis of slavery in §57 of the *Philosophy of Right*—to give an ontological or logical answer to the problem of servitude. Instead, it offers a properly ethical exhortation to its reader, telling us what we must affirm if we are to be free and able to do all that our beings are capable of. Overcoming a state of servitude is not a logical problem, but involves instead experimentation, invention, and the configuration of new potentialities of free expressivity from within the confines of any singular, historical situation. To discover one's essence is above all a political problem that requires the invention of new sociopolitical structures.

If for Spinoza the problem of slavery had remained an abstraction, Hegel is able to formulate his ethical injunction concretely, in light of the Haitian Revolution. To say that in a world where "a wrong is still right," where slavery exists and is still called "just" by the master class (slaves are putatively better off than their African brethren, they are fed, housed, and "civilized" by their masters, and so on), to say in his final comments that slavery is a "valid" and "necessary" wrong, is for Hegel only to repeat what he has been arguing all along: in the world as it existed prior to 1791, slavery is necessary only as a brutal fact of *ideology* (*Naturwesen*), enforced by violence and terror as an incontrovertible, eternal reality that is indeed necessary ("you will work or die, and in any case you'll die like an animal soon enough"), but that is *not true*. True would be the capacity of the human mind to grasp our immanent, undeveloped possibilities denied by the violence of an unfree society; truth would occur through the actualization of human freedom as a concrete, egalitarian universal in the world. Such a truth, Hegel tells us, can be attained only by the forceful negation of a merely "natural," unthinking existence, through the rational and imaginative construction of human freedom as something never before seen on the face of the earth, in human history: a free nation actualizing the principle of universal emancipation. In a word, the state of *Haiti*. Though he never names it, in 1820 Hegel could have been referring to nothing else but this world-historical and previously unimaginable event that ignited and scandalized all of European society for decades.

### A Miraculous Intervention?

In what sense can the Haitian Revolution be called a miraculous event? In one, precisely: The Haitian Revolution was an immanent human undertaking that, against all expectations, caused an unpredictable break not in the laws of nature, but merely within the reigning norms of "natural" historical causality as the eighteenth-century North Atlantic world

## 125  Penser la Révolution Haïtienne

understood them.[76] It was, as Peter Hallward has observed, "one of the most profoundly improbable sequences in all of world history" (2004b). The miracle, in this view, was not one of divine intervention, but rather a decisive rupture in the predictable sequence of events in the modern world-system of agricultural capitalism. As the culminating event of the Spinozian Radical Enlightenment, the Haitian Revolution lays waste to the contemporary faith in miracles. Following Spinoza, the Haitian Revolution, like the French Revolution and the events of May '68 that Alain Badiou rightly celebrates, should be understood as an effect of historical necessity whose logic and rules contemporary observers were incapable of grasping.

The conceptualization of freedom as the (political) appearance of the new received its clearest expression in a short but dense 1968 text by Hannah Arendt: "What Is Freedom?" The Haitian Revolution, and not the American events Arendt celebrated in *On Revolution,* in turn serves as the historical event that best illustrates her attempt to "politicize" the concept of freedom. Arendt's Nietzschean thesis is that, though the problem of freedom is perhaps the archetypal subject of political philosophy, the Christian tradition since Augustine that links freedom with the will and psychological interiority has made it impossible for us to think of freedom as political action. Arendt maintains that we have lost the original Greek understanding of freedom as indissolubly linked with human action. Instead, freedom as interiority first arose as a philosophical problem for Augustine, following Epictetus and Paul, in the late Roman period, precisely when the conscious human transformation of the world—"action," in Arendt's terminology—became increasingly impossible. As the scope of human political action became foreclosed, these thinkers bestowed on the subject a compensatory freedom in its capacity for infinite imaginary freedom, leaving the political world untouched.

In place of the Greek understanding of freedom as human action, Augustine substituted the putatively "free" interiority of the individual will in a "conscious attempt to divorce the notion of freedom from politics" (Arendt 1968, 147). Like Nietzsche's *Antichrist,* Arendt's essay argues that this fateful linking of freedom with the will increasingly determined our modern understanding of freedom up to and including that of democratic liberalism, ironically offering an enfeebled, apolitical understanding of freedom for those moderns who endlessly celebrate representational liberal democracy.

This depoliticized freedom of the individual will is divorced from active intervention in the world, living on beyond Augustine in the splendid isolation of its autocratic interiority in every self-same consumer of Western democracy. The result is the isolationist, depoliticized, libertarian-individualist tendency particularly prominent in the North American understanding of freedom: freedom is strictly equivalent to the freedom to be free *from* political life, to be left alone by the government to cultivate one's garden (149). Where Arendt differs from Nietzsche is in her denegation of the Will-to-Power as merely one more manifestation of this solipsistic interiority, instead opening the field of her reflection to encompass the political, social world of intersubjective human activity.

In contrast to this neo-Carthusian modernity she decries, Arendt understands human freedom not negatively, as the freedom of the isolated, modern, Christian individual, but instead as the positive "freedom to call something into being which did not exist before, which was not given, not even as an object of cognition or imagination, and which, therefore, strictly speaking, could not be known" (151). Arendt argues, crucially, that human action is free only insofar as it occurs under the conscious guidance, not of the intellect or the will (both phenomena of psychological interiority for her), but rather following what she calls "principle": a rational construct that "becomes fully manifest only in the performing act itself" (152).

Already, it should be clear how relevant Arendt's understanding of human freedom is to any interpretation of the Haitian Revolution. Insofar as these events were a mere phenomenon of individual desire (say, Toussaint's Will to Power in Pierre Pluchon's tendential reading), they remain mere historical curiosities. Nor was the Haitian Revolution a simple phenomenon of the intellect. Such was the Encyclopedists' understanding of human freedom and the impossibility of slavery: a mere intellectual thought exercise content to construct the logical impossibility of slavery while the latter proceeded unimpeded as the political and historical reality of Enlightenment political economy. The Haitian Revolution is of consequence insofar as it was a fully manifest human action, an intervention based upon *principle* in the Arendtian sense, in which human freedom as a universal and undivided concept could "become manifest only in the performing act itself": a political action, the destruction of slavery and the construction of a state ordered by the rational principle of universal human autonomy.

Though Arendt never even mentions the Haitian Revolution in her book-length celebration of the *esclavagiste* American Revolution (*On Revolution*), it was the first world-historical event to enact such a notion of universal human freedom not as a mere idea of the Enlightenment, nor as the hypocritical, cynical compromise of a "free" nation economically and socially growing rich off slave labor (France and the United States), but as a principled human act of universal emancipation in consonance with reason. The creation of a politico-cultural sphere of human action free from slavery in the nascent Haitian state was, for all its subsequent limitations, a founding attempt to refuse the logic of sovereignty, of violent domination of the will of one (group, leader) over others, in favor of what Arendt compellingly calls "virtuosity": the improvisation of heretofore unimaginable human social relationships. This Haitian rejection of the logic of sovereignty for sociopolitical virtuosity, perhaps the greatest creative act in all of Black Atlantic politics, largely failed the test of viability it faced in 1804. Though independent Haiti did manage to resist the threat of recolonization by France, it was from its inception infected with the militaristic, terrorist logic of tyranny and plantation-based labor of the Napoleonic slave era. In its short appearance in the world, however, it was truly a miracle of human creativity.

The Haitian Revolution was an expression of human spontaneity, the creation of a slave-free social structure unimaginable not only to the countless defenders and apologists of Enlightenment slavery but for slavery's critics as well. Not Condorcet, not Raynal, not Grégoire, but only Toussaint, Sonthonax, and the countless Haitians who contributed to the universal abolition of slavery in 1804 were able to imagine and construct the immediate and total elimination of slavery as social reality. The miraculous freedom of 1804 lay in the spontaneous creation of utterly new sequences in human history such as decolonization and universal abolition. It was a fracture in the apparently "natural" development of the modern world-system via slave labor, miraculous insofar as it was an immanent "interruption of some natural series of events, of some automatic process, in whose context they constitute the wholly unexpected" (168). This intervention in history showed freedom to be not so much a natural possession of humans (natural right), but rather a capacity for action. "Man is free," Arendt writes, "because he is a beginning" (167). The realm of human social experience is, for Arendt, as much dominated by automatic processes as the natural world. In contrast, "the periods of being free have always been relatively short in the history of humankind" (169).

To call the Haitian Revolution a "miracle" is merely to view its unfolding from the perspective of the dominant, slaveholding society that its example eventually helped destroy. In a centuries-long process that in many respects continues to the present, the imagined inferiority of Africans had been "naturalized," made to appear as a "fact" as much through discursive representation as through the violent restructuration of colonialist European society.

A total network of guilt and shared responsibility spread through the early-modern world-system like the molecules of sugar sweetening one's coffee; like the sweetness of sugar itself that covered the stench of rotting provisions, the exponentially expansive consumption of sugar was a classic phenomenon of alienation. The European consumer came to see the consumption of sugar, unknown before 1000 AD as a natural, unquestioned phenomenon (Mintz 5). The social conditions of the production of sugar were conveniently hidden an ocean away. The Haitian Revolution exploded the mystified "naturalness" of this contingent structuration of what was in fact a transnational, global society. "Every new beginning," Arendt writes, "breaks into the world as an 'infinite improbability,' and yet it is precisely this infinitely improbable which actually constitutes the very texture of everything we call real" (169).

Though Arendt's argument is compelling in its basic thrust, the limitations of her short article are nonetheless glaring. Though it is structured upon the Kantian binary distinction between a realm of nature and a realm of human freedom, she merely palms the contradictions of this dualism that Kant struggled ceaselessly to theorize. Arendt takes as a given precisely the distinction that most urgently needs to be explained: how to differentiate between a natural sequence of causation and a free human intervention into that sequence. How, for example, to determine whether the articulation of universal emancipation in Saint-Domingue was a "natural" development of Enlightenment thought or a miraculous intervention of human freedom and political imagination? Was it readily predictable as a sort of controlled social experiment, through the Pavlovian exposure of slaves to the speeches of Robespierre and the documents of 1789? Or was 1804 a purely unpredictable creation of human imagination, innovation, and improvisation? The answer that this book hopes to provide, of course, is that it was all of these, but that only a complexly rendered examination of the smallest historical details, of the dialectical interpenetration of predictable sequences of causality and unpredictable events, can take one beyond the facile schematic abstraction of politically correct dichotomies.

# 4 Beyond Jacobinism
## Hegemony and Universalism in the Haitian Revolution

### Haiti and the Global Colonialist System

THE MOST famous and widely read account of the Haitian Revolution is undoubtedly the Trinidadian Marxist C. L. R. James's 1937 study *The Black Jacobins*. In it, James famously put forward a compelling account of the events in Saint-Domingue from 1791 to 1804 that led to the declaration of the autonomous nation of Haiti. James situates these events firmly within the eighteenth-century Age of Enlightenment and Revolution, drawing attention both to their fundamental place in the development of the modern world-system of agricultural capitalism (Saint-Domingue as the *center* of France's extraction of surplus profit from slave labor) and to their essential uniqueness.[1]

In part a result of his dual position as black Caribbean subject of colonialism and subject to a liberationist, anticolonial communism, James is perhaps the first commentator to envision the Haitian Revolution as a sequence of world-historical (as opposed to merely peripheral and secondary) events of global modernity.[2] In light of James's analysis, the Haitian Revolution appears today as the first traumatic announcement of a radically decentered modernity only now (in the increasingly extensive globalization of a new century) becoming fully apparent. Saint-Domingue formed an absolutely *central* element in what has since James's time come to be described as a "world-system." It was by 1789 the world's most technologically advanced, highly efficient producer of colonial products (Blackburn 1988, 163). The system in which it operated was an international, transcultural network of labor and production, one that organized a global "commodity-chain" (Wallerstein) to create both commodities (sugar, coffee, indigo) and surplus profit for the North Atlantic powers. At the same time, this world-system generated an array of cultural innovations typified by the development of the New World Creole plantation cultures.[3]

The triangular slave trade of the post-Renaissance Atlantic world is perhaps the archetypal example of such a global commodity-chain. From this world-systemic perspective developed in the work of Immanuel Wallerstein, Europe no longer stands as the autonomous generator of the Modern World, in a process that would have gradually radiated out from a center to await today its completion (Habermas), but, instead, the construction of the modern world-system since 1492 appears increasingly as inextricably linked to global colonialism. In this view, Europe gradually passed from its status as a Western periphery overshadowed by the Ottoman-Muslim center to hegemonize the *management* of this new world (that is, transnational-capitalist) system (Dussel 13). While the North Atlantic nations increasingly (from the Renaissance to the present) abrogated the global planning, distribution, and reinvestment of capital, labor, and profit to themselves, other tasks such as the extraction and transformation of raw materials were delegated to subaltern (so-called "peripheral") colonized peoples and zones of this network.

Seen from this world-system perspective, Saint-Domingue was not "peripheral" but, rather, *differential*. In his 1983 article "Three Instances of Hegemony in the History of the Capitalist World-Economy," Wallerstein writes that the "structure [of this early-modern world-system] is that of an axial social division of labor exhibiting a core/periphery tension based on unequal exchange" (254). Such a simplistic, binary model of a single core/periphery, I am arguing, fails to do justice to the possibilities of radical dehierarchization and multiplication inherent in world-system theory itself. In other words, viewing post-Renaissance capitalism as a differential global structure logically places one outside the participant standpoint that has striven to hegemonize the vision of Europe as center for the past four centuries.

There were and continue to exist many powerfully exploitive hierarchies within this system, but a world-systemic viewpoint should lead us beyond reducing these to a binary, politically correct conflict between a valorized (subaltern) periphery and a stigmatized (North Atlantic) center. World-system analysis should rightly "provincialize Europe" (Chakrabarty), putting into question facile West/non-West, center/periphery binaries, forcing us instead to view post-Renaissance agricultural capitalism as a transnational, differentiated *system* bearing multiple centers and peripheries. Global colonialism was—and continues to be—a system, and as such must be understood to extend throughout an entire geopolitical network. Though this system certainly depends upon multiple economic, racial, and political hierarchies, a systemic perspective implies that each element in this total division of labor is essential; consequently, our judgment of a phenomenon such as slavery in the Enlightenment must call into question the entire system that enabled such an injustice, while we celebrate the transnational system of critique that eventually destroyed it.

From this systemic standpoint, what made the Haitian Revolution so terrifying for European hegemony over the modern world-system was not simply that it destroyed the world's most productive site of surplus colonial profits, a surplus upon which European expansion in the eighteenth century depended; moreover, as a social *revolution* that radically altered the balance of power and hierarchical structure of a colonialist society, the overthrow of the slavery-plantation regime in 1804 threatened this division of labor between center and the peripheries of the new global system.[4] "The freed slave," Daniel Maximin has written, "no longer takes the stance of opposition, but of one whose conquering of freedom has *decentred* the master and displaced the site of mastery" (27). The former Haitian slaves asserted their right to *manage* the process of modernization. In other words, the Haitian Revolution was not merely an event emanating from modernity's *periphery*, as theorists of globalization would have it. More than that, to an important degree it succeeded in *displacing* the center of modernity. In this way it redefined certain fundamental parameters and hierarchies of modernity not only for a small peripheral island but *for the entire world-system*, both in theory (as a defense of political egalitarianism) and in fact (as a bid for decolonization and full control *to manage* autonomously the process of modernization). This dual threat helps explain the necessity for the substantial long-term expenditure of political, economic, military, and ideological resources on the part of the North Atlantic powers to destroy the Haitian bid for managerial hegemony over the process of modernization (as well as the need to constantly reassert the ideological vision of Haiti as "the poorest country in the Western hemisphere").

## The Concept of Black Jacobinism

In *The Black Jacobins,* James described "from below" the radical revolution that first overthrew this world-system based upon slave labor. James drew particular attention to the productivity and transformational capacities of popular and systematically disenfranchised populations that actively appropriated and refashioned the political egalitarianism theorized by Western modernity, an ideology that had by 1791 infiltrated every level of French colonial society.[5]

In *The Black Jacobins,* James's dual gesture is immediately rendered in the book's title: the Haitian Revolution was on the one hand a singular event, a "black" revolution of the enslaved unique in world history in both the transformational compass of its goals and its astonishing success. At the same time, James's title announces, these revolutionaries were full and active participants in revolutionary Western modernity; they were "Jacobins" of the Caribbean. What might James have wished to communicate with this ascription?

The concept of Jacobinism is notoriously fluid, and James never explicitly spells out what he means in attributing the epithet to Toussaint and his colleagues. Over the past two centuries, Jacobinism has variously signified the indivisibility of national sovereignty, juridical and political centralization, the abstract equality of all citizens guaranteed by the rule of law, the role of republicanism in reforming society, and the nationalist drive for sovereignty and politico-military independence (Furet 1992, 243). While James draws our attention to the eventual *dérapage* of Toussaint's revolution, a process superficially akin to the late-Jacobin oligarchy that usurped the place and name of the people, this belated and limited moment in the Haitian Revolution cannot be taken to characterize the fundamental importance of the event as a whole for James.

Clearly, James instead wished to draw our attention to the radical legacy of a French Revolution that demonstrated to the world that, even in the most rigidified and atavistic societies, a disenfranchised multitude of subjects can become agents able to effect "the transformation of man and the world" (Furet 250): "The transformation of slaves," James writes on the opening page of *Black Jacobins,* "trembling in hundreds before a single white man, into a people able to organize themselves and defeat the most powerful European nations of their day, is one of the great epics of revolutionary struggle and achievement" (ix). *The Black Jacobins,* written in the opening moments of the decolonization movement, is clearly an invocation to the possibility for subaltern populations to take control of their destiny. James's narration fashions historical proof of this process and testifies to objective progress in human society itself, where "the prevailing standards of human liberty are infinitely more advanced and more profound than those current in 1789" (James 375).

Such an understanding of the "Jacobinism" of Saint-Domingue not as fealty to a party model, but as the real and historically demonstrable possibility any human community has to bring about its emancipation, implies that we must continue to interrogate the notion of a French "influence" on events in Saint-Domingue. If such an understanding of Jacobinism and its attendant notion of human autonomy were defining features of the

Haitian Revolution, this would imply not the passive reception and copying of a metropolitan political model, but rather the autonomous and active reformulation of the parameters of human freedom signified to any unfree population by that guiding, yet shifting, norm of any and all revolutions: *liberté*. The process of this reformulation, I wish to argue, is best understood as a colonial instance of the struggle for politico-symbolic hegemony first theorized by Antonio Gramsci and more recently developed in the writings of Ernesto Laclau.

### The Struggle for Ideological Hegemony

James's attention to the ideological "Jacobin" dimension of the Haitian Revolution is as famous in Haitian historiography as it is unechoed: with the exception of Eugene Genovese's 1978 study *From Rebellion to Revolution,* historians of the revolution have shied away from elucidating the link between the ideologies of 1789 and 1804. In France, where studies of Napoleon's defeat and the loss of the most profitable colony in history have been rare to nonexistent, Pierre Pluchon's monumental biographies of Toussaint Louverture set the tone in tracing the genealogy of the latter's eventual turn to tyranny. In Pluchon's disparaging view, any links of the Haitian Revolution to French ideology would lie merely in the connection between the Jacobin Terror and its colonial variation in Toussaint's eventual imposition of forced, albeit paid, labor. American historiography, however, has in recent decades begun to examine Saint-Domingue as an autonomous insurgency, shedding light on what Carolyn Fick called in her pioneering 1991 study the "revolution from below." The effect of this reorientation away from a historiography of leaders such as Napoleon and Toussaint Louverture to the insurgent agency of the multitude, while necessary and beneficial, has had the secondary effect of discounting anew the role of ideological influence in Saint-Domingue.[6] This tendency to ignore the role of ideological influence most likely arises from a perspective that celebrates the autonomous agency of the disenfranchised; in such a light, any influence of France upon these colonial events would seem to imply a merely passive receptivity on the part of the former slaves.

In fact, attention to the archival traces of the revolution in Saint-Domingue shows that the ideology of universal human rights encapsulated in the *Déclaration des droits de l'homme* was fundamental. We lack, however, the theoretical means to understand this influence as something other than the passive reception of a pure Platonic idea formed in Paris, or conversely, as the raw, preconscious expression of insurgent action unmediated by symbolic constructs. The concept of hegemony, understood as the struggle for control or dominating influence over symbolic capital, offers a means to reconfigure the explanatory apparatus available for understanding the Haitian Revolution. A hegemonic interpretation of 1804 would take into account the instigatory role of ideas while fully attending to the contestatory nature of their development and dispersion within a complex field of social actors.

While the concept of hegemony—inherited from Gramsci and given a poststructuralist turn in the work of Laclau and Mouffe—has played a fundamental role in the attempt to renew Marxian thought in the aftermath of the disintegration of state socialism since 1989, its configuration has often remained Eurocentric, failing to take into account the implications of global colonialism and a transnational politics of the multitude. This limitation is conspicuous in *Hegemony and Socialist Strategy*. Laclau and Mouffe conclude their analysis by casting the events of the French Revolution as the direct antinomy to the rise of the decentered, multiple, and contestatory social movements that have appeared throughout the world since 1968. The French Revolution, for Laclau and Mouffe, was "the last moment in which the antagonistic limits between two forms of society presented themselves" (Laclau and Mouffe 151). Such a reductively binary vision of events is sustainable, if at all, only by maintaining a strictly Eurocentric perspective on the French Revolution. Seen from the Caribbean, however, the diverse effects of the fall of the Bastille took on a very different air; in refusing the parochialism of Laclau and Mouffe's characterization of the French Revolution, I hope to show that their theory of hegemony nonetheless offers a persuasive means of extending our understanding of the Haitian Revolution.

The concept of hegemony introduces a series of fundamental modifications to the understanding of progressive political practice.[7] To focus on the struggle for hegemony over the concept of emancipation—which in the language of 1789 I am identifying as the French/Kreyol doublet *liberté/libete*—is to underline the degree to which the realm of the political extends to social struggles not reducible to any putatively primary reality such as the economic mode of production. The result of this shift is that no single group such as the proletariat or bourgeoisie can claim ontological dominance in any revolutionary sequence. Instead, we witness an infinite "chain of equivalence" of groups—in 1789, the philosophes, the *Tiers état,* slaves, Jews, women—continuously refiguring the ongoing struggle for emancipation. The final consequence of this shift, as Simon Critchley points out, is a turn to a discursive understanding of social action: "Insofar as social identity," writes Critchley, "loses all points of anchorage within an allegedly deeper reality, identity is the outcome of a discursive construction" (4).

Laclau has gone on to develop the concept of hegemony, in part in response to criticism articulated by Slavoj Žižek. In books such as *New Reflections on the Revolution of Our Time* (1990) and *Emancipation(s)* (1996), Laclau theorizes insurgent subjectivity as being constituted by a *lack* within a structure. Subjective identity is in such a view neither purely passive, fully determined by objective processes of structuration, nor the unhindered, Promethean activity of a transcendental subject-creator. Instead, activity occurs through a process of *identification* with this constitutive lack (Critchley 6).

To figure political action as a process of hegemonization reconfigures the traditional understanding of the relation between singularity and universality. The universal is no longer to be understood as the plenitude of an Enlightenment ideal, radiating outward from a transcendental point of perfection to illuminate humanity, but is instead fundamentally devoid of concretion, naming an impossible fullness that would ground an emancipated society. Universality is in this view a void on the horizon of the social, never fully instantiated, but always informing the struggle of different social actors to embody its promise. The immediate implications of this reformulation of hegemony are enormous. This is so not only for postmodern political practice since 1968, as has been widely recognized, but equally if not more so for an event such as the Haitian Revolution.

Laclau is the contemporary political theorist to have described most clearly the interdependency of the singular specifics of any situation and the universal norms of human rights. In *Emancipation(s)*, Laclau offers a theory of the historicization of any abstract universal such as human freedom. In his formalist understanding of the universal, in which "the universal has no content of its own" (15), Laclau at first only vaguely gestures to unspecified "new discourses of liberation . . . beyond emancipation" (13). In "Universalism, Particularism, and the Question of Identity," however, he explicitly historicizes this formalism. As I am arguing was the case in the Haitian Revolution, Laclau observes that "the universal emerges out of the particular not as some principle underlying and explaining the particular [by subaltern subjects attaining some preexistent human essence], but as an incomplete horizon suturing a dislocated identity. . . . It is one thing to say that the universalistic values of the West are the preserve of its traditional dominant groups; it is very different to assert that the historical link between the two is a contingent and unacceptable fact which can be modified through political and social struggles" (28, 33).

Laclau's example is telling: "When Mary Wollstonecraft, in the wake of the French Revolution, defended the rights of women, she did not present the exclusion of women from the declaration of the rights of man and citizen as a proof that the latter are intrinsically male rights, but tried, on the contrary, to deepen the democratic process by showing the incoherence of establishing universal rights which were restricted to particular sectors of the population" (33). Likewise, in Saint-Domingue, this process of "widening the spheres of [universalism's] application" (34) transformed both the revolutionary world and the very concept of the universal itself. Attention to the universalism of a specific historical case such as the Haitian Revolution can hope to show *how and to what degree* "without the emergence of the universal within the historical terrain, emancipation becomes impossible" (13).

As theorists of the universal as a void without positive content, Laclau and his interlocutor Žižek continue to fetishize the subaltern, disenfranchised subject. Yes, the universal necessarily operates through lack, void, and absence, but against them, one must affirm unequivocally the universal possibility of *all* humans to participate in such a hegemonic struggle to reformulate the parameters of emancipation. No less than Toussaint, one thinks of more privileged subjects such as Robespierre, Sièyes, and Schoelcher, each of whom displaced the hegemony of universal human rights to further encompass the void or lack that was colonial slavery. Only, for the latter, the *mode* of this operation was exactly the reverse.

If the disenfranchised (Olympe de Gouges, Toussaint) needed to *affirm the void* or absent plenitude they inhabited as the true and positive site of universal rights, Robespierre or Schoelcher (as free, white, male, Western European holders of positive rights) actively *voided the affirmation* of their positions of privilege.[8] They did this by displacing the focus of universal rights from themselves to the enslaved, and in the process exercised, no less than Toussaint, their human capacity to singularize themselves (as radical exceptions in relation to their complacent milieu of liberal "abolitionists" [Condorcet, Grégoire, Tocqueville] so ready to compromise the political project of universal emancipation).[9] If the universal "comes to exist ... *only* in a structural element which is structurally displaced," one must nonetheless affirm that *all* humans have the capacity to undertake such a displacement; the modality of such an undertaking will simply be different considering whether one is already a privileged bearer of rights or the subject of their lack (Žižek 1999, 224; my emphasis).

A concrete (yet incomplete) universal appeared in Haiti in 1791 precisely because slaves perceived the contradiction between a universal of which they could conceive and the incompletion of its merely existing first trial run of 1789.[10] This is the element of concretion that attention to postcolonial history and experience can bring to an abstract notion of the universal as infinite deferral and incompletion. Because new forms of violence appeared in Haiti in 1804, should Haitian slaves have followed Condorcet's advice in his 1781 pamphlet *Réflexions sur l'esclavage des nègres* and remained passively enslaved for another generation or two, until the white masters decided they were "ready" for freedom? The problems of social violence in Haiti both under Toussaint and since 1804 are enormous and cannot be ignored. My point here is that they bear their own particularities and problems, dimensions that are emphatically *not* the same as those of violence under the system of the officially vetted, state-based slaveholding plantocracy of pre-1793 Saint-Domingue.

## The Struggle for Ideological Hegemony in Saint Domingue

As the previous chapter noted, in its construction of a dialectic between the universal and the particular, the Haitian Constitution of 1805 asserted the universal equality of all humans ("All mortals are equal"), while simultaneously affirming human "diversity," or what I am calling singularization ("so many kinds of different beings . . . scattered . . . over the surface of the globe") (cited in Fischer 231). This was no insurmountable aporia, but reflected instead the necessary interdependence of universal truth claims with their determinate, historical instantiations. Moving beyond the more limited civil rights of the American and French revolutions, the Haitian Revolution articulated true universalism as an eminently *political,* and not merely reflective, process. As such, the conflict initiated in this struggle for autonomous self-definition was properly hegemonic, an attempt to implement politically highly specific and often incompatible visions of *liberté/libete*.[11]

The struggle for symbolic hegemony was decisive in the singular unfolding of the entire Haitian Revolution. When Haitian slaves demanded their human rights in 1791, they did not simply play by the rules of the Parisian bourgeois in demanding that the conception of those rights should merely be expanded to include African slaves under their rubric. Human rights, in the hegemonic revolutionary Parisian discourse of the period 1789–93, were themselves constituted through the active exclusion of slaves, and could thus not simply admit slaves under their concept without that concept itself being radically transformed.

At the same time, the slaves of Saint-Domingue made strategic use of the absent plenitude of a *universal* (*liberté/libete,* emancipation, *liberté générale*), precisely to make their intervention more than a mere claim for recognition within the categories of the dominant system.[12] In so doing they made apparent what had remained invisible in the celebration of liberty in 1789: that this loudly proclaimed liberty was a deception and mere semblance, the hollow posturing of so-called representatives of the people, their "democratic illusion" underwritten by the slaveholding sugar-production system.[13] Only the active, litigious, uncompromising refusal of the noncoincidence of a subaltern people with its ideal self-understanding (*liberté/libete*) could hope to dissipate the self-satisfied Parisian illusion of France as the Promised Land of the Rights of Man.

Saint-Domingue offers a paradigmatic instance of a hegemonic struggle to determine the contents of a signifier (*liberté/libete*) whose meaning becomes the grounds of ideological struggle. In addition to his tactical military genius, Toussaint effectively hegemonized the symbolic dimension of the revolutionary struggle in Saint-Domingue. The abstract signifiers "liberté" and "égalité," to be found at the head of all revolutionary correspondence, here took on a novel dimension, functioning quite literally as empty, floating signifiers, pointing visually to the very real lack or absence of freedom (slavery) that determined and radicalized the entire Haitian Revolution (figure 3). The absolute and abstract universality of the truth claims of *liberté* put forward by the *Déclaration des droits de l'homme* took on special meaning in Saint-Domingue, where they revealed a merely negative absence of freedom amid ongoing slavery.

This hegemonic process of subaltern struggle is precisely the opposite of the Deleuzian concept of a *becoming-minoritarian*. Rather than a "becoming-different", one witnesses in Saint-Domingue an attempt to become the same.[14] In a world structured by differences ("you are slaves, I am the Master"), the struggle to recognize an immanent Truth of identity ("we are all subjects to a universal right, indifferently") turned the events in Saint-Domingue into a radical intervention to restructure the ontological grounds of a society.[15] The emancipatory process in Saint-Domingue was a struggle for the slaves of Saint-Domingue to become identical not in an ontic sense (to become white, French, European, or the Master), but rather the hegemonic effort to ground their (ontic) becoming-singular—their becoming Haitian in 1804—upon a single transcendental field of human possibility prior to any becoming-singular. It was the

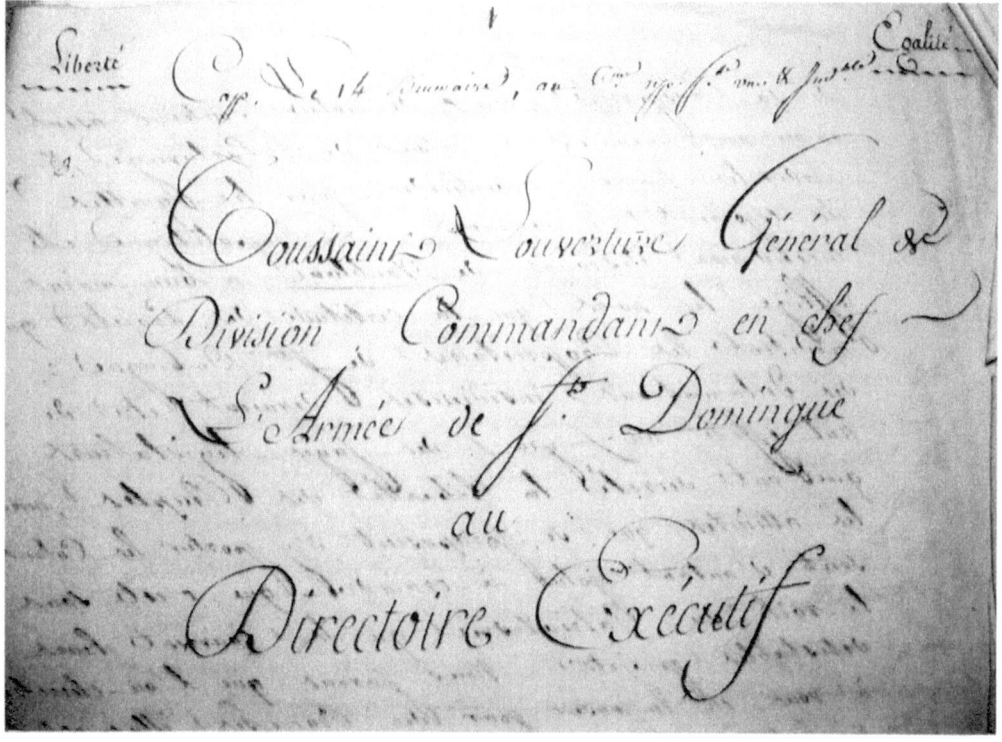

Fig. 3. Portion of letter of Toussaint Louverture, 14 Brumaire, Year 6 (November 4, 1797), with the headings "Liberté" and "Egalité." (Document conservé aux Archives nationales, Paris)

struggle to transform themselves from an uncounted mass of anonymous slaves to being counted among the autonomous nations of human society. Such a becoming-singular of an individual or group, unlike a philosophy of multiculturalist particularism, was necessarily grounded upon a prior ontological possibility, the possibility of becoming subjects to a universal right to freedom.

This struggle for politico-symbolic hegemony and the attendant self-fashioning of new subjectivities along the perimeter of the Atlantic world took form as a paradigmatic instance in Western modernity of what Laclau has called "populist reason." Laclau's formal analysis and defense of the "political logic" of populist reason emphasizes the degree to which any concept is constantly transformed by multiple, conflicting demands as it moves through various cultural contexts (2005, 14). In Laclau's phenomenology of populist reason, a populist sequence arises in the strategic aggregation of a series of differential claims for justice that coalesce into an "equivalential articulation" (74). In Saint-Domingue between 1789 and 1791, a series of demands for the social and political rights of a variety of actors (mulattoes, free blacks, and both Creole and *Bossale* slaves) remained frustrated by the maintenance of slavery and institutionalized racism. This had the effect of separating this population from the metropolitan beneficiaries of the rights of man, and drove them to subsume the diversity of their claims under the absent fullness of the signifier *libete/liberté* located at "the limit of what was representable within" that society (81).

Laclau's analysis of the formation of populist reason describes how, following a sociopolitical disruption such as 1789, a series of disjointed, local revolts can come to coalesce into a single revolutionary sequence, (temporarily) subsuming a diversity of claims for justice within a single articulation (77). In this process a segment of society makes a political claim for its own *privileged* status within society. The white planter class was the first to put forward its own (differential) claims for autonomy to Paris in the wake of 1789, but it was rapidly refused the right to such claims by the numerically superior slaves, and forced to assume its proper place as the class bearing antagonistic, illegitimate (because non-universal) rights. In its place, first the mulattoes and free blacks, then finally the slaves themselves, made bids for hegemony in the rapidly developing struggle.

Within this emergent popular subjectivity, the primary equivalence established was the coalition formed between a diverse mulatto and free-black Creole population, on the one hand, and the rural, African-born *Bossale* slaves, on the other. This strategic alliance in the face of slavery and racism subsumed a series of radically divergent understandings of the precise meaning of *libete/liberté* in the first years (1791–96) of the revolution. Once slavery itself was eliminated, however, this alliance rapidly divided between the various elites (military, Catholic, plantocratic, mulatto, mercantile) and the egalitarian claims of the rural population. It quickly became apparent that the desires of the excluded *moun andeyo* could not remain in dialogue with the newly emergent elite, but instead took up a place not only exterior (*andeyo*) to elite Haitian society but beyond the compass of representability and, to an important degree, even comprehensibility within the emergent norms of transnational Atlantic capital and liberal individualism.[16]

Prior to this division, however, in the period of 1791–95, the unification of these subaltern populations occurred in the face of the overwhelming imperative to eliminate slavery. The crystallization of a series of differential demands into an equivalential sequence culminated in August 1793 with the explicit articulation of the concept of *libete/liberté* by Toussaint Louverture. In his public affirmation of August 29 that "liberty [must] reign in St. Domingue," an emergent populist reason attained specification under an absent universal. The concept of liberty, first put forward in the Declaration of the Rights of Man of 1789, became the "common denominator" that "embodies the totality of the series" (Laclau 2005, 95). The highly charged, privileged signifier of *libete/liberté* enunciated by Toussaint successfully attracted the radical investment of an entire population behind this initiative. It came to represent that desire in a constitutive process of improvisatory invention; it sparked an affective force of attraction and desire that coalesced into a variegated "volonté générale," a process that sustained itself (in the *Bossale* population in particular) through the many years of the struggle for Haitian independence to culminate in independence in 1804 (110).[17] Another way of formulating the legacy of 1804, then, is to say, following Laclau, that a concept (the philosophes' Enlightenment abstraction of liberty) was driven beyond the limits of European provincialism to become an empty signifier that Haiti bestowed upon the modern world, one that we have not ceased to fill with ever-changing, divergent contents in the ongoing political struggle to determine and actualize human rights (183).

## Hegemony and the Paris–Saint-Domingue Continuum

If the idea of a general, universal emancipation from enslavement is the founding and determinant idea of the Haitian Revolution, we should not conclude that it characterized the events in Saint-Domingue uniformly from the first revolt of 1791 to the final declaration of independence by Dessalines on January 1, 1804. Rather, the idea of general emancipation gradually came to predominate the revolutionary events in their many twists and turns over thirteen long years.

When the slaves of Saint-Domingue revolted in the summer of 1791, they joined the struggle to assert hegemony over the drive for emancipation that had determined the events of the French Revolution during the previous two years.[18] This process was exemplified by the Abbé Sièyes's famous declaration from January 1789: "Qu'est-ce que le Tiers État?—Tout." In this moment the particular claims of a section of French society had bid for universal status. This class then gradually asserted its hegemony over the drive for emancipation, and in the process actively excluded other groups—Jews, women, slaves—from occupying such a hegemonic position.[19] The meaning of terms such as *droit naturel* and *liberté/libete* was in constant flux during the revolutionary period, repeatedly redefined by those subjects who felt themselves to be excluded yet understood themselves unequivocally to be subjects of universal rights (Hunt 1996, 23). Within this context, while a very few lone individuals in France struggled in vain to assert slavery and universal emancipation as a central and defining process in the revolutionary period (Marat, Mirabeau, Robespierre),[20] it was only the revolutionaries in Saint-Domingue who would succeed in this endeavor.

In Saint-Domingue, the call for *liberté générale* by the revolting slaves gradually came to predominate over more limited demands for ameliorative improvements in working conditions. For Boukman, the Kreyol signifier *libete* referred to a vaguely godlike, anthropomorphic force with which all slaves could immediately identify. When encouraging slaves to join the revolt he helped instigate, he invoked this *libete* repeatedly with the phrase "Couté libete li palé nan Coeur nous tous" ("Listen to the voice of Liberty that speaks in all our hearts") (Fick 93).

When Vincent Ogé defended the civil and political rights of mulatto property owners in Paris in 1789, his rhetoric, though excluding slaves from the category of humanity, emphasized the constituent, inspirational power of a concept whose inherently universal scope implied the fundamental transformation of the (ancien) regime of power that limited freedom to an elite oligarchy: "Sirs, *this word of Freedom* that one cannot pronounce without enthusiasm, *this word* that carries with it the idea of happiness, is this not because it seems to want to make us forget the evils that we have suffered for so many centuries? This Freedom, the greatest, the first of goods, is it made for all men? I believe so. Should it be given to all men? I believe so again."[21]

The original goal of the August 1791 revolt was to force an end to the practice of whipping and to win three free days per week from the *grands blancs* (Bell 2007, 32). As early as the fall of 1791, however, in the earliest months of the Saint-Domingue revolution when most rebels were merely calling for improved working conditions and continued to invoke the authority of Louis XVI, the *Philadelphia General Advisor* reported that one group of slaves had made the request to a French officer that "all the slaves be made free."[22] Another group, the paper reported, had asserted before the insurrection even began that the slaves "wanted to enjoy the liberty they are entitled to by the Rights of Man" (cited in Dubois 2004a, 105). In a similar vein, a letter signed by an inhabitant of Saint-Domingue named "Nicoleau" from September 19, 1791, asserted in alarmist fashion that the colonists should "renounce the principles of the National Assembly that the rebel slaves have called for; they have sent representatives to demand the rights of man."[23] A letter from Jean-François dated September 4, 1791, a mere week after the initial revolt, asserted somewhat vaguely that "we are only after our dear liberty" and closes with an oath "to win or to die for liberty" (Bell 2007, 37). Though this "we" may indicate no more than the rebel leaders such as Jean-François Papillon himself, its very ambiguity points the way to the future radicalization of this claim.

News of the August 29, 1791, slave revolt first arrived in France in November of that year. Already since late October, rumors of a revolt had been front-page news in the *Moniteur Universel,* reflecting the central importance of Saint-Domingue to France's economy. When confirmation did arrive, the November 2 issue of the *Moniteur* reported that "among the different letters received from Saint-Domingue, some report that the blacks are singing songs of liberty." On November 7, in the first direct confirmation of the revolt, a letter to the *Moniteur* from P. de Cadusch, president of the Assemblée générale de Saint-Domingue placed the blame for the revolt upon Enlightenment philosophy: "Our slaves are armed to destroy us, and philosophy, which appeared made to console men, brings us only despair."

A letter from the rebels in the North to Blanchlande dated September 1791 asserted that "we are only striving after this dear liberty, this precious object. . . . We shall have no other motto than to live free or die for liberty" (Madiou 110). Another letter of September 27, 1791, from a "captain presently in Cap Français" asserted, "In the Northern Province, . . . the rallying cry is the word liberty."[24]

In contrast to these documents, at the same moment in October 1791, Jean-François assured his French secretary, Gros, that he was not fighting for *"liberté générale"* but merely for the plantation managers to be banned from the colony: "In taking up arms, I have never pretended to fight for general liberty, which I know to be an illusion, as much due to France's need for her colonies as for the danger in granting to uncivilized hordes a right that would become infinitely dangerous to them, inevitably bringing about the destruction of the colony."[25] When three civil commissioners arrived from France, Jean-François and his cohort Georges Biassou, in a letter of November 12, 1791, proposed that they would end the revolt if the commissioners agreed to "grant freedom to the number of leaders that we take the liberty to designate to you" while they cynically proposed in return to "pursue the blacks . . . wherever they will take refuge" and to return them to slavery.[26] At this early point in the uprising, the concept of *liberté/libete* at work in this letter is merely rhetorical, a seemingly empty phrase addressed to the French ("que nous prenons la liberté de vous designer"). Implicitly, it signifies to its readers freedom as pure ideology, the mere cynical manipulation and usurping of power by an elite at the expense of the mass of slaves.

The letters Jean-François and Biassou wrote to the commissioners in these months following the first uprising are intriguing, however, in their rhetorical manipulation of the word "liberty"; again and again these former slaves invoke their "liberty," as if to implicitly assert their autonomous humanity to their correspondents in a semi-coded and formulaic fashion. "We have taken the liberty to write to you . . . [*Nous avons pris la liberté de vous écrire*]"; "We take the liberty to request of you . . . [*Nous prenons la liberté de vous prier*]"; "Allow us to take the liberty . . . [*Permettez que nous prenions la liberté*]," they repeat again and again, but only in the end to request a limited emancipation of an elite, or that slaves' working conditions merely be improved.[27]

While the concrete demands of these letters remained timid and limited, this constant rhetorical invocation of liberty served to announce the approach of a moment when these former slaves would call for and be willing to die for a general and unlimited emancipation. The letters written between the slave leaders and the metropolitan French government offer traces of a complex and variegated manipulation of the content of the abstract signifier *liberté/libete*. These early letters by leaders such as Biassou and Jean-François shied away from any explicit linking of "liberté" and the "general" emancipation of slaves.[28] Instead, they used the term only in a secondary fashion, drawing on a highly subordinate and restricted meaning of the term: the "right or permission to do something."

Six months later, in July 1792, a group of insurrectionary slaves in the Southern Province were still calling not for universal emancipation but for three free days per week and the elimination of whipping (Dubois 2004a, 128, 135). At the same moment in the north of the island, however, Jean-François, Biassou, and Toussaint (writing under the pseudonym of his then fourteen-year-old nephew Belair) suddenly aligned themselves with the cause of General Emancipation; in July 1792 they wrote to the Colonial Assembly and commissioners that since the Declaration of Rights declared that "men are born free and equal in rights," they should grant "general liberty for all men retained in slavery" along with a general amnesty.

This letter, discovered by Natelie Piquionne, completely reconfigures the ideological chronology of the Haitian Revolution.[29] In its constant reference to the concepts of an undivided humanity (the writers are "men like yourselves"), both human and natural rights, and general emancipation, the letter is extremely revealing. Piquionne rightly observes that it both cuts short Pierre Pluchon's denial of the role of general emancipation in Saint-Domingue and nullifies C. L. R. James's and Aimé Césaire's efforts to distinguish the role of this universalist ideology in the actions of Toussaint from the self-serving moderation of Jean-François and Biassou (136–38).

Though Jean-François and Biassou would soon end up trafficking in slaves across the Spanish border, this letter marks Toussaint's henceforth unequivocal and unwavering commitment to universal emancipation based upon natural human rights, the imperative around which he would orient without exception his many seemingly Machiavellian actions in coming years (Bell 2007, 43).[30] Toussaint was indeed a leader "capable of absolute treachery, absolute ruthlessness, and absolute hypocrisy"; all these qualities, along with those of logical clarity, rhetorical brilliance, military genius, and the like, were expressed to the highest degree and without reserve to achieve the conditions he thought necessary for his community's initial and continued emancipation from slavery (Bell 2007, 106).

Moreover, the textual citation of the 1789 French *Déclaration* in the July 1792 Declaration demonstrates, no matter what its authorship, the circulation of a universalist human rights ideology in Saint-Domingue well before Sonthonax's 1793 publication of the 1789 document.[31] The document bases its claims on the universalist pretensions of the rule of law instituted since 1789: "We are black, it is true, but tell us, Gentlemen, you who are so judicious, what is the law that says that the black man must belong to and be the property of the white man? . . . We can neither see nor find the right which you pretend to have over us, nor anything that could prove it to us, set down on the earth like you, all being children of the same father created in the same image." The unassailable logic of their argument is the strict equivalency of the doctrine of natural rights: "We are your equals then, by natural right."[32] Suddenly, the precise content of "liberté" had been radically altered; no longer a mere "taking of liberties," the term now takes on its primary and most radical meaning: "the state or situation of a person who is not absolutely dependent upon someone else (opposed to *esclavage, servitude*)" (*Dictionnaire Robert*).

This confusing situation of multiple and conflicting demands only became focused through Toussaint and Sonthonax's unqualified support for general emancipation in August 1793. By then, with the increasing success of the slave revolt, free citizens, including many whites, were already calling openly for "les Droits de l'Homme" and "liberté générale" as a means of rallying the slaves to fight for the Republic. On August 24, 15,000 free men voted for the emancipation of the slaves in the north of the island, and on August 29 Sonthonax decreed a partial abolition that applied only to this northern portion of the island's slaves. The radicality of Sonthonax's gesture lay in the fact that he made no provision in this decree for an intermediary period in which former slaves would gradually weather the transition to freedom, but instead instated abolition instantaneously (Dubois 2004a, 163, 165).

Though Sonthonax in this manner asserted the hegemony of the concept of General Emancipation, Toussaint Louverture soon usurped his dominant role in this process. Clearly, neither Sonthonax nor Toussaint can be said to have "caused" general emancipation in Saint-Domingue. Carolyn Fick points to a historically specific and unusual confluence of factors that made it possible to abolish slavery universally for the first time (1990, 162). These included the idea of general emancipation, the revolutionary Jacobin ideology of Sonthonax, and the political necessity of freeing the slaves to avoid losing the colony to Britain and Spain. Sonthonax, as Robert Stein has argued, was a committed abolitionist who, perhaps alone among his French contemporaries, was prepared for a universal and *immediate* abolition. Fick, however, draws our attention to the simple fact that without the radical, uncompromising, and widespread revolt of the multitude of slaves, the performative gesture of enunciating a proclamation would have had little effect, and "Sonthonax's proclamation may have fallen into something of a void" (163).

Though Sonthonax played an important role in quickening the pace of general emancipation in 1793, recent evidence points to the fact that it was Toussaint who organized and led the slave revolt from behind the scenes from its very beginning in the spring of 1791. At the secret instigation of plantation owners opposed to the island's autonomy, he may have brought together Jean-François, Biassou, Boukman, and Jeannot Billet to start an uprising (while he remained in the background) that quickly overran the northern plantations.[33] In his famous letter of August 25, 1793, Toussaint then publicly asserted both the central place of the struggle for "liberté générale" in the slaves' revolt and his hegemony over this demand: "The idea of this general liberty for which you are fighting your friends, who was it who established the basis of it, aren't I the original author?"[34] The impressive fact is that Toussaint already possessed, in this his first public statement, a *logic* of universal rights whose scope of address was not a class or race, but all humanity. In this logic of absolute rights, claims of equality are reduced to subsidiary, *political* processes.

"Liberty," Bell observes, is in Toussaint's analysis "a right given by Nature; equality is a consequence of that liberty, granted and maintained by this National Assembly" (2007, 103–4).

As a white French man who had never known slavery himself and who had publicly *defended* slavery and the plantation system upon his arrival in Saint-Domingue in September 1792, Sonthonax could never achieve total legitimacy in the fight for hegemony over the process of general emancipation. Though it was certainly a tactical decision, upon their arrival in Saint-Domingue, Sonthonax and his fellow commissioners publicly celebrated the slaveholding plantocratic order. The *Journal Politique de Saint Domingue* of September 19, 1792, reported that when a "deputation of colored citizens" came to greet the commissioners, the latter "responded to them that they only knew of two classes of men, free ones and slaves."

Sonthonax then publicly reaffirmed this standpoint in a speech the following day:

> Citizens of all classes, the Civil Commissioners announce to you that they only recognize in St. Domingue two classes of citizens, the free and slaves, that they view slavery as absolutely necessary, and the slave as the only agent employable for cultivation.... They protest before the Supreme Being, in the presence of all citizens that they have come to enforce the respect of these principles, and that they are willing to give their lives, if necessary, to defend them."[35]

Sonthonax was in fact no defender of the ancien régime, his defense of slavery clearly a tactical decision to give him time as he moved toward the goal of abolition. Still, one could imagine many other options open to him besides making such an explicit and public defense of slavery and the social order based upon the distinction between free men and slaves. Though he did eventually abolish slavery, and though he had earlier published vocal and explicit vituperations against slavery in *Révolutions de Paris* and elsewhere, Sonthonax would always be speaking for others, bestowing freedom from above upon passive subjects (Stein 20–25).

When Sonthonax wrote to Toussaint in June 1794, enjoining the latter to come over to the side of the French Republic, he did so in the language of rights and general emancipation; his paternalistic, condescending tone, however, barely hides the fact that it is Toussaint who by then controlled the game in Saint-Domingue.

> As long as liberty had not been proclaimed, you could have been excused and even right to have spilled the blood of your tyrants.... But since France

has authorized us to declare you free, since August 29, the solemn day of the proclamation of your Rights, those who refuse to serve France are the blindest of men. . . . [France] has forever banished slavery by declaring that a man is not a commodity and that he can neither sell himself nor be sold. . . . *Vive la Liberté Générale*.[36]

It would not be long before Sonthonax, who by the time of his second commission in Saint-Domingue (May 1796 to August 24, 1797) could accomplish little without Toussaint's support, would be sent back to France by the latter.

Somewhat ironically, Toussaint himself had been free and a land- and slave-owner since the mid-1770s. It was only on August 23, 1793, that Toussaint publicly expressed his unequivocal support for general emancipation, and on August 25 that he made his famous declaration: "I am Toussaint Louverture. . . . I want liberty and equality to reign in Saint Domingue." From this point on, Toussaint made the cause of *liberté générale* the central point of the revolution itself, tactically asserting its dominant hegemony in the face of the French Assembly's reticence, assuring through his military and rhetorical skills that the assembly would by 1794 address the cause of the abolition of slavery.

## The First Dissidents

When Toussaint publicly announced his devotion to the cause of "liberty and equality" on August 25, 1793, and even before when the rebel slaves Biassou, Jean-François, and Belair (and most likely Toussaint) drafted their letter of July 1792 to the Saint-Domingue General Assembly and French Commissioners, they effectively became the first political dissidents of the modern era. Their rhetorical gesture was precisely that which would come to typify the act of modern dissidence from Haiti to Helsinki: to invoke the rule of law and right as it has in fact been formulated and promulgated by the oppressor himself, and to hold him to the letter of these claims.

> You Gentlemen, [they wrote in their letter of July 1792] who pretend to subject us to slavery—have you not sworn to uphold the French Constitution of which you are members? What does it say, this respectable Constitution?—what is its fundamental law?; have you forgotten that you have formally vowed the declaration of the rights of man which says that men are born free, equal in their rights; that the natural rights include liberty, property, security, and resistance to oppression? So then, as you cannot deny what you have sworn, we are within our rights, and you ought to recognize yourselves as perjurers;

by your decrees you recognize that all men are free, but you want to maintain servitude for four hundred and eighty thousand individuals who allow you to enjoy all that you possess.[37]

As a formal contestation of human rights abuses grounding its claims upon the legal and moral doctrines of their oppressors, the Haitian Revolution can rightly be called an incipient phenomenon of "dissidence" precisely in this modern sense.[38]

What is dissidence? Dissidence, defined as "public opposition to the laws, norms, and structures of a political regime," is not determined by the social status of a dissident, whether the dissident is rich or poor, black or white, an active participant in a political elite, or the excluded of a society. It is not defined by whether the dissident resorts to force or subscribes to a philosophy of nonviolence. Dissidence is defined, above all, by an individual or group's critical action under the guidance of some universalizable transcendental norm. This norm specifically allows one to bypass the contingent limitations of a given situation. Such a norm need not be magisterial on the order of the Universal Declaration of Human Rights or the Helsinki Accords. It can be something as simple as the transcendental definition of what a bus or a diner is: "buses transport fare-paying passengers along a specific route" or "a small, inexpensive restaurant where customers eat at the counter or in booths." Reference to such definitions allowed Rosa Parks, for example, to construct a dissident action that remained faithful to the transcendental definition of a bus, beyond any contingent situation: a bus is not a site for the racial classification of humans or their molestation, but a means of transport for human beings.

Parks's action points to a second necessary characteristic of dissidence. Many individuals and groups base their critical actions on transcendental norms, from the Nazis' critique of racial degeneration to the actions of a country that invades another unilaterally in the name of Democracy in the face of universal condemnation. For an action to be dissidence, its regulating norm must be universalizable to all humanity (this disqualifies the Nazis); second, the actor must also find means of action that in and of themselves instantiate that norm to some degree.

Rosa Parks did not kill southern racists in the name of free access to the city transit system, nor did she mount an invasion of Mobile's city hall; she simply sat on the bus in accord with her rational understanding of the concept "public transport." Similarly, any dissident action in support of human freedom or democracy must proceed so that it symbolically (and to that extent actually) furthers that end in a universalizable fashion, rather than destroying or bypassing universal norms of human rights in the name of Truth. If all humans were free to sit on buses as a means of transport, human freedom would be furthered in some small measure. If all human communities invaded one another in the name of freedom or democracy, however, the effect would be the total destruction of democracy and human freedom.

Václav Havel, whose 1974 essay "Power of the Powerless" is perhaps the most compelling theorization of modern dissidence, characterized the latter as a fundamental intervention within the domain of symbolic activity in a totalitarian society (and the slave plantation was no less "totalitarian" than Havel's Czechoslovak Socialist Republic); in other words, dissidence occurs as a struggle for ideological hegemony in a public sphere completely subordinate to a terroristic dominant ideology (Soviet-Marxism for Havel, slavery within the colonial plantocracy).[39]

In contrast to the universal ideological alienation of a totalitarian system, Havel proceeded to isolate the fundamental phenomenon of his intervention: the possibility that within a political systematization of lies, any human individual might choose to "live in truth" (*žít v pravdě*). Though the slave-based labor system of the eighteenth-century New World plantations was infinitely more dependent upon raw physical violence than that of Havel's totalitarian state (and thus necessitated the resort to violence on the part of the slaves), their fundamental similarity lies in the dissidents' struggle for hegemonic domination of concepts such as "Liberty" and "Truth." In the face of the systematic assertion of lies as truth (*Pravda*, as the ideological organ of the Soviet state called itself), the dissident asserts the "force of truth [*silou pravdy*]" (149). This truth is no mere idea; though it can take the form of the "conceptual thought" of the intellectual, it could just as well for Havel be a "rock concert" or a "student demonstration," "refusing to vote . . . or a hunger strike" (151).

In Saint-Domingue as in the Soviet Bloc, dissidence was a phenomenon not of contestation among the enfranchised (whether Jacobins and Montagnards in Paris, or Communist Party members), but precisely of the excluded and uncounted, of slaves and the "Plastic People of the Universe."[40] Dissidence, Havel wrote, "is a community that is *a priori* open to anyone," a movement that "originate[s] elsewhere, in the far broader area of the 'pre-political,' where living within a lie confronts living within the truth" (156). The dissidents of Saint-Domingue, perhaps even more than those of Prague and Gdansk, had no possibility of struggling for an alternance of political parties within a system predicated upon their disenfranchisement from the human race.[41] To act as a dissident and live within truth is not to form a loyal opposition, but instead to refuse participation in the totality of a social system.[42]

Finally, the common feature of all modern dissidence is the focus on universal human rights and the rule of law. Their efficacy depends upon the demonstration of the incongruity between the actions of an immoral state that calls itself the Truth and the universal norm of a right to freedom under the rule of law. The creation in 1789 of a society grounded not upon divine right but upon universal human law/rights (*droit*) created the conditions for the invention of dissidence—as distinct from phenomena such as revolt or critique—by private individuals such as Olympe de Gouges and Biassou, Jean-François, and Toussaint Louverture.[43]

The inspired perversity of dissidence is that its practitioners do not *invent* a moral code that they then hold up against a purely evil system, but instead turn the system's own code against itself. It is the totalitarian system itself that authorizes its own destruction. Dissidence in its distinctly modern sense became possible only when a *political* system based upon the divine right of kings and its legal manifestation in the *Code Noir* was replaced by a system founded upon the Rights of Man (rather than, say, the *moral* system of the Old Testament). In revolutionary France under the rule of the "incorruptible" legalistic purity of Robespierre, slavery offered precisely this point of what Havel called a system's "maximum mendacity." When forcibly confronted with this mendacity by slaves who refused to let the question of their humanity be sidelined, the self-appointed guardians of liberty, equality, and fraternity had, paraphrasing Havel, "no other choice" than to abolish slavery, against their own interests: "Because they [the Czechoslovak government] cannot discard the rules of their own game, they can only attend more carefully to those rules" (190). The Thermidorian reaction and Napoleon's subsequent reimposition of slavery simply confirm Havel's point, insofar as they could only pursue their agenda by abandoning the basic "rules" of 1789 and 1791.

Finally, Havel's analysis reveals the intensive relation between singular experience and universal right at the heart of the phenomenon of dissidence. The universal, in this view, arises not from its abstract affirmation by the bureaucrats of terror (whether Saint-Just or Gustav Husák), but instead as the self-differentiating articulation of human freedom by the uncounted—housewives, immigrants, students, the homeless, GLBTQ citizens, slaves: "Historical experience teaches us that any genuinely meaningful point of departure in an individual's life usually has an element of universality about it. . . . It must be potentially accessible to everyone; it must foreshadow a general solution [*obecneho řešení*] and, thus, it is not just the expression of an introverted, self-contained responsibility that individuals have to and for themselves alone, but a responsibility to and for the world [*odpovědností ke světu a za svět*]" (194).

This "general solution," the universal emancipation of humanity grounded upon a common potentiality to self-determination and perfectibility, is the legacy to the modern world of the Haitian Revolution. It has continued to inform the Haitian struggle for *libete/liberté* beyond 1804 and into the twentieth century. Most famously, the 1919 "Caco" revolt of Charlemagne Péralte against the U.S. Marine occupation was explicitly formulated as a dissident action that grounded its actions upon transcendent, universal norms. Péralte's July 1919 letter to the French consul in Port-au-Prince justified anti-U.S. resistance by the very principles of national self-determination put forward by Woodrow Wilson himself at the end of World War I:

> Contrary to the principles generally agreed to by civilized nations and to the rules of international law, the American government, taking advantage of the great European war, has intervened in the affairs of the small Republic of Haiti. . . . Today our patience is at an end and we demand our rights, unrecognized and flouted by the unscrupulous Americans. . . . In this day when, at the conference for peace among the civilized nations, they have sworn, before the entire world, to respect the rights and sovereignty of small nations, we demand the liberation of our territory and the right of free independent states, as recognized by international law. . . . We are prepared to make any sacrifice to liberate Haitian territory and create respect for the principles adopted by President Wilson himself, concerning the rights and sovereignty of small nations. Please note, Sir, that the American troops, by virtue of their own laws have no right to wage war against us. Sincerely, Charlemagne Péralte, Commander-in-chief of the Revolution, and 100 other signatories. (cited in Arthur and Dash 221–22)

Unlike the revolution of 1804, Péralte's act of dissidence, like so many others in modern history, was quickly and violently crushed by occupying forces who paid no attention to the norms of autonomous determination inscribed in their own constitutions (Millet). The memory of such strangled acts of dissidence lives on, however, to inform the political unconscious of our present era of transnational empire.

## 5 Toussaint Louverture, the *Moun andeyo*, and the Transcendental Conditions of Political Autonomy

### The Philosophy of the Haitian Revolution

THE EXAMINATION of the Enlightenment philosophy of natural and human rights in previous chapters offers a diverse series of theoretical tools with which to sound the political philosophy of the Haitian Revolution and Toussaint Louverture in particular in its fullest depth. As a concrete philosophy of praxis instantiated through intermittent, historically situated symbolic interventions, the Haitian Revolution offers no "philosophy" in the scholastic sense. To interpret the philosophical tenor of the Haitian Revolution means to assess critically the meaning of its various symbolic texts—as much the tactical decision of its actors to sacrifice all to the cause of universal emancipation as their actual letters, speeches, decrees, laws, and constitutions.

The philosophical richness of these diverse historiographic texts remains to be elaborated, such that one could then speak properly of a "philosophy" of the Haitian Revolution, much as Bernard Groethuysen spoke of a *Philosophie de la révolution française* in 1956. Carolyn Fick is no doubt correct to remind readers that the movement of events in Saint-Domingue was impelled above all not by events in France, nor by nominal leaders such as Toussaint, but instead by the steady, overwhelming assertion of the desire of a largely anonymous population of former slaves to live in a free society. Leaders such as Toussaint could only nurture and give direction to a desire that preexisted their intervention. Such an assertion, however, tells us little about the historically specific form the Haitian Revolution took. It is in this sense alone that one may be justified in focusing on a figure such as Toussaint, who, in dialogue with contemporaries such as Sonthonax, Jean-François, Robespierre, Diderot, and the *Déclaration des droits de l'homme et du citoyen*, was instrumental in focusing the revolt around the non-negotiable criteria of universal rights and the rule of law in a society free from slavery.

The singularity of the Haitian Revolution stands in this light as the furthest-reaching attempt of the Age of Enlightenment to ground social revolution upon the universal, ontological moral principles of human autonomy elaborated by the Radical Enlightenment. The obvious postmodern, identity-based retort that would condemn such a claim as betraying the singular (African) nature of the Haitian Revolution is no more than a tendentious, politically correct regression to neo-Negritude. Toussaint Louverture, though born of African parents, was a product of both the Age of Enlightenment (as much the development of a global sugar economy based upon slave labor as Raynal and Robespierre) and Afro-American culture. No doubt certain elements of African culture were sustained in his personality (his status as *docteur feuilles,* for example); still, to read the entirety of his surviving symbolic enunciations (letters, proclamations, speeches, laws) is to grasp the startling penetration of Enlightenment moral philosophy in his every action.

From the very first surviving testimony of his actions after 1791, we witness the remarkable transformation of Toussaint from an active participant in the slaveholding culture of Saint-Domingue into the instrument of that culture's total and absolute destruction in the name of the universal law of human autonomy. Toussaint Louverture, a free black since 1776, was himself a slave owner previous to 1791. This remarkable fact leads Pierre Pluchon to dismiss Toussaint's later invocations of General Liberty as the hollow posturing of a power-hungry "profiteur du régime colonial" (cited in Piquionne 135). More accurately, the fact of Toussaint's pre-1791 status as slave owner testifies to the extraordinary transformation of his entire worldview.[1] Speaking of the slaves of Les Platons in 1792, Carolyn Fick has described what must have been a general phenomenon throughout the island: "An irreversible transformation had occurred in the lives of these slaves. In less than a year, many of them had traveled the distance from obedient servant to armed auxiliary of mulattoes and free blacks in a movement that was not of their own making, finally to emerge as agents of their own freedom, and on their own footing" (1990, 150).

From his earliest interventions in the slave revolt in 1791 until his death in 1802, Toussaint submitted his actions to a concern for the transcendental rule of law. The first mention we have of Toussaint occurs in Gros' "Historical Account of the Events" from December 1791. After describing the opportunistic desire of Jean-François and Biassou to claim liberty only for themselves and 300 of their followers, Gros mentions in passing how "Toussaint à Bréda" saved the author from certain death at the hands of Biassou; instead, Toussaint forced Biassou to put Gros to trial before the law: "He [Biassou] was obliged to put us to trial, and to go before a court martial."[2] Toussaint's mentor Laveau shared this concern for the rule of law, and undoubtedly helped reinforce its primacy for his mentee. A proclamation by Laveau of 24 Vendemaire an 3 (Nov. 16, 1794) reiterates the replacement of the rule kings by the rule of law that followed 1789: "You have emerged from slavery, you are French citizens, henceforth having no other masters than God and the law."[3]

In a declaration of September 7, 1798, published in the *Moniteur Universel*, Toussaint made clear his commitment to the universal rule of law. He offered a general amnesty for plantation (and former slave) owners; in so doing, he placed concern for the law above the spirit of vendetta and retribution. "The spirit of humanity must predominate over all other considerations," Toussaint wrote. "Wishing to ally this concern with the security of a country that has been too often compromised, guided by my love for liberty, I promise, in the name of the French government, a generous amnesty, security and protection."

The publication of Toussaint's 1801 Constitution has too often been understood, even by sympathetic interpreters such as James and Césaire, in what we might call Napoleonic terms: as a mere moment in the consolidation of power by a now-uncontested leader who increasingly and tragically betrayed the ideal of emancipation for the neoslavery of forced plantation labor. The publishing of the 1801 Constitution, however, was in many respects the culmination of Toussaint's decade-old attempt to reorient the society of Saint-Domingue away from the arbitrary violence of slavery and to ground social relations upon the universal, abstract law of human autonomy.

It is 1801, not 1804, that constitutes the founding moment in the history of postcolonialism. This was the moment in which a colonized society first became an autonomous society, in the sense not only of a society that gives itself its own laws[4]—the same could be said of the slaveholding societies of America in 1776 or France in 1789 and, indeed, of Nazi Germany in 1933—but autonomous in the more limited Kantian sense of a society in which such auto-constitution is specifically governed by a criterion of universality. In the long and complex history of the struggle for a self-constituted society, amid landmarks such as 1776, 1789, 1848, 1917, 1956, 1968, and 1989, the date of 1801 can rightfully take pride of place as the moment in human history in which a society not only composed itself but did so, for all its secondary contradictions and shortcomings, upon the constitutional basis of undivided universal human rights.

Toussaint constructed the "Ceremonial Program for the Proclamation of the Constitution" (July 8, 1801) as a public celebration of this instantiation of the rule of law in Saint-Domingue. Attentive to the cultivation of moral consciousness that he had witnessed in the development of his own personality in the years since 1789, the constitution he formed for Saint-Domingue grounded liberty upon a single criterion: freedom from slavery. The program offered a public examination of the distinction between a regime of arbitrary force and a democracy: the submission of all, Toussaint claimed, must be to the rule not of a leader or master, but to abstract law based upon universal human right, a law that takes the concrete form of a constitution.

In his desire to cultivate the moral consciousness of those he governed, Toussaint was concerned above all to assure the presence at the event of "all the teachers and their students," in order to "hear the proclamation of the Constitution." Toussaint's goal was avowedly to "penetrate every spirit with affection and respect for the Constitution which must consolidate public liberty."[5] The freedom Toussaint imagined in this constitution was "public": slavery is an entirely social institution, and its abolition and positive absence in turn depended upon instituting new social relations. Not the inward happiness or absence of suffering of individuals, the single goal of Toussaint's politics was to institute the conditions of freedom within society such that individuals could realize their inherent human possibilities. In consequence, the public nature of freedom necessarily implied for Toussaint the education of the population of Saint-Domingue.

The ceremony itself stressed the link between a society existing under the rule of universal law and the conquest of human autonomy. In his opening speech, the president of Toussaint's assembly, Borgella, underscored the replacement of an arbitrarily imposed system of laws with a constitution: "The Metropolis, . . . had forced you to submit to a Law that [the inhabitants] had neither made nor consented to."[6] Toussaint's own speech further pointed to the transformation he intended for the population of Saint-Domingue, from heteronomous objects of the arbitrary whims of the Métropole, to the autonomous, enlightened (in the Kantian sense) constructors of their own Law.

Addressing them as if they were a newly formed nation ("Peuple de Saint-Domingue"), he celebrated the constitution as the guarantee of public freedom: "Oh you, my fellow citizens of every age, state, and color, you are free, and the Constitution that has been given to me today must make this freedom eternal." Toussaint called upon all assembled to submit, not to a king, nor to an assembly, nor even to Toussaint himself, but instead to "submit to the Law alone; it will never cease to be your protector and guardian. . . . Swear . . . before the Supreme Being and myself that you will submit to these Laws, which must contribute to your happiness and consolidate your Liberty."

The ambiguous nature of these exhortations is nonetheless patent. It is Toussaint, as governor, who would decree and institute these laws, proscribing all critical disagreement and the option of revolt, arbitrarily and autocratically imposing his will upon his fellow citizens in the absence of even the most minimal democratic structures in the system his constitution sought to implement.[7] In point of fact, Toussaint had simply replaced a distant autocracy with a homegrown one. The single difference is that this system was erected not upon divine right, but upon universal human rights; as such, and unlike the laws of the ancien régime, the entire paternalistic and exploitive empirical political system the 1801 Constitution calls for in its subsidiary articles (6–77) is a priori *invalidated* by their betrayal of the grounding, unqualified right to human autonomy articulated in Articles 3, 4, and 5.[8]

Four days after the events celebrating the publication of the constitution (July 12, 1801), Toussaint issued a general amnesty of prisoners in which he again made clear that the transformation of society he intended was from one based upon arbitrary violence to the rule of law: "The island of St. Domingue has finally obtained the benefits of a Constitution. . . . Until today the colony has only had uncertain Laws; the time has come where positive Laws shall clearly fix the rights and duties of all Citizens."[9] A declaration of June 29 asserted another dimension of the rule of law, attacking the corruption of public officials who had been charging citizens illegally for various public services: "As a public servant [*homme public*], I must render Justice, as for all my actions, without charge to all individuals." These speeches and decrees all attest to Toussaint's fidelity to the institution of the rule of law in Saint-Domingue. His faithfulness to this imperative stemmed from a single point: the domination of the rule of law constituted in his view the sole means of formalizing and codifying the total elimination of slavery. His constitution of 1801 was the summation of this desire to institute socially the total abolition of slavery—not as the personal whim of one leader or class, but rather as the absolute and rational grounding of a society upon universal human right.

Though it is unclear to what extent the form and content of the constitution can be directly attributed to Toussaint (his secretary general, Pascal, played a significant role in its composition [de Cauna 199]), it is certain that Toussaint oversaw every word of what was undoubtedly the most important document of his public career. It borrowed much in content, style, and form from the French constitutions of 1791 and 1793 (Fischer 264) and from the Thermidorian Constitution of 1795 in its ban of slavery, while going beyond all of these earlier documents in its ontological fidelity to unqualified universal emancipation. While transparently promoting the consolidation of Toussaint's personal power (the constitution made him governor of Saint-Domingue for life[10]) and inaugurating a Haitian recourse to *caporalisme agraire* (agrarian militarism), the historical importance of the 1801 Constitution lies in its attempt to base, for the first time in world history, a decolonized society upon the rule of law and social justice.

One should avoid overpersonalizing the 1801 Constitution; it reflects not only the limitations of Toussaint Louverture and his indubitable desire for power but also those of postslavery Saint-Domingue society as a whole. The document's contradictions reflect the fundamental division between what Trouillot has called the Haitian "nation" that desired assurance of continued freedom from slavery, and the "state," which "inherited the social and economic institutions from colonial times, [institutions that] required a regimented labor force" (Fischer 269). Toussaint Louverture merely condensed this contradiction between nation and state in the antinomies of his own person, in the contradiction between an absolute fidelity to the universal abolition of slavery and a defense of paternalist, militaristic forms of agrarian plantocracy in the name of the state and independence. This conflict was structurally endemic to Saint-Domingue/Haiti, and was not a mere matter of Toussaint's personal psychology; from 1801 until the general abolition of slavery throughout the North Atlantic world, "freedom from slavery could be guaranteed only through independence. The transnational ideology that lay at the foundation of Haiti thus had to be disavowed even by those who owed their liberty from slavery to it" (Fischer 271).

Though we may rightly reject the constitution's nearsighted defense of obligatory, large-scale plantation labor (Articles 14–18), this is only a tactical and secondary defense (the *means*, Toussaint believed, to ensure continued emancipation), not the foundation of the constitution itself. For Sibylle Fischer, the tension between individual liberty and paternalist authoritarianism inherent in the 1801 Constitution arises from the text's multiple authorship, "in committees that would have included men trained in France and illiterate former slaves" (228). It is unlikely to the point of impossibility, however, that Toussaint would have allowed the text to make its ringing defense of phallocratic authority had he not subscribed to this vision of Saint-Domingue's reality. Instead, the document initiates a Haitian politics of predatory and messianic republicanism (Fatton 11) while inventing a novel form of republicanism that rejects absolute property rights in the name of an unqualified human right to freedom from slavery.

While it goes on to reassert patriarchal authoritarianism, Toussaint's 1801 Constitution is based upon a single, universal criterion: human autonomy. The universal abolition of slavery ("Art. 3.—There can exist no slaves on this territory, slavery is forever abolished there. All men are born, live and die free and French") as well as other secondary rights of autonomy (the institution of meritocracy and the destruction of privilege, equality before the law, guarantee of due process) form its ontological ground.[11] Fischer considers this the fundamental and most original dimension of its articulation. Fischer points out that the document has no preamble or equivalent to the 1789 Declaration of the Rights of Man and Citizen, and it is impossible that this omission can be an oversight on Toussaint's part. "The issue of slavery," Fischer comments, "is thus addressed not as a part of a list of individual or social rights . . . but as part of a title dealing with 'inhabitants', that is, as an aspect of the political constitution of the colony" (264).

Fischer proposes that the changing content of universal rights affirmed in the various French constitutions of the 1790s must have been profoundly troubling for observers in Saint-Domingue committed to the absolute and unassailable eradication of slavery. Her analysis of "the radicalness of Toussaint's approach" underscores the paradoxical nature of his initiative: in refusing to articulate a separate, timeless, and universal statement of human rights, the 1801 Constitution instead integrated that statement into the body of the document as its principle article. Such a formulation implies that for Toussaint, the universal, unqualified human right to freedom could not remain a timeless abstraction; instead, Toussaint was intimately aware of the fragile status of human rights in the geopolitical context of the 1790s, and the constitution was thus a political and historical initiative, "the indispensable foundation of the geopolitical entity called Saint Domingue" (264).

Toussaint's 1801 Constitution moved beyond the abstract, theoretical universalism of Enlightenment antislavery to historicize and politicize the struggle for human rights. Its most radical gesture, Fischer shows, was to have made of human rights an eternally contested point of political intervention and defense, while simultaneously universalizing those rights by making them independent of citizenship and applicable to all men, no matter what their color (266). Paradoxically, "by admitting territorial limitations" on freedom (limiting the ban on slavery to the geopolitical space of Saint-Domingue), "the Saint Domingue constitution gains a higher degree of universality" than those French constitutions granting only citizens the benefit of "universal" rights. "It is through the unlinking of the rights of liberty from any question of citizenship that the universality lost in the first moment [of mere citizenship] is restored in the moment that it applies to 'all men'" (266).

In this sense, the 1801 Constitution is utterly incommensurate with an ancien régime supported by the economics of slave labor. Property ("sacrée et inviolable") is subsidiary in this document to respect for the natural law that makes it impossible for any human being to own another. The inviolability and respect for property is subordinate to the universal ban on slavery that inaugurates and grounds the constitution.[12] As a secondary right, this defense of property cannot include the possession of one human being by another. In its ontological focus upon unqualified freedom from slavery, the 1801 Constitution necessarily posed the codependency of liberty and equality much more radically than in Paris in the 1790s. Only if all humans are understood to be fundamentally equal could they all be free from enslavement.

The contradictions of this document, however, begin at the level of its ontological grounding. The focus on geography, on the territorial expanse of Saint-Domingue, in its opening paragraphs underscores the fact that a universal ban on slavery can become manifest only in a determinate situation, in a particular, empirical, and contingent site. Indeed, the formal structure of the first three articles of the constitution manifests such contradictions: its ontological ground (the universal ban on slavery) necessarily refers back to its own (empirical) ground. The latter both qualifies the constitution's universality (only within the geographical expanse of Saint-Domingue) and allows it to become an embodied, singular universal, an empirical reality unknown in any nation in 1801. More accurately, one might conclude that these two elements, one an abstract universal and the other a concrete singularity, each form the poles of the singular universal that was Saint-Domingue in 1801, a country constitutionally freed from slavery.

Toussaint's 1801 Constitution is the first in Western modernity to resolve the contradiction between universal human rights and the defense of private property. As Florence Gauthier has shown, the French Declarations of the Rights of Man and Citizen (1789, 1793) left this contradiction unresolved. On the one hand, the natural right of all human beings to their freedom is inalienable and universal; on this point the American, French, and Haitian revolutions all agree. If this is so, however, the right to property must be a subsidiary, secondary right that can be sustained only insofar as it supports the primary human right to "life, liberty, and the pursuit of happiness." Here, as the introduction to this volume showed, both the American and French revolutions came up short. The right to property cannot be absolute in a democratic state based upon natural right. When it infringes upon human rights (as in the case of slavery, where one human would constitute the "property" of another), it must be limited.[13]

From 1789 to the definitive abandonment of natural right in favor of property in the Thermidorian convention's Constitution of l'An III (1795), this contradiction remained unresolved. Both universal natural right and the social right to property were contradictorily posited as absolutes.[14] Before Toussaint's 1801 Constitution, the only attempt to resolve this contradiction had been Robespierre's "Project for a Declaration of the Rights of Man and Citizen," submitted to the convention on April 24, 1793. This proposal explicitly sought to subordinate the right to material property to natural human rights (the right to existence, to liberty, and to the fullest possible development of one's human faculties) (Gauthier 82). "The goal of all political association is to defend the natural and imprescriptible natural rights of man, and the development of all his faculties." The right to property, Robespierre maintained, "can prejudice neither the security, nor the freedom, nor the existence, nor the property of our fellow men. All possessions and traffic that violate this principle are illicit and immoral" (Robespierre 123, 120). Four months before Sonthonax's emancipation proclamation of August 29, Robespierre's draft explicitly condemned slavery as an illegitimate extension of the right to property (Gauthier 74).[15] For Robespierre, society has only one goal, a raison d'être that grounds and determines all other secondary considerations regarding its structure: to realize the right of all humans to self-preservation, freedom, and self-realization. Though the Jacobins adopted his proposal on April 21, 1793, its original subordination of property rights to natural right was eliminated in the final, compromised declaration adopted by the convention on May 29.

Prior to 1801, the foundation of a society based upon an unequivocal, uncompromised fidelity to human rights never occurred in the Age of

Enlightenment.[16] Toussaint's Constitution of 1801, in its defense of the plantation system (in this sense regressing, like the Thermidorian Constitution of August 22, 1795, far behind the French Constitution of 1793), is consequently antinomical, its subsidiary clauses standing in radical contradiction to the foundation of the constitution itself. This makes the 1801 Saint-Domingue Constitution a truly deformed document. Appended to its founding principle of human autonomy is an utterly antidemocratic system that subjugates individuals to a series of authority figures: the Catholic religion, a paternalistic family structure, the plantation system, and the unlimited authority of Toussaint himself.[17] While founded upon the principle of universal human autonomy, the means it chose to structure society to achieve that end instead reinstituted every form of heteronomy the Age of Enlightenment had called into question.

## Beyond Enlightenment Universalism: Militarist Plantocracy versus Stateless Egalitarianism in Revolutionary Saint-Domingue

The limitations of Toussaint's politics of *liberté générale* have been readily apparent to both his critics (Pluchon) and defenders (James, Césaire). His increasing recourse to forced labor after 1796 unarguably betrayed the Spinozian tradition of the Radical Enlightenment and, more directly, the revolution he had helped to focus upon the single criterion of undivided, universal freedom. Historians will no doubt continue to debate whether this political choice was warranted, given the need to rebuild the colony's economic base to assure the continuation of the abolition of slavery, or a mere regression on the part of Toussaint into relative tyranny and personal alienation from the multitude of former slaves. This attempt to reimpose plantation labor should not be understood, however, as the mere personal initiative and psychobiographic "failure" of Toussaint; it was structurally necessitated by the ever-increasing division of Saint-Domingue into state and nation, and the process he initiated would recur repeatedly under Dessaline, Christophe, and Boyer, until the Haitian peasants' determined refusal to participate in wage-labor and to allow the reimposition of a state apparatus became so insurmountable that the elites were forced to abandon any hopes of reimposing large-scale agriculture and instead turned to the expropriation of export duties levied on the peasants' coffee crops.

General perception rarely admits that the Haitian Revolution was in fact one of the most successful and progressive in world history. Not only, as this book has argued, did it elaborate and implement the world's first process of decolonization. It was also the only revolution in the Atlantic world to successfully undertake radical land reform. Unlike other Latin American states in the nineteenth century, Haitians, from 1796 on, effectively refused the postslavery reconstruction of the plantation system sought by the revolutionary elite from Toussaint to Christophe, avoiding tenant and for-hire farming for a land-owning elite and forcing the distribution of small tracts to the peasantry, such that Haiti remains largely unique as a modern nation of "minifundia" (Lundahl 1979, 264).

Lundahl's 1979 study *Peasants and Poverty* describes in detail how Haitian peasants rejected the attempts to reimpose forced plantation labor that began under Toussaint, Sonthonax, and Polverel in 1796 and continued after independence in 1804.[18] Lundahl argues that Pétion's initiation of redistribution was both a political maneuver to avoid alienating the numerically dominant black underclass in his mulatto republic, as well as a response to the realities of changing world-systemic commodity production. After 1804 the large fixed capital and labor requirements of sugar production were no longer available, world prices decreased repeatedly, and "the plantation economy simply collapsed" (273). In a highly militarized society wrought by civil war and the constant threat of invasion, land redistribution was the solution to ensuring that soldiers received their wages in one form or another.

The effects of this reform largely determined the subsequent course of Haitian development: since the elite possessed no latifundia-type income base (as in other Latin countries such as Brazil), they turned instead to taxation of exports and/or political power to embezzle national funds.[19] The struggle of "state against nation" (Trouillot) that characterizes Haitian politics since the 1790s is in large measure traceable to this process.

This process has important theoretical dimensions as well, however, for it forces one to confront the charge that a universalist moral theory in the Spinozian-Kantian mold—one that I am arguing characterized Toussaint's vision of the revolution—is in fact radically exclusionary of any moral vision other than its own. The abstract Enlightenment formalism of universal rights that Toussaint made his own, in other words, would in this view exclude all moral exteriority and difference; any other vision of moral action than Toussaint's would have been violently and radically denied in the struggle for power in 1790s Saint-Domingue. In Michel-Rolph Trouillot's words, "The major weakness of Louverture's party, and the fundamental contradiction of his regime, was the leadership's failure to face the fact that the goal of unconditional freedom was incompatible with the maintenance of the plantation system" (1990, 43).

Following the reformulation of the concepts of freedom and equality that occurred in their relocation from Paris to Saint-Domingue in 1791–93, the struggle for the hegemonic power to determine the content of these concepts continued apace. Toussaint unambiguously believed large-scale plantation agriculture to be, as he put it in a letter from 1797, "the only thing that may give Saint-Domingue back its old splendor" (cited in Lundahl 1979, 260). Increasingly in 1790s Saint-Domingue, however, the now-free former slaves contested Toussaint's concept of freedom. In a letter from Toussaint to Laveaux from February 1796, the black general described how he debated with a group of rebellious citizens in Port-de-Paix over the exact meaning of the freedom they had attained. Could freedom admit to multiple interpretations, or was it defendable in Saint-Domingue only via the large-scale plantation labor, under duress if necessary, of all citizens? Neither Toussaint nor anyone else in power in Saint-Domingue—not Sonthonax, Laveaux, Rigaud, Dessaline, or Christophe, with the possible exception of Moïse— envisioned a social model for the island based upon small-scale, self-sufficient farming (Stein 145). Could freedom include the right to tend only one's own garden, or to live in the forest, as a maroon free from society's norms and strictures, or even the freedom simply to sit and watch the grass grow while sipping *clairin*?

Carolyn Fick has drawn attention to the crucial period of October 1793–May 1794 when there occurred a relatively free and open transition from slavery to a quasi-sharecropping system of obligatory labor enforced by Polverel's work code, published on February 7, 1794. During this intermediary period, the slaves in the southern region of Saint-Domingue that Polverel oversaw were free to undertake a spontaneous self-organization of their newly conquered freedom, and from the little documentary evidence we possess, it is clear that they did so without hesitation. They refused the reconstitution of the postslavery nation in subservience to a coercive state apparatus, and asserted the radical egalitarianism of a subsistence economy able to produce labor-free time in abundant surplus, time reappropriated as the most valued possession of those formerly forced to labor for others from dawn to dusk. They did so in an environment that required no more than two days work per week for subsistence (Blackburn 1988, 8).

In a clear refusal of the large-scale plantation system under which they had been enslaved, these free citizens quickly restructured their daily lives with the goal of maintaining their own self-sufficiency. Fick's description of this process is impressive, and deserves to be cited at length:

## 165  Toussaint, the Moun andeyo, and Political Autonomy

On some plantations, [the former slaves] took advantage of the absence of the owner and the relative state of abandon in which he left his plantation to expand the size of the small lots, or kitchen gardens, provided for them under slavery for subsistence. Thus, they began cultivating portions of the plantation property as their own. They helped themselves to the uncultivated fruit of the land such as wood, fodder, and other products that grew spontaneously and that existed abundantly in a natural state. They helped themselves to the plantation rations and sold what they could at the market. They freely used the horses and mules belonging to the plantation, both for personal pleasure and to carry their stolen goods to market. On some plantations, the workers had, in effect, taken over the land for their own purposes. As they were organized in brigades, each group would cultivate that portion of the land assigned to it, and the workers would then sell the products that were superfluous to their needs. (1990, 168)

The total transformation of society in Saint-Domingue in this period meant as well a unique and autonomous redefinition of the meaning of human freedom by the *Bossale* participants in the revolution: "Freedom for the ex-slaves would mean the freedom to possess and to till their own soil, to labor for themselves and their families, with no constraints other than their own self-defined needs, and to sell or dispose of the products of their labor in their own interest" (1990, 180). Land of one's own, sufficiently large to nourish a family and perhaps produce a small surplus for local markets, was then and has remained till today the predominant measure of freedom for the vast majority of the Haitian nation.

No human community has ever needed a code, theory, or bureaucratic direction to begin constructing an autonomous society.[20] In contrast, the bureaucratic code of Polverel was aimed precisely at crushing and regimenting all such self-organization. It paternalistically told laborers what was "the work expected of them, as well as the allocated earnings due to them" (Fick 1990, 171).[21] It sought to replace the autonomous use of the universal, emancipatory faculty of reason with the hierarchal and violent logic of *instruction:* "To cut back one day of work per week is to cut back one-sixth of the year's work and therefore diminish revenues by at least one-sixth. Suppose that a sugar estate gives, most years, three hundred *milliers* of sugar in profit through regular work of six days a week. The share of the landowner would be two hundred *milliers;* yours would be one hundred *milliers*" (reproduced in Hunt 1996, 140). The slaves' insight, one that radicalized the entire eighteenth-century logic of "Enlightenment," was to have grasped immediately the universal truth that intellectual *capacity* is one and universal (though circumstances may destructively limit its development and expression), and, second, to have understood that the unfolding of this universal intelligence in any singular instance is itself the process of emancipation: thought as a universal attribute of humanity, freedom its immanent expression. Polverel, no longer concerned with *emancipation,* now wanted simply to put blacks in their place; instead of enlightenment, he began a program of instruction of the putatively ignorant that was mere intellectual *abrutissement.* "Africans," he concluded, "you have been educated." In other words, I, the *maître,* have now returned you to your proper and natural place (of subservient ignorance, as mere laborers).

The lesson of the Haitian Revolution is that the struggle to create an autonomous society, to promote the often competing demands of liberty and equality, and to minimize or eliminate various forms of physical and symbolic violence and exclusion will always remain an unfinished *political* struggle, one never resolvable by reference to any theory or doctrine. The self-organization of the free citizens of Saint-Domingue after 1793 began the construction of a newly autonomous society in a moment of open, unsettled structural fluidity. These actions stand in direct contrast to the militaristic, antidemocratic, and paternalist authoritarianism of Toussaint's 1801 Constitution. Its appearance was contingent; the protean Toussaint, with his creative genius and personal experience of slavery (and slave owning), could conceivably have once again reinvented himself, and come to see beyond the limitations of his militaristic worldview, creating a novel social structure that would sustain and expand the intimations of an autonomous Bossale society emerging all around him in the 1790s.

Toussaint, however, never admitted to such possibilities. When he addressed the rebels of Port-de-Paix in 1796, he linked their freedom from slavery to their passive submission to both the laws of the French Republic and plantation labor. "I mounted my horse," he wrote to Laveaux, "and entered into the circle where, after having reproached them for the murders they had committed, I told them that if they wished to conserve their liberty they would have to submit to the laws of the Republic, to be docile subjects, and to work" (Laurent 314). Though divided by birth (as a Creole native of the island) and status (as a formerly slaveholding *ancien libre*) from his predominantly African-born listeners, Toussaint possessed a politico-theatrical genius for adapting his speech and behavior to the expectations of his audience. When writing to the Parisian *Moniteur,* he and his secretaries carefully crafted letters in the language of the philosophes. Here, before a crowd of African Bossales, he staged a traditional *palabre,* with himself, on horseback, occupying the position of paternalist authority.[22]

The rebels replied to Toussaint that their rights had not been respected, and that in their part of the island, unlike Toussaint's, they were treated unequally in comparison to whites and mulattoes: "On your side [of the island] . . . the whites and mulattoes who are with you are good and are united with the blacks. One would think that they are brothers born of the same mother. That, my general, is what we call equality." To be discriminated against as they had been, they cry, "is not to be free" (316). Toussaint, however, refused this differential logic (here one is unfree, unlike the North) in the name of a single universal logic. "All the reasons you give me appear just, but were you to have a house full of them [*mais quand même vous en auriez plein une case*] . . . you would still be in the wrong because you made yourselves guilty in the eyes of God, the law, and men." Toussaint stood before his *confrères* not to promote the immanent self-fashioning of an egalitarian society, but as the embodiment of three transcendental universals (divine law, positive law, and the natural law of all humankind) that allowed for no exceptions. If we are to believe Toussaint, his persuasive power won them over, and to a one "they responded to me that they were wrong . . . and would commit no more misdeeds and would be wise and obedient" (317).

The story of Toussaint Louverture and the Haitian Revolution is one of a massive transformation of both society and consciousness. Toussaint Louverture accomplished this transformation in his own person, from the slave and then slave owner that he was prior to 1791, to become one of the great protagonists of human emancipation (alongside figures such as Gandhi and King). Much in Toussaint's character can be explained by his extreme and even rigid fidelity to moral law: when those who had erred, such as the "rebels" of Port-de-Paix, proclaimed their renewed faith in Toussaint's republican moral universe, he was inevitably forgiving. When faced with insubordination that conflicted with his moral vision, he was invariably ruthless. "Fascinated by duty," observes Gérard Laurent, "he was insensible to pity [in cases of indiscipline and disobedience]. No entreaty could move him when it required the transgression of a law or a principle" (154).

While one could add many later and much harsher anecdotes regarding the turn to forced labor by Toussaint (to say nothing of his successor Henry Christophe), the logical parameters are sufficiently clear in this early polemic over the substance of freedom in postslavery Saint-Domingue:

could such freedom admit of multiple interpretations, or must it fall under the violent erasure of difference inherent in an abstract, categorical logic that linked autonomy with human labor in a hierarchical society? We undoubtedly have here an early example of the self-destruction of enlightenment: when Toussaint refused to look beyond the given (military/plantation-based) world he knew, the process of enlightenment that had taken him in a few years from being a black slave owner to the defender of universal human rights began to grind to a halt. In refusing to bring the critical spirit of enlightenment to bear upon Saint-Domingue society after he came to dominate the island in 1796, Toussaint came to stand for the eventual regression of that society behind the universal norms he had previously brought fully into practice for the first time in world history.

Toussaint's refusal to consider the viability of a Bossale, minifundia-based society is readily understandable. As Madison Smartt Bell has pointed out, Toussaint was a Caribbean-born *Creole* who had never known the small-holdings and subsistence-based agriculture typical of much of Africa. Toussaint had known firsthand every dimension of the life of the plantation, however, from that of slave to land- and slave-owner after 1776. He had been fully inscribed by 1789 as a subject of the Atlantic world-system of agrarian capitalism. From his exile in the Fort de Joux, he recalled his net worth in 1789 as precisely 648,000 francs. Toussaint knew exactly what it would take to make that system economically viable after 1791. Toussaint's repeated demonstrations of support for returning *grands blancs*, though always qualified by the imperative of defending a slavery-free system, loudly proclaimed to all Saint-Domingue society his divided allegiance (Bell 2007, 146, 201, 274).

By 1801 Toussaint had come to give a quite singular meaning to the concept of universal emancipation. Rather than the destruction of plantation slavery and its replacement by the self-organization of the Haitian peasantry, universal emancipation in 1801 implied for him the economic reconstruction of the island with forced plantation labor. Furthermore, this social structure demanded, in his view, the unquestioned submission of all to his own unlimited authoritarian rule. Perhaps Toussaint justified this authoritarianism to himself by his increasing belief in the story he had never ceased telling publicly since 1793: that it was he alone who had first, unwaveringly, and successfully defended their freedom. In any case his accession to power had, by his own admission, finally come to control him. Though he recognized that the promulgation of his 1801 Constitution and its de facto proclamation of independence would most likely provoke Napoleon to invade, that it would destroy any hope for the quasi-Federation status for Saint-Domingue both desired in their more objective moments, Toussaint's strategic rhetorical genius was no longer in force. He admitted as much to his envoy Colonel Vincent, writing that he was unable to restrain himself from unilaterally promulgating and then sending to Napoleon as a fait accompli this new constitution.[23]

In contrast to Toussaint's steadfast dedication to a militaristic, plantation-based model of human freedom, the Bossale community of Saint-Domingue developed an egalitarian society that would effectively refuse this elite social model for the next century and a half. The Bossale community of Saint-Domingue clearly perceived the constitution of an autonomous transcendental state mechanism—so ardently sought after by the military elite from Toussaint to Christophe—to constitute a threat to be avoided at all costs. From 1793 on, they instituted their human rights prior to the existence of any state apparatus that would have paternalistically granted those rights to them, disproving the current wisdom that the instantiation of human rights necessarily depends upon a functional system of nation-states for enforcement. Instead, they immediately acted to construct a system that Gérard Barthélemy has rightly called an "egalitarian system without a state," one that would secure and maintain their freedom and equality, a system that functioned within the world-system itself as the latter's unassimilable, indigestible other.

This process of self-organization was an act of escape from any system that would exploit their surplus labor by incorporating them within a regime of commercial consumption and dependency on wage remuneration. Since it quickly proved impossible for the Bossale culture to impose any structural limitations and dependency upon leaders such as Toussaint, limitations that would keep power away from an oligarchy and firmly located with the peasantry, the ruse of the *moun andeyo* was simply to withdraw from direct combat into the self-regulating egalitarian system described by Barthélemy (30–68).

Though almost entirely self-directed and conceived, this egalitarian impulse of the Bossale community was nonetheless largely coherent with libertarian Radical Enlightenment traditions from Spinoza and Van den Enden, through Radicati and Robespierre. Though the recognition of a stateless system as something other than barbarian underdevelopment would await subsequent theorization, Spinoza, in the *Tractatus Politicus*, explicitly justified a radical egalitarian land distribution such as that which would occur in Haiti after 1804: "Land and other assets belonging to it, are effectively the public property of the commonwealth, that is, they belong by right to all who have united and are therefore able to protect it."

Publicly owned land is essential "as the basis for [the people's] defending their collective power and freedom" (cited in Israel 272).

In his 1990 study *L'univers rural haïtien*, Gérard Barthélemy describes how Haitian peasant society, which has always appeared to the outside world as a regressive, aberrant failure of the process of development, in fact has long represented an organized, systematic refusal to adopt this model. Instead, Haitian rural society is an "egalitarian system without a state" (Barthélemy 28). It is precisely this sustained construction of a large-scale *stateless* community that distinguishes Haitian Bossale society from all the major political forms of modernity, whether representative or monarchic democracy, fascist, or bureaucratic socialist.[24]

Following Pierre Clastres, Barthélemy argues that Haitian rural society should not be understood as a failure, but instead possesses a highly structured social system whose accomplishments are simply invisible or incomprehensible to the outside world. Clastres analyzed this process as an active appropriation of labor-free time in Amazonian subsistence economies, refiguring it not as lack (of civilization, surplus capital, and so on) but as the active constitution of societies protecting themselves from the development of a separate state apparatus that would seek (through violence) to alienate, exploit, and expropriate a maximum quota of labor from a community.

Similarly, the goal of the Haitian Bossale community, in the face of the constant threat represented by elite culture and its fealty to the dominant North Atlantic model of wage-labor and surplus profit accumulation, was to maintain a state of equilibrium in the rural community that would prevent the resurgence of hierarchical power structures and social inequality. Consequently, Bossale culture strove systematically to harmonize social relations without recourse to transcendent authority such as representative, constitutional government, police, or codified legal systems. In short, the goal was to institute a society "outside of all [constituted] politics" (Barthélemy 29).

The mechanisms Haitian Bossale society has developed to achieve this goal since acquiring independence in the 1790s have long appeared, to the eyes of outsiders (Haitian or not), as testimony to a failure to adopt the dominant, North Atlantic social habitus. These mechanisms include an education that limits the development of autonomous individuality in relation to Bossale society, as well as the cultivation of comportments based upon suspicion, fear of the Other, jealousy, and envy (32–33). Similarly, a whole series of social rituals enforce the constant redistribution of wealth to prevent accumulation and maintain economic equality (33).

The generalization of the practice of sorcery (*Wanga*) and the constant threat of its invocation in insular communities regulates intersubjective behavior in the absence of an objective juridical apparatus (35). Labor takes the form of either self-subsistence or unremunerated work for the commons (*Combites*) (37).[25]

The interdependent practices of Catholicism and Vodun, in turn, play differentiated roles in this maintenance of a structure of egalitarian equilibrium. The universalism of Catholic subjectivity and rituals, for Barthélemy, offers a destructured, atemporal political interface for relations with the world outside the Haitian countryside, while the Vodun cult of ancestors (*Loas-héritage*) sustains a sacralized, organic relation to the rural environment (43). In turn, various social "strategies" support Bossale egalitarianism: the refusal of technological innovations ("technical precarity," 48); the strategic subdivision of property with each generation, and the nonexistence and/or hypercomplexity of cadastral apparatuses (51); various strategies of passive (emigration, seduction, dissimulation, complication, dispersion, erosion, dissuasion, derision) and active (*Cacos*) resistance to the outside world allow the maintenance of Bossale egalitarianism in a state of dynamic equilibrium without endangering its functioning. This system, a legacy of the Haitian Revolution, functioned in such a state of dynamic equilibrium from the late 1790s to the 1960s, until the destruction of the Haitian (natural and social) environment under the regime of Papa Doc undermined its viability.

The development and long-term viability of this stateless egalitarianism and refusal of contractual wage labor relations may appear as no more than a curiosity, a Luddite blip in the ever-more-encompassing reach of Western consumerism and its founding ideology of liberal individualism. And yet, in a period in which global humanity is already being forced to address the havoc this secular mythology has wreaked upon the earth, we may well be obliged not only to moderate certain "excesses" of consumer and business behavior (while leaving the system functionally intact) but also, if we are to survive on the planet, to call into question the global politico-economic structures that perpetuate and reinforce the culture of "boundless" consumption and progress. As such, the long-term sustainability of Haitian stateless egalitarianism—and notwithstanding the externally determined ecological disasters Haiti has known (deforestation, Creole pig massacre)—is of interest to all who believe that the coming shift from unlimited consumerism to an ethics of global responsibility (Jonas) will require fundamental changes to the sociopolitical system that has brought us to the brink of disaster.

Given the immediate historical context of a slave-labor-based world-system, from the moment Napoleon abandoned the revolutionary ideals of 1789 and decided to reinstate French slavery, it is doubtful that an entire nation composed solely of small farmers could have remained free from slavery beyond 1802. Whether or not this is true, the crucial point is that even when Haitians did defeat the French in 1804, the global political context that so feared the Bossale vision of an anarchist, minifundia-based freedom quickly and systematically undermined (by refusal of diplomatic recognition, embargo, and the like) any incipient autonomy of the Haitian state, reducing it to the empty rhetorical posturing of a largely worthless constitution. No true freedom, one that would allow for the sustained development of both liberty *and* social equality, was ever possible for Haitians in such an unfree totality as was Western modernity in 1804.

During the early years of the Saint-Domingue revolution (1791–96), the shared imperative to abolish slavery allowed for the strategic composition of a radical populist movement uniting the black and mulatto elite with the numerically superior Bossale community. The Enlightenment thought that Toussaint Louverture absorbed into the core of his being after 1789 had radicalized the struggle for the universal freedom from domination of the people of Saint-Domingue, uniting a diverse community under the empty, absent signifier of *libete/liberté* in a true expression of populist reason. After 1796, however, the fundamentally conflicting visions of freedom of these two communities—one dedicated to imposing the individualistic freedom of the wage-labor/consumerist individual, the other dedicated to a fully egalitarian, subsistence-based, stateless community—quickly divided Saint-Domingue between (elite) state and (Bossale) nation.

The construction of stateless egalitarianism by the *moun andeyo* thus indicates the final level at which the Haitian Revolution took shape as a phenomenon of the Spinozian Radical Enlightenment, making Haiti, like the philosophy of Spinoza itself, an unassimilable anomaly within the modern world-system. In its refusal of all forms of transcendental authority and the Hobbesian transfer of rights to an elite, Bossale society constituted a purely Spinozian political phenomenon perhaps unique in Western modernity. Freedom for the Haitian rural community was not, as it clearly was for Toussaint Louverture, their Kantian subjection to an authoritarian transcendental law. Bossale society was not founded upon a social contract; instead, its stateless egalitarian system called for its own constant renegotiation to maintain the community's absolute dedication to the expression of an uncompromised egalitarian freedom.

When, as for Spinoza, the expression of our powers of thought are understood to be indivisible from all other modes of physical expression, freedom is no longer a preexisting interior choice or consent to subject oneself to an authority—a master, a representative government, a constitution, a law. Instead, freedom only exists as its actualization and expression within the realm of all-encompassing nature, of which humans are only a part. Either a body (and the thought of that body, insofar as "mind and body are one and the same thing" for Spinoza) expresses itself freely or it does not. Haitian Bossale society refused all forms of delegation and representation of power as a new servitude masquerading as freedom itself.

Like the political philosophy of Spinoza, this society stood in starkly critical relation to liberal individualism and its ideology of individual acts of free will. This was a society that refused to accept the claim that to consent to the delegation of rights to a sovereign is to make a "free" decision to subject oneself to authority. Bossale society was not based on a model of the subject's interiority, its free will and consent, and in consequence refused—as Warren Montag has written of Spinozian politics—"the entire juridical apparatus of laws and rights for which [these concepts] serve as a foundation."[26] Instead, what mattered in Bossale society was the constant readjustment of the disposition of bodies to maintain an egalitarian freedom in dynamic equilibrium with an unfree outside world.

Freedom is not an eternally preexistent, ready-at-hand "natural" right; the ideology of a timeless natural right dear to Toussaint Louverture served from this point of view merely to justify new forms of servitude, "producing retroactively the foundation that gives [subjection to authority] its legitimacy" (Montag 50). To the *moun andeyo*, the claim Toussaint made for their submission could only appear as the ruse of a new servitude that attempted to lure them into accepting anew the regulation and control of their bodies and productive power. The contrast between the immanent structuration of this vernacular society and Toussaint Louverture's dedication to plantation labor, the abstract formalism of constitutional law, and his unwavering insistence that all subjects be bound by these structural limitations, could not be starker. The laws of Bossale society remained immanent, never inscribed in a constitution or decree, but instead only existed in their actualization, in the process of their constant externalization and expression as the activity of an oral community.

Bossale society was not based upon liberal individualism, but worked instead to *combine* powers (*coumbite*) to maximize the expressive potential of the community. As Spinoza argued, a single being is by itself incapable of expressing its fullest potential. Only when recognizing its place and determination within the order of nature and acting in concert with others is that singular potential able to realize itself freely in prospectively infinite forms of vernacular creativity. "In order to achieve a secure and good life," wrote Spinoza in the *Tractatus-Theologico-Politicus,* "men had necessarily to unite in one body. They therefore arranged that the unrestricted right naturally possessed by each individual should be put in common ownership and that this right should no longer be determined by the strength and appetite of the individual but by the power and will of all together" (cited in Montag 1999, 67). A free community does not alienate its rights in an illusory decision of the "free will," but instead strives to maximize the power of each, bearing "common ownership" of their powers. The freedom of Bossale society, in its antagonism to liberal individualism and wage-labor, could exist and survive only through this shared combination of the singular forces of each individual. Societies, like individuals themselves, are to be understood in this view as infinitely complex entities built up from composite assemblages of forces, assemblages that in turn maximize the expressive capabilities of every member (Montag 69).

While the philosophy of the Radical Enlightenment announced the universal elimination of slavery, it also contained the theoretical seeds of the human and social dysfunction of post-1804 Haiti. This occurred for Haiti not in some essentialist, teleological dialectic of enlightenment necessarily leading to barbarism, but only insofar as its population—divided between an elite that favored a plantation-based labor state and a nation desiring to maintain their small-holdings land plots—never reached a consensus on how the latter might be sustained in the capitalist world-system of the time. Instead, the Bossale community managed to survive for the next century and a half through passive and (occasionally) active resistance to the liberal world-system, in a strategic withdrawal of *maronnage* to the Haitian hills.

The recognition of the unique and significant contributions of this Haitian egalitarian social system must be emphatically distinguished from any romanticization or aestheticization of rural life, poverty, or the like. Haiti's outrageously elevated rate of infant mortality or the persistence of AIDS and malaria is to be universally decried. Such secondary effects of Haitian rural poverty and isolation within the liberal world-system, however, must be distinguished from the unique social structures invented in rural Haiti since 1804.

On the other hand, one must also recognize that the egalitarianism of the Haitian *moun andeyo* forces us to interrogate what this study has heretofore taken as an unambiguous value: that the furthering of the process of singularization and the realization of the inherent potentiality of every human individual is an objective, ontological good. To what extent, one might well ask, is this value a mere reflection of consumerist, individualistic liberalism, rather than a universally objective value? For Haitian rural society, as Barthélemy rigorously underscores, stands as well for the systematic minimization of the modes of expression of its individuals, this in order to maximize internal social equality. Is equality necessarily to be achieved at the price of liberty, or does what Balibar has termed *égaliberté* exist as a viable option for modern societies?

One might properly describe Haitian Bossale society as a social assemblage dedicated to the systematic *externalization* of singularity. This is the contradiction of the unique achievement of the *moun andeyo*: the construction of this singular and exceptional totality in the modern capitalist world-system has been effected through the *internal* suppression of the possibilities of individualistic expression on the part of its members (28). Was the violence of this suppression the price to be paid for Haiti's pariah status in the modern world since 1804? In other words, was the contingent marginalization of the Haitian state merely reflected internally as social violence? Or is this suppression of individuality a universal feature of any social structure that would ensure egalitarianism in the face of an ontological human tendency of every individual to strive for self-singularization?

To understand the foundation or ontological ground of human rights as an indeterminate, yet universal, possibility to "singularize" social existence, while allowing one to retain the notion of the human as an indeterminate opening onto possibility, still, necessarily, remains a problematic and, indeed, aporetic proposal. Such a vision of the "human" and of human rights as was put forward in the Haitian Revolution operates its own structural exclusions. The former slaves of Saint-Domingue forcibly broke through their prepolitical situation of exclusion from the domain of right, to become political subjects of universal rights. They constructed for the world not one, but two, unique and previously unimaginable forms of political "dissensus"—that is, a contestatory reconfiguration of the ontological parameters of social existence (Rancière 2004, 304). For Toussaint Louverture and the various elites who followed him after 1801, liberty meant the universal, uncompromised abolition of chattel slavery for the first time in world history, a freedom inscribed through the construction of transcendental social mechanisms (constitutional, juridical, military, religious, paternal, moral) to ensure the enforcement of that prescription within a nation divided between an "enlightened" elite and an "unenlightened" peasantry. For the Bossale community, freedom meant instead the construction of an undivided, stateless egalitarianism, with its own attendant forms of violence: the systematic suppression of the expression of individuality among its members to assure the reproduction of social equality.

The former slaves of Saint-Domingue demonstrated through an active process of political subjectivation that the attribute "Man" of 1789 was not *only* an ideological falsehood of the bourgeoisie's bid for power (Marx), but that as a previously inconceivable interjection into the (symbolic) economy of the eighteenth-century world-system, in its very formalism it retained an operative efficacy. The positive efficacy of this abstraction ("Man") opened a gap or interval in that century, a gap inherent in the inadequation between the slaves' active and ongoing depoliticization and exclusion (through the dehumanization of slavery) and the universal rights of man, a process enacted through their isolation from the normative consensus on slavery of the Assemblée nationale.

For all this, we remain here, necessarily, with the same old question (the rights of *whom?*), now displaced to a new limit. What about those, I would ask in closing this chapter, who are unable to engage a process of dissensus (Rancière), of those unable to construct "a new beginning" (Arendt)? In short, what of those who may, potentially, be capable of their own singularization, but prove unable to do so? What are the rights, for example, of those in a vegetative coma? Of those cut off from society in maximum security prisons or extradited to third countries beyond the reach of lawyers and the global media? To say nothing of animal rights, and of the ecological world as a whole? Is it enough simply to say, following Spinoza, that their rights extend (only) as far as their power to act? In this sense, the foregoing analysis must be seen as no more than a prolegomenon, one that opens onto the true problem of the twenty-first century: what are the rights of all—not all humans, or even all living beings or the planet, but simply of all, without qualification?

Here, at the end, in speaking of the rights of all without distinction, we risk returning to the beginning point of all (human) reflection, what Hegel called determination (*Bestimmung*), in which undivided Being passes over from its own nothingness devoid of determination into Becoming. In this case, my hope and wager here has been that reflection upon the Haitian Revolution, today, can lead into a new process of political Becoming, a process of political subjectivation and an imperative of responsibility that we are now only beginning to envision.[27] An egalitarian politicization of us *all,* insofar as *everyone,* to some degree, is excluded from the "universal" consensus: from the (functionally alienated) titular bearers of economic, social, and political power, to the stateless and rightless mere humans from Saint-Domingue to Auschwitz and Guantanamo, to those unable to autonomously singularize their existence, to nonhuman animals, and to the biosphere itself. A politicization that refuses the red herrings of cultural difference and pseudo-tolerance to ask instead how we can become subjects to a process of universal emancipation. We must fully develop the capacity we find ourselves bearing to critique the grounds of our own existence, to imagine other possibilities, and to move beyond the given and all constituted authority. This remarkable possibility that formed the spirit of the Radical Enlightenment can, indeed must, continue to constitute and reconstitute the singularity of our being-in-the-world.

# Conclusion
## Remembering 1804

Tout moun se moun.
—Jean-Bertrand Aristide, *An Autobiography*

Nothing that has ever happened should be regarded as lost for history.
—Walter Benjamin, *Theses on the Philosophy of History*

WHAT CAN it mean for us, two centuries on, to remember the end of the Haitian Revolution and the declaration of the independent nation of Haiti in 1804? It might first of all mean something like an injunction to remember the losers of history, those sacrificed in the triumphant march of history. In the case of Haiti, this might mean not so much remembering a failed attempt at global colonization as recalling as best we can all those who found themselves caught up in the grinding machinery of the Napoleonic war machine, the victims of an arbitrary and subjective decision to make war, a decision taken by a leader who came to power in a bureaucratic coup d'état. It might mean remembering those who enlisted in his army in a combination of economic necessity and patriotic fervor to defend the universal democratic ideals of the French Republic, only to find that hope betrayed, to find themselves sent overseas as cannon fodder in a unilateral and offensive war to reassert the global hegemony of a colonizing empire.

The ideologies of tolerance and multicultural difference are wrong not in the absolute, but because they are fundamentally conservative and seek to preserve islands of privilege in a sea of iniquity. If our world were a just one, they would perhaps be valid imperatives; in a context of global systemic and direct violence, we must find new ways to affirm our *in*tolerance of injustice, exclusion, and violence, and to identify the ways we enable these processes. We must, as Haitians have repeatedly in the past two centuries, *politicize* this intolerance for injustice. The forms this process of politicization will take cannot be known a priori; infinitely varied according to their sites of enunciation, they encompass the radical intolerance of Gandhi, Patočka, and King, local and global struggles for public sphere hegemony, and the uncompromising anti-imperialism of Toussaint and Fanon.

Any contemporary attempt to understand universal emancipation needs to include, perhaps even to begin from, a site such as Haiti, which has demonstrated over the last two centuries the insufficiency of any project that would consider the "Third World" through mere cursory references to a few canonical theoretical texts (Said, Spivak). If we are witnessing today the constitution of a global mass democratic movement in sites such as Seattle, Genova, Porto Alegre, Paris, and New York, these first-world events confront an already constituted state of (relative) law and order.[1]

The events in Saint-Domingue offer an eloquent rebuttal to the postmodern shibboleth that all (political) representation always leaves out a remainder, an excluded, minoritarian Other, what in Deleuze's words constitutes "a non-represented singularity which does not recognize, precisely because it is not everyone or the universal. 'Everyone' recognizes the universal, but the singular does not" (Deleuze 1968, 74). Though excluded from political representation in 1789, the slaves of Saint-Domingue drew precisely the opposite conclusion to this postmodern politics of "difference": that they were subject to a universal right.[2]

What can the postmodern vision of the rule of law as always-already (rather than potentially) alienating mean for a place such as Haiti (or Rwanda, or the Congo . . .), where the rule of law too often cannot be said to exist at all, places where law is not the complex relation of individuals and communities to a universally valid norm, but where law is instead no more than the direct expression of violent domination: whoever has the machine guns and torture chambers is right?[3] Like many other postcolonial states, Haiti has all too often in its two-hundred-year history been subject to the deformalization and derationalization of law into a semipermanent state of emergency characterized by the arbitrary and unpredictable wielding of raw power.[4] Repeatedly, the history of Haiti has demonstrated the radical insurgency of unfree subjects against the forces of violence and domination, but the fact that Haiti is the greatest historical instantiation of the insurgency that theorists such as Hardt and Negri rightly celebrate has never been enough to ensure that those subjects can realize their full human potential as autonomous, creative subjects, that after their insurgency they will not be taken out of their beds at night and assassinated or thrown into jail without recourse to justice.

When slaves overthrew the archetype of the constituted law of the master, the *Code Noir*, they showed that a just state of law does not refer to the hierarchical imposition of discipline upon a subaltern population by a sovereign elite. The true rule of law was glimpsed only in the suspension of its violent (ancien régime) caricature; a just rule of law appeared in this moment, when a society struggled to define the parameters of its freedom, autonomously. This rule of law as justice cannot be reduced to a perpetual eschatology, *à venir*, but is the expression of what Benjamin called revolutionary or "pure" violence that overthrows a regime of disciplinary, mythico-juridical state violence, opening a space for juridical improvisation (see Agamben 62). A true rule of law occurs in such moments of invention when a subject gives itself its own laws, rather than accepting those of mere authority or tradition; when a society constitutes itself, imaginatively, autonomously. The Haitian Revolution shows us that the rule of law can only occur in a society in which sovereignty has become *banalized*, such that all, universally, can give the law unto themselves.

Since the concept of sovereignty has traditionally been linked to the power of a *state* to command its subjects, a "banalization" of sovereignty would imply

1. the reappropriation of the power to legislate and construct social existence from the state to social actors (individuals, collectives), that is, a maximum coincidence of the Multitude and the unalienated power of political decision making, with no distinction between rulers and the ruled;[5]
2. consequently, the *desublimation* of the state as transcendent law-giving force, the destruction of its monopoly on legislation, and the reappropriation of this power by the multitude;
3. the *politicization* of so-called civil life and the erasure of the public/private distinction upon which the modern state founds its powers; and
4. the *multiplication* of what has traditionally been conceived of as an *indivisible* (state-centered) power, and the consequent reappropriation of legislative or "constituent" power (as well as the powers of judgment and execution) by a multitude (as opposed to a unified "people" subject to a General Will) of subjects.

If historical awareness of the Haitian Revolution has amounted, in the words of the January 2004 Debray report to the French government, to a "singular absence," the task of any rememoration of the events of 1791–1804 would be to bear witness to this revolutionary sequence. And yet the Haitian Revolution does not exist, as one of the handful of books published on Haiti in the year of its bicentennial of independence put it.

Haiti has too often been perceived in Western modernity as a lack, as pure negativity: as violence, destruction, poverty, political dysfunction, dictatorship, and exploitation. One wonders who could have conceived such a perfect dumping ground for our disavowed imperfections and failings, as though these things existed only in this periphery of the Atlantic world. The task of any remembrance of the Haitian Revolution must surely be to bring into question this perfect scenario, one that leaves those outside Haiti miraculously cleansed of any guilt in the ongoing subjection of the Haitian multitude.

One example of such blindness is the 2004 report of the committee headed by Régis Debray to Dominique de Villepin, *Haïti et la France,* which presents an overview of Franco-Haitian relations since 1804 and offers a series of recommendations to the French government. The report does call attention to France's slaveholding past, asking: "How many French know that the Declaration of the Rights of Man and Citizen was *initiated* in Paris, but instantiated [*accomplie*] in Saint-Domingue, where human rights became, almost without our knowledge, truly universal?" (18).

Released in the months before the French-supported overthrow of Aristide, the report then goes on, however, paternalistically to call upon Haitians to "assume their share of responsibilities in the incredible degeneration . . . of the richest colony in the world . . . to an African [*sahélien*] level of malediction" (20).[6] It then proceeds to reduce the question of the repayment of Haiti's 90 million franc payment to France for recognition of its independence, extorted from the country in 1826 and among the primary causes of its economic underdevelopment, to a "propaganda campaign . . . without juridical foundation" (21, 23). Could it be that current French and transnational juridical norms are not fully developed? Such a simple question eludes the authors of the report, for whom the question remains a terrifying (in its rightful claims on French responsibility?) "Pandora's box" (25). The report hypocritically describes the seemingly unlimited "good will" of French aid projects in the face of Haitian "failures," "waste," and "egoism" (28–29), and laments over the "painful . . . trauma" of Dessaline's massacre of the last French planters in Haiti (32).

In a different vein from such bureaucratic cynicism, in the attempt to place the Haitian Revolution within the flow of linear time, one witnesses historical experience and understanding disappear in much contemporary journalism on Haiti. Though few major media sites noted the Haitian Bicentennial on January 1, 2004, when U.S.-sponsored violence quickly escalated there in the following months, even the slightest attempt to place these events in historical perspective magically disappeared.[7] Instead, the evocation of some nature-based, eternally recurring Haitian cycle of violence, ever-renewed, ever-same, became a magic incantation in American and French media seemingly intent on the active "otherization" of Haitian violence, convincing us that such things only happen there, in what was endlessly labeled as the "poorest country in the Western Hemisphere."

When an article actually attempted to provide some sort of explanation, its impoverished thinking was palpable, and the lack of any desire even to try to understand was paraded as insight. On February 24, 2004, a *New York Times* editorial stated that "abrupt and violent changes of government have been a regular feature of Haitian politics over the years and are among the main reasons that Haiti has never developed stable democratic institutions." Through the magical incantations of first-world pundits, effect miraculously becomes historical causation, and Haiti is returned safely to its eternal, natural state as the land of "abrupt and violent changes"—that is to say, a place devoid of human control over our social destiny, our political existence—and where violence can instead surge forth at any moment like the hurricanes, earthquakes, and volcanic eruptions that mark the Caribbean submission to natural time. As though the United States bore no particular burden in Haiti's two-centuries-old political dysfunction, as though we hadn't actively supported the French imposition of a ransom for political recognition in 1826, a ransom that left the country by 1880 paying 80 percent of its gross national product to finance the loan it took from France itself. As though the U.S. Marines had left things better than they found them after occupying Haiti twice in the last century to "democratize" this country.[8]

## Contemporary Reformulations of the Haitian Public Sphere

While the North Atlantic media continue to present Haiti as "the poorest country in the Western Hemisphere," Haitians themselves continue to participate in the transnational, oral public sphere of debate on human rights that they helped create in the Age of Enlightenment. For proof, witness Jonathan Demme's documentation of the remarkable life of Michelle Montas and her husband, Jean Dominique, in his film *The Agronomist*. Filmed over the course of a decade and a half, from 1986 to Dominique's assassination in April 2000, Demme's documentary explores the parameters of the contemporary oral public sphere that Dominique and Montas articulated through their dedication to the radio station Radio Haïti. In the 1950s and in the early years of the Duvalier dictatorship prior to Dominique's intervention, radio was not a "news media" but rather mere "entertainment" and diversion, both for the Haitian elite and for the disenfranchised Haitian masses. Radio Haïti doggedly persevered through the Duvalier dictatorships and the various crises of the 1990s in its dedication to presenting and disseminating information within a context of massive political repression. After the departure of Duvalier in 1986, an independent, critical news media emerged to play a key role in the development of a multiplicity of grass-roots democratic initiatives, concretizing the promise of a truly autonomous public sphere of debate (Dupuy 2007, 58).

The opening moments of the film neatly describe this conflict between radical political oppression and the commitment to a free and open public sphere (00:29–1:18). "For the freedom of the press, Radio Haïti at the service of the Haitian people," the station announces to its public. *The Agronomist* stages a complex mise-en-scène of the populist credentials of Jean Dominique. For us to accept Dominique's role in a Haitian oral public sphere, we must be absolutely convinced of Dominique's populist bona fides. The film thus spends considerable energies in representing Dominique's ties to the Haitian population. Though coming from an elite family, Dominique describes how his father instilled in him pride as a Haitian amid the first American occupation of Haiti ("You are Haitian; my great-grandfather *fought* at [the battle of] Vertières [in the Haitian Revolution]; never forget that you are Haitian"). His sister goes on to describe how their father took him out into the countryside to encounter the realities of the Haitian population (12:25–13:06). A specialization in agronomy, as Dominique presents it, was taken as an opportunity to try to "do something about this *awful* situation" of the Haitian peasantry. Dominique soon spent six months in jail for his early social agitation.

His early work developing Haitian cinema was likewise an attempt to develop cinema as a forum open and accessible to Haiti's largely illiterate public (17:58–18:42). In presenting Alain Resnais' *Night and Fog* in his cinema club in the 1960s, Dominique early on mobilized the particular, hidden potentialities of an oral public sphere within a historical context of political repression and denial of freedom of the information. Recall from chapter 2 Habermas's definition of a public sphere based upon three criteria: (1) private individuals (2) coming together in a public setting (from a coffee house to the Internet) and (3) exercising their universal human faculty of reason *autonomously*.

## Conclusion

In watching this "militant, anti-fascist film," Dominique comments, "everyone realized that Auschwitz *was* Fort Dimanche." Here, we witness in action the operation of autonomous reason on the part of a disenfranchised, supposedly uneducated population. Dominique, the film tells us, did not have to impose his own transcendental explanation of the film as a vanguard, enlightened intellectual leading an ignorant population forward to a state of consciousness that he had already achieved. Rather, Dominique is presented as a mere vehicle or conduit for information; his public, in turn, then reflects logically and autonomously upon this material, through a process of comparison, abstraction, extrapolation, and interpretation rigorous in its pure, mathematical perfection: "Everyone realized that Auschwitz *was* Fort Dimanche"; Auschwitz = Fort Dimanche (19:05–19:50).

Upon his purchase of Radio Haïti, Dominique's first innovation was to initiate the presentation of news in Kreyol, abandoning the elite language of French. In this manner Radio Haïti immediately sought to include the mass of illiterate Kreyol speakers, creating in a single stroke a mass-based oral public sphere. In addition, Dominique underlines another characteristic of an *oral* public sphere, a characteristic that exceeds the Kantian and Habermasian emphasis on natural language and the written word. An oral language contains a whole range of signifiers less specific than words in their logical precision, but which nonetheless are able to convey definite information to a knowing population versed in their sonorous manipulation.

In a context of political repression and censorship, such slippery and shifting signifiers take on a heightened importance in conveying meaningful, critical information. Dominique's respectful and celebratory documentation of the Vodun ceremony of Saut d'Eau not only captured the dynamic, fugitive beauty of a stigmatized and oppressed Afro-American cultural creativity but also transmitted as well, to knowing listeners, an "expression... of resistance against them, against the *Diab* [Devil]! If you listen carefully, Who is the *Diab*? Who is 'them'? It was the Macoutes" (20:48–21:14).

Dominique describes how, during the era of Jimmy Carter's presidency, the members of this public sphere were able to profit from the Duvalier regime's dependency on foreign aid to press the claims of universal human rights. The dissident members of the Haitian oral public sphere were able to hegemonize public debate around the signifier of "human rights" in order to increase, through publicity, the regime's vulnerability to international critique by the Carter administration and organizations such as Amnesty International. "We profited from [this possibility]. We went faster, further, giving speech to the people."

When Radio Haïti began reporting on events in Latin America, Michelle Montas relates, Haitians again exercised their critical reflection to draw the parallel between the overthrow of the dictator Samosa in Nicaragua, events in Iran, and Baby Doc. "Of course they said, 'Aha, Somosa looks like Jean-Claude.' 'Aha, the Shah of Iran looks like Jean-Claude. There is something familiar.' And more and more, through foreign news in Kreyol, the outside world opened to their minds. But also, the inside world, because they were *quick* to understand that when a bunch of Nicaraguan people said 'No!' to Somosa, they were not only Nicaraguans [in question]. . . . Every [bit of] information, even about the garbage in the street, was seen by the Power as opposition" (28:11–28:56).

Demme projects Dominique's links to the people through a veritable sensualization of human intelligence, expressed through that most sensual of languages, Kreyol. "Every morning, you have to *smell* the enemy! . . . I smelled something out there, in the heart of the country, thought the Macoutes and the Duvaliers have squeezed, ransacked and broken the people's backs, still, something remained down *deep*, and it was about to blossom" (29:31–30:10). Dominique describes his encounters with the peasant rice farmers of the Artibonite Valley, and their eventual refusal to cooperate with the extortion of the Duvalier government. Dominique, as an elite outsider to their concerns, gradually had to come to win their trust, to show that he was one of them and on their side. "Peasants don't talk easily. The peasant I was talking to gave me a little piece of the story, and stopped. And they went to listen, to test my own [fidelity]. Then when I came back to them, they said, 'Ok, you are good'" (31:30).

The testimony of Charles Suffrard, an Artibonite rice farmer, is crucial to the film's rhetorical construction of Dominique's linkage to the Haitian population. As a child and young man, he tells Demme, "I used to listen to Jean Dominique. I used to soak up everything he said." Suffrard, though a peripheral figure in the film's visual diversity, is a key figure in its representation of Dominique as a direct and faithful link to the Haitian masses. A furtive image of a Haitian peasant walking across a mountain ridge, with only a small battery-operated radio in hand, further encapsulates the flows of a network of information moving between Dominique and the Haitian masses, through the medium of Radio Haïti (44:30).

The other key figure in this filmic representation of a functioning, critical, and autonomous oral public sphere is Jean-Bertrand Aristide. The film dwells extensively on Aristide's early speeches, his lack of fear and liberating will to speak the truth. Aristide's Sunday sermons, in turn, were recorded and distributed throughout the country through another vehicle of this oral public sphere, the cassette tape. In its later sequences the film goes on to portray an Aristide alienated from the free and autonomous public sphere he helped create. Demme dramatically includes footage of Aristide's call for disarmament, a sequence that seems to signify the destruction of autonomous reflection by Power, and the imposition of a monological, dictatorial will: "I am the head of state!" Aristide yells. "Et je veux! Et je veux! Et je veux! Et je peux! Je veux, et je peux! C'est fini!" (1:03:33–1:04:04). The circularity of the logic is total, the exclusion of communication, reflection, debate, brutally devastating.

Amid growing turmoil and attacks, Dominique reasserted, in the weeks before his assassination, his faith in the power of the public sphere to defeat the forces of violence: "Here, I have no other arm than my journalism. My microphone and my unshakable faith as a militant for true change! . . . I end with Shakespeare: 'The truth will always make the Devil's face blush!'" (1:10:38). As Demme shows Dominique's ashes being cast into the Artibonite Valley, *The Agronomist* casts its final, most compelling image of the unity of Jean Dominique with the Haitian people and land, a unity that underwrites the organic functioning of an articulate, resolute, highly conscious public sphere of oral critique that has characterized Haiti from at least 1791 into the twenty-first century.

## Progress and Human Rights since 1804

It is only because the human mind can conceive of the universal, without ever entirely grasping it, that we have progressed toward a universal ban on slavery or the tentative extension of civil rights to subjects based on "race," political status (refugees), or sexual orientation or gender (gay, lesbian, and transgendered citizens). This is not to claim that there has been progress in an absolute sense. Such a claim would be hollow and meaningless in the face of the many historical failures and ideological manipulations of the idea of human rights.[9]

Has there been any progress in implementing universal human rights since 1789? A whole tradition of critique says no, from Edmund Burke's *Reflections on the French Revolution* (1790), through Heidegger (the critique of "the they" and "publicness")[10] and Carl Schmitt (*Crisis of Parliamentary Democracy*), and on to contemporary theorists such as Alain Badiou (*Ethics*). These critics point to events such as the degeneration of the ethical idealism announced in 1789 into the Terror of 1793 and the guillotine. In Haiti both the Napoleonic French army and the rebel slaves resorted to terrorization and every form of torture imaginable to them.[11] From the hamstrung and economically impoverished nation that resulted from the Haitian Revolution to the impotence of a Declaration of Human Rights and a United Nations powerless to stop the Rwandan genocide or war in Iraq, whether there has been any progress remains an open question.

Immanuel Kant asked the same question about the French Revolution in his 1798 text "Contest of the Faculties," and responded that it was precisely not the subjective violence of the Terror that should retain our attention. Rather, Kant claimed, the progress brought about by the French Revolution lies in its construction of a universal idea of freedom, an idea that negated the local, communitarian politics of race, ethnicity, and nation to interpellate all those innately endowed with the capacity to understand its logic.[12]

Kant asked the question, "Is the human race continually improving?" In offering a positive answer to this question, Kant presumed precisely what remains first to be demonstrated: that humanity in fact exists as an actual totality. Kant maintained that one can in fact obtain a "prophetic" vision of human history "if the prophet himself occasions and *produces* the events he predicts" (177). He found just such an event in the French Revolution: for all its violence and bloodshed, its "misery and atrocities," it aroused a "sympathy" that proved "a moral disposition within the human race" (177). Kant's analysis is fundamentally idealist; in refusing to consider whether the violent destruction of the ancien régime constituted historical progress, his political analysis remained merely speculative. Instead, the Haitian Revolution went beyond Kantian idealism to show the true power of the concept of *libete/liberté* when it successfully overthrew the ultraviolence of plantation slavery.

The Haitian revolutionaries who had labored as slaves, making cane grow in the fields and transforming it into sugar and rum, knew all about labor and "producing an event [one] predicts." Farming is perhaps the prototypical event in the history of humans' domination of nature, mastering its unpredictability through the imaginative power of human reason to conceive of a nonexistent project (to avoid starvation by growing food in the coming season) and to implement that project. The violence of the slaveholding plantation system, of course, transformed this bucolic vision into a living hell. In response to this attempt at dehumanization, Haitian slaves, certain in their own humanity, conceived of another project and worked to "produce" that event: universal emancipation from slave labor. This labor of productive, intersubjective human reason was at once a historical process leading to independence and a philosophical event that pointed to the *auto-production* of Haitian autonomy.

In 1793 Toussaint Louverture moved beyond the politics of local revolt to pose the concept of "émancipation générale" as defining the revolutionary sequence in Saint-Domingue. In this moment Toussaint suddenly brought contingent, local, historical events into relation with their foundation, the eternity of a singular truth, precisely in the attempt to make that eternity realize itself *in time,* that is to say, historically.[13] The true progress effected by Toussaint and his colleagues occurred not in battlefield violence and destruction, nor even in the development of successful guerrilla war tactics, but in the symbolic domain.

This universal progress occurred as the transformation he effected in the meaning of *libete/liberté,* in the struggle against the sedimented meanings of a word he did not invent, to reinvest it with new implications, as much as in the actualization of that new understanding in the destruction of plantation slavery and the production of a constitution and a free nation. While Toussaint eventually betrayed the truth of those concepts when he forced his nation back to the plantations, we can only recognize this failure precisely because a truth had been posed in its timelessness. Such a critique would be absurd in the case of a mere local revolt to obtain a garden plot behind one's shack, or to have Saturdays off from slave labor. Instead, the guiding concept of general emancipation that Toussaint put forward illuminates his subsequent historical limitations.

Both Toussaint and Christophe saw labor as an ontological absolute whose development (more work) would lead automatically to the autonomy of their subjects. The ordering of Haitians back to the plantations was a tropicalization of the Enlightenment fetishization of labor seen as the ahistorical, ontological creator of value (Locke, Smith, Ricardo). Haiti, ever a land of extremes, most clearly shows the limitations and dramatic shortcomings of a production-based economy devoid of any ethics of self-limitation. The ecological and human catastrophe resulting from the destruction of Haiti's indigenous forest since 1804 testifies to the obvious need to critique any production-model of human experience; it is this ongoing critique, rather than any univocal affirmation of progress, that constitutes the advancement of the dialectic of enlightenment.[14]

The singularity of the Haitian Revolution in the modern world-system complexifies any simplistic dismissal of 1804 as an idealistic failure to instantiate universal human rights. How then can we understand the place of the Haitian Revolution in the global progress of human rights since the Enlightenment? Jacques Mourgeon's brief yet dense study *Les droits de l'homme* offers an overview of the historical development and instantiation of human rights, attacking in particular the idea that there has in fact been any absolute progress in the implementation of human rights since 1789. If, Mourgeon claims (and he cites no statistics), since 1945 the number of underdeveloped countries has increased from 77 to 133, the number of individuals living below the poverty line, hunger, infant mortality, and illiteracy have all increased (50), if massive cases of genocide have continued unabated, if all this and more is true, is one then justified in concluding that no progress has occurred in propagating human rights?

Such a pessimistic conclusion conflates what I think are two separate issues: the (always partial and contingent) advancement of human rights in any specific case and the critique of subsequent new and different forms of their denial that arise with historical events. It passes over the fact that many historical changes have occurred precisely because in places such as Saint-Domingue, the claims of human rights were pressed and imperfectly advanced. Viewing human rights from the standpoint of a jurist, Mourgeon claims that the utility of human rights exists only when they gain obligatory force from their inclusion in a constitution (68). Such a claim ignores a decisive intervention such as that of the slaves involved in the Haitian Revolution. The slave with a copy of the Declaration of the Rights of Man in his shirt pocket (Parham 34), like Toussaint Louverture before the drafting of his own 1801 charter, had no constitution to enforce their claims, yet these claims nonetheless brought about enormous historical change.

Marcel Gauchet, in a similarly jaded appraisal of the progress of human rights, has argued that our contemporary period since the global events of 1968 is characterized by the gradual weakening—and virtual collapse after 1989—of the various master narratives of political liberation, both on the left (as socialist utopia) and the right (as political liberalism). These have been replaced, he argues, by a global, neoliberal freedom of consumerist choice in an information-based society. The discourse of universal human rights, "the organizational norm of collective consciousness" in the contemporary period, is for Gauchet simply the ideological apology for this lack of political vision (330). Faced with the collapse of the ongoing struggle to create a just society (collapse of trade unions, of communism, of national borders before the incursion of global capital and its demands for systemic restructuration), Gauchet concludes that the discourse of human rights exists merely to supply a good conscience to universal political acquiescence.

## Conclusion

Limiting political intervention to questions of human rights, in this view, is to excise questions of social justice for a fetishistic focus on the isolated, violated individual. Such a focalization is certainly false insofar as it ignores the historical conditions that tied the appearance of the modern individual to the transformations in social relations characteristic of global modernity. For Gauchet, this relation is antinomical: "This is the constitutive contradiction of modern democracies: no free and participating citizenry without a separate power concentrating within itself the social universal" (20).

There is no inherent link between a society that claims to guarantee individual human rights and the creation of conditions that might best realize those rights. Undoubtedly, the contemporary regime of human rights tends simply to function as a palliative that addresses only the grossest violations of human dignity without ever calling into question the wider social conditions of systemic violence that allowed these to occur. The defense of human rights is formally empty: it invokes no particular political regime (Liberal democratic? Communist? Anarchist?) and instead institutes, at the level of political discourse, a systematic short-circuit between the law and the individual, independently of any specific sociopolitical form.

Such critiques of the regime of human rights are applicable to the case of the Haitian Revolution insofar as the ideology of human rights functioned as the dominant political discourse there as well. In an odd historical conjuncture, the primacy of human rights discourse appears retrospectively in both the 1790s and the 1990s. Crucially, one might argue, the dependency on a logic of universal human rights in the Haitian Revolution both allowed for the short-term success of this sequence (1791–1804) and left it vulnerable to the (neocolonial) processes inimical to Haitian political and economic autonomy after 1804. Though the ideology of universal rights gave those who had directly experienced the unfreedom and suffering of slavery an unparalleled impetus to complete their revolution no matter what the cost, such an ideology said nothing about how a society freed from slavery should then be constructed. In this sense what had been a struggle to instantiate the very real, positive freedom of a society without slaves in the 1790s quickly became a hollow, negative freedom after 1804, once that minimum guarantee had been achieved.

Without a positive image of how a universally free society might be constructed within the preexisting complexity of the early-modern world-system, the revolutionary elite of 1804 simply fell back upon the only model they knew, the plantation structure of large-scale and forced labor that produced a handful of commodities for the global agricultural world-system.

Similarly, Haitian peasants' categorical refusal to return to the plantation after 1804 was an attempt to implement a contrary model of small-plot subsistence cultivation. The Haitian singularization of the Enlightenment may have received its impetus from the ideal of universal rights, but what sort of a singularity that new nation would become was precisely a political question; here, the formalism of universal rights could only begin to *orient* (but never finalize) the subsequent process of reflection on how an autonomous society should and might be constructed.

Haiti is critical for understanding the "Structural Transformation of the Public Sphere" as a global phenomenon, a realm extending beyond the provincial confines of early-modern Europe for one final reason: It was Haiti that precociously announced the hollowing out of a robust Enlightenment public sphere of debate into what the Frankfurt School famously dubbed the "Culture Industry." One might conclude that the Enlightenment global public sphere that I have described in earlier chapters in fact proved unable to develop and sustain in Haiti the complex debate over the meaning of human rights occurring in France from 1789 to 1794.[15] In its place there remained by 1804 only an empty formal and negative criterion for the structuration of Haitian society: no slavery allowed. Slavery, at least since Toussaint and Polverel forced Haitians back to the fields, was only to be taken in the most limited, technical (and cynical) definition of the term.

In the face of Gauchet's critique, however, it should be clear by now that the Haitian Revolution nonetheless bears an enormous difference from the contemporary reign of human rights discourse in late capitalism. If, in the contemporary context, the discourse of human rights endorses the withdrawal of individuals from participation in the construction of the political project to construct a just society, Saint-Domingue witnessed precisely the opposite progression between 1791 and 1804. The Haitian Revolution was a mass-based project to instantiate the constituent rights of the multitude; here, human rights discourse functioned as a call to political subjectivity, a call to become subjects of universal human rights and to overthrow the slaveholding society that systematically denied those rights. As such, and for all its limitations, it continues to offer the depoliticized contemporary global human rights regime a historical countermodel.

### Haiti and the New World Order

To remember Haiti two centuries after its independence is to bear witness to its testimony—a testimony not, as the 2004 Debray report would have it, to an imminent threat of Haiti contaminating other countries (as a consequence of poverty and political dysfunction) (16). No, the scandalous singularity of the Haitian Revolution stands before us as if to demand from us a call akin to that of Zola's "J'accuse!" It reminds us precisely of a world of unfathomable structural violence and terrorization, where torture was the daily coin of existence. It reminds us that Haitians were the first in world history to demonstrate that the torture of human beings, like slavery, is never the isolated "mistake" of a few "bad apples." Slavery and the torture that supports its functioning are systems that are themselves predicated upon a global system of enablement, one that encourages them, one that governs its daily function through their incessant recapitulation. There are more slave laborers in the world today—at least 27 million—than at any other moment in human history.[16] The Haitian Revolution demands that we bring into question the system of our daily existence that enables such slavery to continue, to interrogate our lives as a constant enabling of this torture insofar as we reconfirm political regimes—however they may describe themselves—based upon violence and a culture of terrorization and fear.

To successfully undertake this rememoration and questioning, even to begin to remain faithful to the singular event that was Haiti in 1804, is to come to grasp, as did the slaves of Saint-Domingue, that we live in such a culture of torture and violence, and that it is right here with us, not far off in some postmodern Heart of Darkness. This culture of violence and fear resides in the Haitian and American families imprisoning children in Florida and elsewhere as *Restaveks*. It is perpetuated by the U.S. multinationals such as Disney and Warner Brothers that systematically exploited Haitian labor into the 1980s (Arthur and Dash 118, 126). It resides in our cultures of ubiquitous citizen surveillance, a culture that eats away at our rights and freedoms on a daily basis; a culture just down the side road off a country highway or behind a brick enclosure in the middle of downtown, in our houses of torture and devastation that we call prisons. It lies in the culture of systematic suspicion and the suspension of rights of political refugees and asylum seekers (Danticat 2007).

To undertake this rememoration and questioning successfully would be to interrogate the systematic attempts of the United States to isolate a Black Republic that was the first in modernity to call for the universal destruction of slavery, a republic that the United States would not formally recognize until 1862, a republic the U.S. Marines would occupy from 1914 to 1934. "In few places in the world," Paul Farmer observes, "are the lineaments of responsibility so easily traced. . . . Rarely, in fact, have two countries been as closely linked as the United States and Haiti.

Haitians are, by and large, fully aware of this historical fact. But citizens of the United States are, by and large, oblivious to these links" (Farmer 42). The United States' multifaceted attempts to systematically weaken, if not destroy, Haitian sovereignty since 1804 are by now well documented. These include the destruction of the Haitian Creole pig population ordered by Jean-Claude Duvalier under pressure from the United States, an act that amounted to the cruel and absurd destruction not only of a unique species but of "a master component of the Haitian peasant's production system," as well as CIA and AID (Agency for International Development) funding of the movement to overthrow Aristide in 1991.[17]

The United States' political and economic elite were terrified of the egalitarian implications of Haitian independence, universal and immediate abolition, and peasant-based land reform and its attendant stateless egalitarianism. Though the reaction-formations of American policy have varied over two centuries, history tells us that this terror has never ceased, living on as a zombified haunting of American foreign policy far beyond the moment it should logically have disappeared in 1862. These formations include the American diplomatic quarantine of Haiti throughout the nineteenth century, the U.S. Marines' support of the 1888 overthrow of the Légitime *régime,* and the monstrous U.S. policy of supporting Duvalier's totalitarian regime in the 1960s in order, in the words of recently declassified documents, "to deny Haiti to the Communists . . . [and to] assure Haiti's support of the U.S. on matters of importance in the OAS, U.N., and other international organizations" (Farmer 74, 93).

More recently—though the classified documents are still largely unavailable—U.S. sabotage of the democratically elected Aristide government in the spring of 1991 ranged from the covert actions of the CIA to the ideological pressures exerted by the U.S. media.[18] Aristide's election demonstrated to a shocked first-world oligarchy the democratic, egalitarian, and nonviolent accession to political hegemony of the disenfranchised, of those with absolutely no qualification to rule beyond this absolute lack of entitlement. In 1991, for the first time since 1804, Haiti stood out beyond its hinterlands to present the world with an image of uncompromised popular enfranchisement, while the United States continued its own long-term descent into democratic enfeeblement that culminated in the scandal of its own 2000 "elections." This process of Haitian democratization would be quickly suppressed, however, by Raoul Cedras's coup of September 29, 1991.

While it may not be immediately obvious why the United States should devote resources to repeatedly destabilizing the political system of a country that poses no discernible threat to its geopolitical power, the repetition of this process over the past two centuries speaks to the fact that Haiti poses some very real menace to U.S. hegemony. Quite simply, as in the Athenian invasion of Melos described by Thucydides, the United States is regularly compelled to intervene politically and militarily to reassert its dominance as an imperial power and to avoid at all costs losing prestige and influence.[19] No state, no matter how small, can be allowed to assert an alternative economic and/or political model to that of the imperial power.

This threat is one of ideological contamination: Haiti has consistently stood since 1804 for the possibility of direct, popular self-determination, of a self-regulated society that rejected the dominant model of representation by the propertied classes and of contractual wage-labor fundamental to this day to North Atlantic capitalism. Jean-Bertrand Aristide has since 1991 represented the promise of what Alex Dupuy has called a "redistributive" democracy, one that prioritizes the egalitarian assurance of economic rights. This is a promise Aristide has taken, in consonance with the tenants of liberation theology, to form the enabling foundation of all other social rights (Dupuy 2007, 19). Unlike other Latin American leaders, Aristide refused to view Haiti as a minoritarian client-state of Washington and its free-trade agenda. Instead, Aristide has always been perceived by Washington (save for a small minority of Black Caucus Democrats) as "a threat to 'order' and 'stability' in . . . the Caribbean region" because of his explicit (if comparatively moderate) liberation theology and defense of Haiti's "downtrodden masses" (142).

It is quite true, as Dupuy has argued, that Aristide never had a chance to put in place the mechanisms of popular debate, decision making, and "control and accountability" that would offer the Lavalas rank-and-file power over the political process (2007, 93).[20] Aristide's Lavalas party never structured itself in consonance with the traditional egalitarianism of the Haitian rural population, but instead united around Aristide's messianic vanguardism. And yet Dupuy's critique never accounts for the Haitian multitude's constant, unwavering support for Arisitide from 1986 to 2004 and beyond (a support the author nonetheless acknowledges).

Haitians, like any other population, are quite capable of recognizing who does and does not accurately represent their interests; to deny this evident truth would be to revert to a neo-Hegelian loathing of the "rabble"—admittedly always a danger in matters of Haitian politics. The Haitian majority's unflagging support for Aristide, no matter what the Washington policy- and opinion-makers and their Caribbean minions may tell them, stems from his ongoing defense of social and economic justice; land, education, and health care reform; and the fundamental and universal cause of basic human dignity. Far from endorsing a totalitarian messianism, Aristide continued, following his internationally vetted democratic election in 2000 and beyond, to assert the imperative to address the basic human needs of "access to health care, education, food, and housing, which he still considered basic human rights" (142). In response, the United States financially and diplomatically supported the antidemocratic militarism of the so-called Coalition Démocratique (CD), eventually managing to destabilize Aristide to the point of his 2004 forced "departure" from Haiti.[21]

A decade ago, amid the turmoil of the Cedras coup, the Brazilian musicians Caetano Veloso and Gilberto Gil wrote a song entitled "Haiti" for their album *Tropicália 25*. The album marked the twenty-fifth anniversary of the counterculture movement that the two had led in 1968 to protest a Brazil of ever-increasing violence and dissolution of the rule of law by successive military regimes since 1964.[22] The song's refrain gives us an answer to the question of Haiti's "singular absence" in the form of a Zen-like refrain: "O Haïti é aqui. O Haïti não é aqui" ("Haiti is here. Haiti is not here"). "Think of Haiti, pray for Haiti," Caetano and Gil tell us, and this thinking must take the form of an active confrontation with the impossibility of our situation, from wherever we find ourselves in the world: "Haiti is not here. Haiti is here."

Rather than describing any events in Haiti, the Brazilian rap Caetano wrote represents the violence and despair he was witnessing in Brazil. It describes police beating blacks at a concert he went to by the Afrocentric, black-pride group Olodum on the very site where slaves were whipped in colonial Salvador da Bahia: the neighborhood of Pelourinho. The song condemns the massacre of 111 prisoners in a São Paulo prison and the omnipresent violence of a Brazilian racism that calls its society a "racial paradise." If we think Haiti is a small island far from us in the Caribbean, a site where we can download violence and misery to assure ourselves that we live in the land of peace and prosperity, or as the Brazilian flag would have it, the land of "Ordem e progresso" ("Order and Progress"), we should think again, because what we think of as Haiti is right here around us everyday.

In Brazil, and throughout North Atlantic society, as we all know. In the United States, for example, where the incarcerated population has long since reached the highest levels of the population in both absolute and proportional terms in human history, higher than the USSR of Stalin's

Gulag. The United States, where the Patriot Act undertakes the deformalization of the rule of law and the installation of an untrammeled state of emergency, a United States pursuing the destruction of universal human rights at home and in Guantanamo, and on and on. If this book has any value at all, it is as an attempt to learn from an event that is to some extent alien to everyone alive today, within and outside of Haiti. Each of us, as individuals and communities, can learn from this example how to begin to construct universal right, not as a repetition of received dogma, but from the resources of our own critical, constituent subjectivities. To think of Saint-Domingue and the nation of Haiti that succeeded it, to remember the violence of the Age of Enlightenment from a distance, our distance, is to refuse to reduce Haiti to the bestialized space of the eternal return of "natural" violence; it is to represent to those of us outside Haiti, the degree to which *that* Haiti is right here in our world. At the same time, it is to renew the Haitian struggle for the universalization of human singularity, as freedom, as beauty, as pleasure, as desire, as understanding, as the freedom to create and communicate, a freedom and beauty that marks Haiti, with Brazil perhaps its only rival, as one of the greatest, freest, and most humane creative cultures in the Western hemisphere.

# Appendix

Chronology of the Haitian Revolution (1791–1804)

THE EVENTS we now call the Haitian Revolution occurred in the French colony of Saint-Domingue between August 1791 and January 1, 1804, when Jean-Jacques Dessalines declared the independence of the new Haitian nation.[1] One of the singular events of human history, the Haitian Revolution arose out of the particular social situation of Saint-Domingue in the years prior to 1791. In the 1780s Saint-Domingue was the principal world producer of the commodities to which Europe had become increasingly addicted since the Renaissance: sugar and coffee. Saint-Domingue was and remains to this day the most economically lucrative colony in world history, and was at the time the richest colony in the Americas. By the time of the French Revolution in 1789, colonists had expanded the number of plantations on the island to nearly 8,000. In a terrain comprising a mere 10,700 square miles (about the size of Maryland), much of it mountainous, Saint-Domingue alone produced a staggering 40 percent of France's overseas trade. This enormous wealth, the product of the forced labor of African and Creole (native-born) slaves, underwrote to a great extent the rise of the commercial bourgeoisie in the port cities stretching from Bordeaux to Nantes and thus, ironically, in great measure the French Revolution itself.

At the time of the French Revolution, the population of Saint-Domingue was made up of some 500,000 slaves, 40,000 whites, and 30,000 members of the intermediate class of free blacks and mixed-race inhabitants. This enormous slave population, coupled with such a disproportion between the enslaved and free populations, was unique in American slave colonies and would prove to be of enormous importance in the success of the slaves' revolution. The dominant white class was itself divided between an elite group of plantation owners and subaltern *petits blancs*, a group made up as much of itinerant sailors as of petty merchants, plantation overseers, and artisans. The free black and mulatto population (*gens de couleur libre*) of Saint-Domingue was notably large for a European colony of the period, yet all were obliged to submit to the systematic racial discrimination of French plantocratic society. Anyone with an African ancestor was subject to the Enlightenment version of Jim Crow laws: banned from political and professional life, they could not mix with whites in public settings. The slave population was heterogeneous, made up of newly arrived (*Bossale*) slaves as well as "Creoles" born into French slavery and fully acculturated into the plantation social structure.

The events of the French Revolution were directly responsible for upsetting the fragile balance of powers that had allowed Saint-Domingue to exist as a functioning, profitable social structure based upon the forced extraction of human labor. While this book pays close attention to the overseas movement and subsequent reformulation of the ideas of liberty, equality, and fraternity, in purely structural terms the French Revolution destabilized in Saint-Domingue, no less than in France itself, the ancien régime political, legal, and police apparatuses. Following the fall of the Bastille, on September 27, 1789, the island's plantocratic *grand blanc* elite formed a colonial assembly that, though divided on issues such as autonomy, sought strictly to reinforce the colony's system of white supremacy and slave labor. By the fall of 1789, free coloreds in Paris were demanding equal rights with whites, while paradoxically defending the bulwark of racially discriminatory laws that separated them as a social class from slaves. On October 22, free coloreds defended their rights before the National Assembly, invoking the Rights of Man. Such actions only antagonized the plantocratic elite, who became increasingly hostile to mulatto claims. This hostility quickly escalated by November into lynchings and pogroms of mulattoes who publicly demanded their civil rights. On March 8, 1790, the National Assembly attempted to dispense with the problem by granting ultimate authority over internal affairs to the Colonial Assembly, asserting in addition that the metropolitan constitution would no longer apply overseas.

This initial period of conflict between the white landowning elite and free nonwhites culminated on October 28, 1790, when Vincent Ogé, a leading voice for mulatto rights in Paris, secretly returned to Saint-Domingue. He organized a group of some three hundred mulatto followers in a revolt whose aim was to bring about by force the juridical equality of his class with whites. Ogé fatally refused to incorporate slaves into his insurgence, and, though it caused an immense panic, white militia forces quickly crushed the rebellion, capturing Ogé and his followers across the Spanish border where they had retreated. Ogé and his fellow rebel Chavannes were then publicly tortured to death in a display of plantocratic terrorism.

Though the French Assembly, with its enormous financial stake in the continued flow of goods from Saint-Domingue, had refused to that point to admit that the rights of man should apply to the French colonies, the torture of Ogé turned French public opinion against the planters. On May 11, the assembly began debating the question of colonial rights, and on May 15, 1791, the National Assembly granted full and equal political rights to the small percentage of mulattoes (some four hundred in all Saint-Domingue) whose parents were both free. This decree consolidated white resistance to mulatto rights, leading in addition to calls for cessation from revolutionary France.

Amid such conflict and division among the two dominant castes in the colony, signs of open slave revolt quickly began to mount in the summer of 1791. On August 14 a large group of slave leaders meet in the Bois Caïman forest, with the slave Boukman as their leader, to set forth plans for a large-scale revolt. Toussaint Louverture, a free-black slave owner much respected in the black community, appears to have played a leading role planning this event, which may in addition have been instigated by white landowners who did not fully realize what forces they were setting in motion. On the night of August 22, 1791, this massive slave uprising began the unfolding of events that would culminate in Haitian Independence thirteen years later. Led by Boukman and another slave leader, Jeannot, the uprising spread across the plantations of the North, where whites were killed in vicious reprisal for the years of torture and abuse of slavery. Fires burned across the Northern Plains for some four days, and in response white militias quickly attempted to cordon off the North from the Southern and Western portions of the colony. This isolation remained effective until 1793. In the following weeks, over a thousand plantations would be burned and looted. Some two thousand whites and perhaps ten thousand blacks were killed by December, with massive torture and execution occurring on both sides.

The ideological and political aims of the rebels were extremely heterogeneous and unfocused in these initial months. Some defended the King of France (who had in fact already fled to Varennes), acting on the rumor that he had issued an emancipation decree. Other leaders, such as Jean-François and Biassou, tentatively asserted their claim for partial, and then universal emancipation based upon the rights of man. During this time, Toussaint remained on the plantation of Bréda where he had been a slave in his youth, and then a free slave owner since 1776, protecting the family of his former master, Bayon de Libertat.

On September 24 the National Assembly, moved by stories of atrocities committed against whites, repealed the May 15 decree. The effect of this act was to set mulattoes once again against whites, thus eliminating the possibility of a concerted reaction to the black uprising. In the South and West, mulatto troops burned the towns of Jacmel and Port-au-Prince. In November, Toussaint, having arranged for the safe departure of Libertat and his family, joined the rebel camp of Biassou, where he served as doctor while already beginning to enforce the rule of law in the treatment of white prisoners. Following the death of Boukman on November 14, Jeannot, Biassou, and Jean-François came forward as the leaders of the revolt. Biassou and Jean-François executed Jeannot, the most violent of the leaders, in late November. On November 29 the first of a series of civil commissions sent by the French Assembly, made up of Mirbeck, Roume, and Saint-Léger, arrived in Le Cap. In December the commissioners made contact with Jean-François and Biassou, who, in a letter of December 10, demanded freedom for themselves and four hundred followers. In subsequent negotiations Toussaint remained in the background in an advisory capacity.

By February 1792 the now Jacobin-controlled assembly was attempting to repeal the September 24 law. In March, Mirbeck was driven out of the colony by white hostility to the commission. On April 4, 1792, the National Assembly reversed itself, once again granting full citizenship rights to mulattoes and free blacks. This law also named a new commission to Saint-Domingue, possessed of both dictatorial powers and six thousand troops and national guards. These commissioners, Sonthonax, Polverel, and Ailhaud, arrived on September 18 armed with a strongly Jacobinist politics to defend the republic. Though Sonthonax publicly reaffirmed the inviolability of slavery upon his arrival, given his previously explicit denunciation of slavery in the French revolutionary press, this appears to have been a cautionary measure leading up to his emancipation declaration of 1793. By December, Toussaint had assembled black troops under his leadership, including future leaders such as Dessalines, Moïse, and Charles Belair, and quickly began training them with French defectors and prisoners.

In February 1793 war was declared between France and Spain, which controlled the neighboring colony of Santo Domingo. Toussaint, Biassou, and Jean-François all went over to Spain, which had promised them personal freedom, though not general emancipation. Spain supplied arms and money, while the French Republican forces, which continued to condone slavery, were withering away, victims of tropical disease and diminishing resources that failed to be renewed from France. In an attempt to strengthen their regime, Sonthonax and Polverel began both to reform the legal code governing plantation labor and to free individual groups of slaves who had experience bearing arms. On June 21 Sonthonax formalized this partial emancipation, proclaiming that "all slaves declared free by the Republic shall be the equals of all men, white or of any other color. They shall enjoy the rights of all French citizens." Finally, on August 29, 1793, Sonthonax, desperate to shore up his Jacobin forces, universally emancipated all the slaves of northern Saint-Domingue. Though he had no authorization to do so from France, Sonthonax's decree is of particular importance insofar as it was the first unconditional, total, and immediate abolition of slavery in world history. No conditions or delays were stipulated to black freedom. The same day, Toussaint issued a statement of his own, calling for the allegiance of all blacks to the cause of universal emancipation. Blacks, not only in the North but in the South and West as well, where slavery remained nominally in force, quickly abandoned large-scale plantation labor for the cultivation of small plots for personal consumption.

Toussaint, who would become a world-renowned figure celebrated by everyone from Wordsworth and Lamartine to Carlos Santana, had been a member of the native-born slave elite prior to 1791. First as a slave, then as a free black, he had worked as a coachman on the Bréda plantation, where he became a fervent devotee of Catholicism. He learned to read and sign his name, but also is said to have spoken fluently his father's Ewe-Fon (Arada) language. He was a master in the traditional use of herbal plants and medicines. Freed by Bayon de Libertat by 1776, when he was approximately thirty, he moved freely between the two worlds of white landowners and black slaves, eventually coming to own both slaves and land. Soon after joining the Spanish cause, Toussaint quickly became the dominant military force in the colony, a position he would reinforce ever more completely until his capture and deportation in 1802. Even at this early date, Toussaint revealed himself to be a military genius who could utterly confuse and overwhelm his French and mulatto opponents. Though unwavering and at times brutal in his defense of the blacks' cause, he was marked by a spirit of justice and fairness, and his actions and proclamations reveal a leader who repeatedly affirmed the rule of law over the spirit of retribution.

On May 6, 1794, Toussaint stunningly, and for reasons still not entirely clear to historians, changed sides with his now sizable army of four thousand men and rallied to the French Republic. On February 4 the National Assembly had formalized Sonthonax's proclamation abolishing slavery; this seems to have been the deciding event for Toussaint, who remained unwaveringly committed to universal emancipation from slavery for the inhabitants of Saint-Domingue from at least August 1793 until his death in 1803. Toussaint's *volte-face*, as it is called, was the defining moment in the Haitian Revolution, aligning the black forces behind the linked causes of universal emancipation and Jacobinism; from then on, this sequence of events took on its particularly world-historical character, becoming a struggle for the unconditional and universal abolition of slavery.

By 1795 Toussaint had driven the Spanish from Saint-Domingue, and in July Spain surrendered to the French Republic. While Jean-François and Biassou stayed on with the Spanish, the cessation of hostilities with Spain increased the level of conflict between mulatto troops and Toussaint's largely black army. On March 20, 1796, the mulatto leader Vilatte captured Étienne Laveaux, the governor of the colony and Toussaint's mentor and protector. When Toussaint dramatically freed Laveaux, the National Assembly promoted him to deputy-governor, then in 1797 to commander-in-chief of the French forces in Saint-Domingue.

Toussaint rapidly dominated events in the colony. When Sonthonax, who had been called back to France to stand trial before the charges of exiled white landowners, returned in May 1796, Toussaint quickly outmaneuvered him. Toussaint was able to rally the slaves against the former liberator turned Thermidorian, who now strove to force them back onto the plantations as nominally free indentured laborers. On August 20, 1797, Sonthonax again returned to France, this time under pressure from Toussaint, who henceforth completely dominated the military and political events in the colony. The French envoy Hédouville, sent by France in an attempt to mediate Toussaint's growing power, was similarly dispatched back to France in October 1798, after Toussaint spread rumors among blacks that Hédouville planned to restore slavery. Upon his departure, however, Hédouville sowed the seeds of future conflict, granting full authority to the Southern mulatto leader Rigaud over Toussaint.

In August 1799 war erupted between Toussaint and Rigaud, a conflict known as the "War of Knives." With ten thousand soldiers behind him, Toussaint was able to defeat Rigaud's forces in a struggle marked by both extreme violence and the unfolding of a profound division between blacks and mulattoes that would continue to plague Haitian politics for decades to come. Dessalines in particular led a total war of utter brutality against the mulatto troops. Rigaud was finally defeated on July 5, 1800, at Acquin. Though Toussaint declared a general amnesty following the war, he allowed Dessalines to continue the massacre of some ten thousand mulatto men, women, and children.

By the end of 1800, Toussaint ruled Saint-Domingue as governor. In October of that year, he proclaimed a general system of forced, military-style plantation labor in an attempt to rebuild the colony's economy. Blacks' laboring status was fixed immutably, made permanent based on their past status as slaves. Though greatly resented by blacks as quasi-enslavement, the system was largely successful in economic terms. Toussaint refused to subdivide the enormous sugar plantations, and drafted the army to enforce his work provisions upon his fellow blacks, implementing corporal punishment for those who refused to work. He welcomed back those white planters who affirmed his rule, and even supported the resumption of the slave trade to supply field hands. The execution of Toussaint's adoptive nephew Moïse in November 1801 for leading an uprising against his labor regime dramatically revealed Toussaint's increasing authoritarianism. Conversely, this period saw an increased enforcement of the rule of law, a reduction in racial conflict, and the incipient construction of an educational infrastructure.

In July 1801 Toussaint issued a constitution that affirmed his status as governor for life, giving him the authority to make and promulgate all laws for Saint-Domingue, simultaneously granting the French government mere consultative status. Though not a declaration of independence, it was more precisely a declaration of juridical autonomy that maintained only a nominal association with the French Republic, now controlled by Bonaparte. When Bonaparte received the Constitution, the infuriated leader, further alarmed by Toussaint's unilateral annexation of Santo Domingo on January 28, 1801, quickly mounted the invasion he had already envisioned to reassert French hegemony via the crushing of Toussaint and the reimposition of slave labor in Saint-Domingue.

Napoleon dispatched his brother-in-law General Leclerc with ten thousand troops to invade Saint-Domingue in February 1802. Toussaint had at his disposal some twenty thousand troops by this time, and ordered General Henry Christophe to burn Le Cap before French forces could land there. In the face of these healthy and well-trained troops, Toussaint, Dessalines, Christophe, and their troops quickly retreated from the cities to the mountain terrain they knew so well, and once again vicious, total warfare broke out between both sides. Faced with early French successes, Christophe defected to the French in April 1802, while Toussaint and

Dessalines surrendered on May 1. Toussaint then retired to his plantation with some two thousand guards. On June 6 Leclerc captured Toussaint in Gonaïves and quickly deported him to France; he was sent to the mountain prison Fort-de-Joux, where he died the next year.

Though the tide of events seemed to have favored the French in the summer of 1802, by May a massive outbreak of yellow fever had already begun decimating the French troops, killing three thousand of them by June. By July Leclerc wrote that he was losing one hundred sixty soldiers to yellow fever every day. The arrival in June of news of the restoration of slavery in Guadeloupe further reinvigorated the black struggle against the French that had continued on despite the defection of the revolution's ostensible leaders. By September 13 Leclerc had lost an astonishing twenty-nine thousand soldiers to fever and warfare, and on November 2 Leclerc himself succumbed to yellow fever. When Christophe and Dessalines rejoined the revolution that had continued on in their absence, the tide decisively turned against the French. With Toussaint removed from the scene, Dessalines united the black and mulatto forces under the threat of general reinslavement of all nonwhites. Though General Rochambeau made a final, genocidal attempt to terrorize the black revolutionaries into submission, England's declaration of war against France in May 1803 eliminated the possibility of his receiving any fresh troops. The English then proceeded to blockade the island in June, and after a series of routs, Rochambeau fled Le Cap on November 10, surrendering to the English. On January 1, 1804, Dessalines declared the independence of the new nation of Haiti, founding a nation based upon the universal freedom of all of its citizens for the first time in world history.

# Notes

### Abbreviations
AN     Archives nationales (France)
CAOM   Centre des archives d'outre mer (Aix-en-Provence)

### Introduction

1. The assertion is strange, insofar as Israel's 800-page masterwork seems dedicated to proving, on the contrary, that there was not one but two pan-European Enlightenments: one moderate, deferential to constituted authority, and another, radical and Spinozian, that "challenged the fundamentals of revealed religion, received ideas, tradition, morality, and what everywhere was regarded, in absolutist and non-absolutist states alike, as divinely constituted political authority" (159). In his epilogue Israel further claims that "there was just one highly integrated European Enlightenment encapsulating a four-way conflict between Newtonians, neo-Cartesians, Leibnitio-Wolffians, and radicals," without ever describing what factor united these warring camps (715).

2. The historiography on the Haitian Revolution is growing quickly. Readers looking for a basic introduction to its events now have a number of excellent choices in English, including C. L. R. James's classic *Black Jacobins,* Carolyn Fick's *The Making of Haiti,* and Laurent Dubois' *Avengers of the New World.*

### 1. Saint-Domingue and the Singularization of Enlightenment

1. Already in 1810, fully 73 percent of the Haitian state's revenues were derived from export/import taxation. This tactic of extraction would be rapidly perfected, to account for precisely 98.2 percent of the state budget in 1881, while only six years later the *entire* government budget came from customs duties (Trouillot 1990, 61). This was a general process that Fanon would first identify in *Les damnés de la terre* as neocolonialism and one that has been analyzed in its Haitian specificity in studies such as Michel-Rolph Trouillot's *Haiti: State against Nation* and Mats Lundahl's *Peasants and Poverty: A Study of Haiti.*

2. Donnelly makes such a defense for human rights to dominate our assessment of any political regime in section 11.8 of *Universal Human Rights* (2003).

3. I will compare the accomplishments of the American, French, and Haitian revolutions on this score in what follows.

4. One could contrast such a view with that of contemporary theorists who, in due deconstructionist fashion, implicitly invalidate any practical intervention because of its inevitable failure fully to correspond to its concept. Judith Butler is content to point out that "slave uprisings that insist upon the universal authorization for emancipation nevertheless borrow from a discourse that runs at least a double risk: the emancipated slave may be liberated into a new mode of subjection" (40).

5. "One cannot create a state on the grounds of universal racial equality and remain indifferent to the continuation of racial slavery elsewhere" (Fischer 237). See Fischer (236–44) on the transnational and universalist implications of Haiti's abolition of slavery, and the vicissitudes of this orientation in nineteenth-century Haitian politics.

6. As in Condorcet's 1781 text "Réflexions sur l'esclavage des nègres," where the philosopher-mathematician argues quite "rationally" for a gradual elimination of slavery over the course of one or two generations (38, 44). For a strong critique of the limitations of Enlightenment universalism in light of the problem of slavery, see Sala-Molins, *Les misères des Lumières*.

7. See Lundahl on the long-term economic consequences of this near total destruction of what in 1789 was the world's most profitable and highly developed plantation colony. Deborah Jenson has pointed out that the revolutionary slaves of Saint-Domingue "seemed to—yet did not—demand universal emancipation" (personal communication, Oct. 26, 2005). I do not wish to conflate two distinct issues in using the phrase "universal emancipation." My claim is not that Saint-Domingue revolutionaries explicitly engaged in a transnational *political* process dedicated to eradicating slavery throughout the globe; this dimension of decolonization was merely implicit in what was necessarily a localized fight against French slavery in Saint-Domingue. It would become an explicit agenda only after 1804, and then in a necessarily compromised and limited fashion—as, for example, the constitutional decree that all humans *on Haitian soil* became free—thanks to the constantly threatened political autonomy of the young nation. Rather, I am arguing that Toussaint and others explicitly and consciously grounded their revolution in a universal principle of practical morality (in the Kantian sense) that guided their endeavor, as in Toussaint's 1797 assertion to the Directory that he would "defend the rights of Humanity for the triumph of Liberty and Equality."

8. Gordon Wood points out, however, that if the patrician American revolutionaries failed to abolish slavery, their egalitarianism created the social conditions in which it immediately became a glaring and impossible-to-ignore contradiction that led inexorably to the Civil War and abolition (186). Similarly, David Brion Davis observes that "if the American Revolution could not solve the problem of

slavery, it at least led to a *perception* of the problem" (1975, 285; emphasis in original). The complex relationship between American slavery and the American Revolution has been the object of extensive documentation. Classic studies include Jordan (1968), Robinson (1971), MacLeod (1974), and Davis (1975).

9. Davis 1975, 77; Bell 2007, 12; Blumrosen 69.

10. Though Jefferson must be given some credit for replacing the right to "property" with the right to "the pursuit of happiness," Zuckert points out that this substitution does not necessarily "signify a rejection of [the right to property]" (60, 65).

11. Vermont, prior to its admission to the Union in 1791, had technically been an independent nation since the end of the Revolutionary conflict.

12. Yale Law School Avalon project: http://www.yale.edu/lawweb/avalon/states/vt01.htm. Accessed Jan. 22, 2007.

13. Cited in Davis 1975, 276. See also Davis 1975, 76, 83; 1983: 276.

14. See Blumrosen, however, for a detailed argument that consciousness of this issue lay at the heart of the negotiations leading from the 1774 Continental Congress to the three-fifths compromise of the 1787 Constitutional Convention.

15. Twenty-five of the fifty-five 1787 Convention delegates actually owned slaves (Davis 1975, 100).

16. Davis 1983: 268; 1975, 104, 125; Blumrosen 220.

17. Robespierre made a similar defense of the right to revolt (against any tyranny, rather than slavery in particular) in his discourse on a new declaration of the rights of man of April 24, 1793 (2000, 127).

18. See James (116) and Césaire, "Les limites de la revolution française" (1960, 171–90), for further discussion of the suppression of the question of slavery in the Revolutionary Assembly.

19. See Franklin Knight (403) for a discussion of the varying interpretations of the Rights of Man among the various free classes in Saint-Domingue.

20. CAOM 87 MIOM 13.

21. David Scott, in his brilliant explication of James's Toussaint Louverture, figures Toussaint as a prototypical Enlightenment intellectual, moved by a Kantian moralistic formalism, "by completely rational ends he has self-reflectively prepared in advance" (2004, 198). Scott's Toussaint is a tragic figure, trapped between the uncompromising moral imperatives to which he holds himself and the inevitable course of a dialectic of enlightenment that leads him, necessarily and following the dictates of his own moral formalism, into a new barbarism (205).

22. Sankar Muthu offers a brilliant critique of this intellectual *doxa* in the concluding chapter of *Enlightenment against Empire*. Recent revisionist descriptions of the multiple, often contradictory "Enlightenments" can be found in Baker and Reill, Jacob (1981), Porter and Teich, and Israel.

23. See Robert Misrahi's preface to the *Tractatus Politicus* on the unity of Spinoza's ontological and political thought. See Vernière (661–64) on the problem of the infinite in Spinoza and its distinction from the radical materialism of

Diderot and d'Holbach. With the exception of Sieyès (Vernière 684), Spinoza's thought, unlike that of Montesquieu and Rousseau, played virtually no explicit role in the political philosophy of the French Revolution. It was instead anonymously reinscribed in an overall climate of thought and via Rousseau's *Contrat social*, with its panoply of (unacknowledged) Spinozian concepts (Vernière 481–86).

24. I have noted "translation modified" for those published translations that I have altered.

25. The Spinozian assertion of universal causality or necessity could conceivably be critiqued as an illusory second, and not first, nature. In such a view the concept of second nature "is the totality of whatever has been so completely trapped by social and rational mechanisms . . . that nothing differing from it can manifest itself. And because there is nothing else outside it, it acquires the appearance of the natural, in other words, of what simply exists and is given" (Adorno 2006, 121). Such an analysis is subject to its own *aufhebung*, however. In fact, the illusion that all is necessary, that there is no (utopian) possibility of an outside or other world, is itself subject to human understanding (via, say, a Marxian critique of political economy). Spinoza argued that the human mind can (potentially) come to know adequately the causes not only of our true ideas but also of all our ideas, true and false (Macherey 83).

26. "With his system," Jonathan Israel writes, "Spinoza imparted shape, order, and unity to the entire tradition of radical thought, both retrospectively and in its subsequent development, qualities . . . [that] were henceforth perhaps its strongest weapons in challenging prevailing structures of authority and received learning and combating the advancing moderate Enlightenment" (230). Israel's argument tends to totalize the Radical Enlightenment around the single unifying figure of Spinoza. My additional thesis is that what Spinoza liberated was precisely a protean, polymorphous potentiality of singularization. This force negates constituted totalities as a potentiality immanent to all humanity.

27. On the social construction of universalism via the extension of laboratory conditions across a network (based on the model of Pasteur), see Latour (273).

28. The quote is from Deleuze 2002, 33. See Jameson 2002; Žižek 2004, 186.

29. And *not* his definition of "singular things," which is relational: "By singular things I understand things that are finite and have a determinate existence" (Spinoza 1999, 116). The finite—that which has definite boundaries or limits—defines itself in relation to what it is not; a singular thing is for Spinoza merely one of the many modes of a single and univocal substance, not the autonomous being Hardt and Negri tend to make of it. Hardt and Negri's attribution of the "singular" to indicate the power (*potentia*) of constituent subjectivity muddles this distinction between substance and the various determinate modes of that substance (*natura naturata*) that Spinoza calls singularities. In a properly Spinozian (though less rhetorically effective) sense, what Hardt and Negri call constituent power is the expressivity of substance, not the "singular." This slippage is especially clear in Negri's discussion of singularity (1991, 63). Though Spinoza clearly reintroduces

elements of transcendence and anthropomorphism to his final conception of God in book 5 of the *Ethics* (Alquié, 98, 390, 397), perhaps the authors of *Empire* would argue that, properly understood, God for Spinoza represents a naturalistic "appropriation of the divinity" that could well go by the name "Multitude" (Negri 2004, 133).

30. See Peter Hallward's *Out of This World* on Deleuze and the historical movement from classical notions of the infinite (Spinoza), to the finitude of autonomous specification (Kant), to the contemporary "counter-actualization" of human finitude (66).

31. Badiou, in his short study *Ethics,* has developed a more transitive understanding of the singular, describing the process of subjectivation as the maximal singularization of individuals in a given situation, a singularization achieved through the "affirmative thought" of what is timeless and "immortal" in human being (33).

32. "The diffusion of ideas," writes Roger Chartier, "cannot be taken as a simple imposition: reception is always an appropriation that transforms, reformulates, and exceeds what it receives. [Public] opinion is no mere receptacle or soft wax, and the circulation of thoughts or cultural models is always a dynamic and creative process" (35).

33. *Liberté/libete* is not so much a concept, that is, the abstract mental representation of an object, but a word or *mot,* taken in its strongest sense: the free linguistic object that directly produces radically new meanings (Dictionnaire Robert).

34. This investigation should remain faithful to Foucault in its attempt to chart "the appearance of objects, types of enunciations, concepts, strategic choices (or transformations that affect those that already exist). . . . In order to analyze such events, it is not enough simply to indicate changes, and to relate them immediately to the theological, aesthetic model of creation (with its transcendence, with all its originalities and inventions), or to the psychological model of the act of consciousness. . . . Archeology tries to establish the system of transformations that constitute 'change'; it tries to develop this empty, abstract notion, with a view to according it the analyzable status of transformation" (Foucault 1972, 171–73).

35. Some scholars have argued that the three-fifths compromise of 1787—the decision to count slaves as three-fifths of a human for representation in the House—enabled the "first blanket prohibition of slavery in the history of the world" in the northern states. This geographically partial emancipation occurred, however, in an area north of the Ohio River where it was unpopular and of little economic consequence (Blumrosen 243).

36. Lundahl (1979) describes in great detail the contemporary use of this highly developed faculty of judgment on the part of the Haitian peasantry in, for example, the process of price determination in the country's network of markets. Unlike the Western consumer's complacent belief that all copies of any given product

will be identical, a highly developed art of judgment and haggling becomes necessary "when qualities and measures [of products] are not homogeneous.... Buyers and sellers can [easily] inform themselves of demand and supply conditions in the market-place [and] every *revendeuse* knows exactly where to go to find the product she wants.... The bargaining situation ... involves comparison of products with those of other sellers, consultations with friends and bystanders, and thorough examination of each item. As a result, the information at the disposal of both buyers and sellers is more or less perfect, and cheating becomes very difficult" (Lundahl 1979, 164).

37. The French "expérience" implies at once the impact of lived-through events on an individual's knowledge as well as the controlled observation of the scientific "experiment."

38. A true democracy is for Spinoza the organization of society such that "all inhabitants, without exception, ... enjoy their rights" (1958, 443, translation modified). If Spinoza goes on to qualify this universalism by excluding foreigners, women, and slaves in the closing lines of the unfinished draft of the *Tractatus politicus* (445), this senile moment of prejudice cannot stand before the unambiguous logic Spinoza articulates everywhere in his writings: as soon as any being has the power to do something, it has the right to. In other words, slaves and women are dependent because they lack the power to act autonomously. As soon as they can do so, they have the absolute right to overthrow their servitude. Only then can society exist in conformity with reason, allowing for the maximum expression of each individual's essential capacity for singularization.

39. Cited in Kramnick 186, 220, 287. Condillac was quick to specify and critique, however, the latent dualism of Locke's attempt to preserve an innate capacity of the human mind to organize sensual experience, one that maintained, Condillac argued, the mind-body dualism that the Radical Enlightenment thinkers, from Spinoza to Diderot, systematically denied (Israel 234, 517).

40. A Haitian farmer, asked to explain his colleagues' systematic refusal to follow the advice of international agricultural "experts," gives a brilliant contemporary example of a faculty of judgment that is opaque to Western arrogance: "If they are going to understand our reasons, these people will have to live where peasants live. At least then they would see why we plant the way we do. If you ask me, there's no-one who doesn't look after his own interests in the place where he lives. If people found that planting in straight lines really worked, they wouldn't be so stupid as to reject the method" (Arthur and Dash 108).

41. Perhaps the sole exception to this tendency was William Godwin's "Enquiry Concerning Political Justice" (1793).

42. Cited in Kramnick 222–23, 27–30.

43. Cited in Sepinwall 134, 67, 95, 99, 95.

44. The term is Rancière's in *Le maître ignorant*. His brilliant biography of the anarchist education reformer Joseph Jacotot is the inspiration for many of the following comments.

45. "Understanding first had to work with the ideas that it had at hand, using them as though they were authentic knowledge, to make them produce all the effects of which they were capable" (Macherey 62).

46. If all humans think, always already, they need only construct that thought, improvising from the immediate situation they find themselves thrown into as humans have from time immemorial: for Spinoza, "The first hammer used by a smith was not in fact a true hammer, no more than the man who manipulated it was a true blacksmith; instead, this was a stone picked up on the side of the road, a 'natural' instrument in itself imperfect, which only became an instrument through the use that was made of it. . . . The true problem is to know what becomes of these ideas that one possesses [habemus enim ideam veram], how they are transformed, in the manner in which one could transform a stone to make of it a hammer" (Macherey 62–63).

47. Jeremy Popkin remains unconvinced of the veracity of this tale, which he calls "perhaps a little too good to be literally true" for those theorizing the "synthesis of "European" ideas about liberty and African beliefs" being forged in the Saint-Domingue revolution (personal communication, Dec. 7, 2007).

48. As the initial antislavery unity forged in the years 1791–96 dissolved in the face of its own success, an array of different claims regarding the proper political formation for this incipient community arose, ranging from the radical egalitarianism of the former slaves' *Bossale* community to Toussaint Louverture's exceedingly undemocratic 1801 Constitution, in which the leader is granted "the reins of government," which "are confided to him for the rest of his glorious life" (cited in Bell 2007, 211). I will return to this theme in chapter 5.

49. This eradication of all difference extended, for example, to the attempt to destroy the regional languages. A "Report to the Committee of Public Safety on Idioms" of 8 Pluviôse, Year II (Jan. 28, 1794), claims that "federalism and superstition speak *bas-breton;* emigration and hatred of the Republic speak German; counter-revolution speaks Italian, and fanaticism speaks Basque. Let us destroy [*cassons*] these instruments of damage and error" (cited in Carpentier and Lebrun 252).

50. The *Liste générale des condamnés* lists among the offenses of those sent to the guillotine: "Jean Baptiste Henry, aged eighteen, journeyman tailor, convicted of having sawn down a tree of liberty, executed 6 September, 1793"; "François Bertrand, aged thirty-seven, publican at Leure in the department of the Côte-d'Or, convicted of having furnished to the defenders of the country sour wine injurious to health, condemned to death at Paris and executed the same day"; "Marie Angelique Plaisant, seamstress at Douai, convicted of having exclaimed that she was an aristocrat and that she did not care 'a fig for the nation,' condemned to death at Paris and executed the same day" (cited in Hibbert 226).

51. For a narrative description of Duvalier's systematic destruction of the rule of law and recourse to torture, see Marc Romulus's *Les cachots de Duvalier,* and the Platform of Haitian Human Rights Organizations for a listing of violations

under the Cedras regime (Arthur and Dash 76–77). For a more systematic analysis of the development and structural singularity of Duvalier's totalitarian regime, see Trouillot 1990, ch. 6 and 7.

52. "In the course of its daily labor, the peasantry never directly confronted the system's ultimate beneficiaries—the top state officeholders, and, above all, the merchant bourgeoisie. Hence, even though peasants might have wondered about the causes of their poverty, they knew few individuals upon whom to place the blame" (Trouillot 1990, 86).

53. Franz Neumann forcefully argues this point in his article "The Concept of Political Freedom." See also Scheuerman (196–97). One should also, of course, remain critically attentive to the ideological use of calls for the "rule of law" by organisms such as the World Bank to justify the imposition of open markets on vulnerable populations (Buchanan and Pahuja).

54. Moreover, the continued elitist compromises of this Haitian pseudo-democratization hobble any attempts at Truth and Reconciliation and "preserve the freedom of the torturers, . . . engendering an ambiguous sense of normalcy . . . built upon the constraining legacy and continued presence of criminals. [This serves to] legitimize the silent violence of daily material deprivation plaguing deprived majorities" (Fatton 154).

55. Fatton 17, 28, 32; Arthur and Dash 162, 172–73.

### 2. The Idea of 1804

1. Habermas, "Popular Sovereignty as Procedure," in *Between Facts and Norms,* 463–90.

2. Peter Hallward points out that "Saint-Domingue isn't even mentioned in Simon Schama's best-selling *Citizens* (Knopf, 1989) or Keith Baker's *Inventing the French Revolution* (Cambridge University Press, Cambridge, 1990), while François Furet and Mona Ozouf were unable to find room in their 1,100-page *Critical Dictionary of the French Revolution* (Harvard University Press, Cambridge, MA, 1989) for an entry on Toussaint L'Ouverture; the entry on 'Slavery' in their index refers only to America's revolution, not Haiti's" (2004b).

3. David Geggus's outstanding *Haitian Revolutionary Studies* is a watershed that reveals how many archives still remain unexplored, pointing to years of future research.

4. As such, it was of course not free of its own contradictions (to be considered more fully in my concluding chapter), the most glaring being the reimposition of forced labor by Toussaint and, subsequently, Christophe, as well as the revolution's failure to fully enfranchise women, whose freedom remained the merely negative one not to be enslaved.

5. "Slaves, women, people of all professions and of all nationalities, all [are to] be admitted, with neither restriction nor privilege" (Badiou 1997, 14).

6. Cited in Davis 1975, 43. Davis observes that the "negative equalitarianism" of "the early Christian view of slavery was of central importance in reconciling

the masses to the existing social order. It constituted the core of an ideology that encouraged hope, patience, endurance, and submission, while reminding the powerful of their own fallibility" (43). On St. Paul and the transformation of Christianity into a universal, global secular force, see Ellen Meiksins Wood (35).

7. See Bell (2007, 186, 194) for examples of the Catholic moralism that Toussaint increasingly propounded in public ceremonies following his accession to power in 1796.

8. "Voodoo was for the slaves a language, a way of expressing and resisting their cultural and religious assimilation. . . . It was the focus for the development of political consciousness so far as it allowed the slaves to be aware that their values were different from those of the whites" (Laguerre 70).

9. The Mande Charter has been handed down since the thirteenth century through oral tradition in the Mande hunter caste (Donso). It is to be distinguished from the later Kurukan Fuga Charter of 1236. The latter first appeared in transcription in D. T. Niane's classic *Soundiata ou l'épopée Mandingue* (1960), while the earlier Mande Charter was transcribed and published in 2003 by Youssouf Tata Cissé. It is upon the latter version that I base my comments. Due to its oral nature, there is still significant scholarly debate over its antiquity and veracity. A number of West African intellectuals, including Djibril Tamsir Niane, Siriman Kouyaté, Raphaël Ndiaye, Cheikh Hamidou Kane, Martin Faye, Mangoné Niang, and Youssouf Tata Cissé have, however, begun to analyze these two texts as predecessors to the European rights documents. My comments are intended as no more than a gloss upon their work, one that points to a dispersion of this subaltern human rights discourse throughout the early-modern Black Atlantic world. For more information on the charter, see Niang 2006. Many thanks to Dmitri van den Bersselaar, Étienne Smith, Stephen Belcher, and Charles Becker for their help in following the current debate in African Studies over the Mande Charter(s).

10. Whether Kant is actually *correct* about the existence of pure a priori judgments is beside the point for the *historical interpretation* I am putting forward here.

11. Robespierre's deductive approach to questions of political rights and slavery follows upon the precocious intervention of Mirabeau into the debate on slavery on August 21, 1789. On this date, mere days after the promulgation of the *Déclaration*, Mirabeau, in the *Lettres du Comte de Mirabeau à ses commettans*, publicly articulated, and with biting irony, the full political consequences to be drawn from this text: "Nous ne pensions pas que le moment fut si proche où la grande cause de la liberté des Nègres, enveloppée dans celle générale de l'espèce humaine, serait solennellement établie, avouée, sanctionnée par l'Assemblée nationale. . . . Aucun [représentant esclavagiste de Saint-Domingue] n'a proposé comme amendement [à la Déclaration des droits de l'Homme et du Citoyen] de déclarer, *les hommes blancs seuls naissent et demeurent libres*. . . . C'est donc ici le voeu non seulement de l'Assemblée nationale, mais celui des planteurs eux-mêmes,

que tout homme, de quelque couleur qu'il soit, a un droit égal à la liberté" (personal communication, Marcel Dorigny, Nov. 30, 2007).

12. For more on this contentious issue in the historiography of Robespierre, see Tallett.

13. To the end, the Robespierrists were, in Georges Labica's estimation, "minoritaires au sein de Jacobins, eux-mêmes minoritaires parmi les Montagnards, lesquels ne disposent d'aucune majorité à la Convention. Ce qui, en effet, en dit longue sur la nature de leur pouvoir" and the long-standing prejudice of their putative "dictatorship."

14. Cited in Alan Wood 2003, 94. Wood describes how it was John Locke who took the decisive step in the theorization of capitalist property rights to enclosure when he formulated a theory of labor that justified the appropriation of colonial lands, occupied or not, whose usage failed to stand up to contemporary English standards of "improvement" (96).

15. Though Robespierre did not know poverty firsthand in his own existence, this fact (along with other petty marginalia such as his style of dress), rather than making his systematic and unswerving defense of the poor "grotesque," as one commentator recently put the matter, makes it instead all the more surprising and admirable (Doyle and Hayden 7). The work of Albert Soboul has analyzed in enormous detail the fundamental contradictions that divided the sans-culotte peasantry from the Robespierriste intelligentsia.

16. Robespierre abandoned this defense of the press in the spring of 1793, however, to the demands of political expediency and power (Gough).

17. "Reason commands how we are to act even though no example of this could be found" (Kant 1996, 371).

18. Paget Henry takes to task a putatively European "universalism" in this fashion in *Caliban's Reason*. Kant, of course, referred explicitly only to the French, and not the Haitian, Revolution. On Kant's understanding of human freedom as inclusive of, and explicitly predicated on, the exercise of reasoned creativity by all humans, figured by him as an explicit anti-imperialism, see Muthu, ch. 4 and 5.

19. This problem is even more prevalent in a book such as Emmanuel Eze's *Race and the Enlightenment*. To think that by presenting the racist writings of Linné, Kant, Herder, Jefferson, Hegel, and Cuvier one has addressed the topic of "race and the Enlightenment" seems to me not false (these thinkers obviously made racist statements and judgments) but a mere half-truth. It does not even cast Africans as passive victims of Enlightenment thought (by, say, investigating what the actual consequences of these racist statements might have been); instead, it completely and utterly silences them, erasing them from any participation in the Enlightenment whatsoever. The locus classicus of this approach to intellectual history, one that shares with Eze's volume a near-total focus on white European thinkers, remains Michèle Duchet's *Anthropologie et histoire au siècle des Lumières*. In a recent talk, Laurent Dubois calls for just such an

"intellectual history of the enslaved," urging historians to "construct a picture of an integrated space of debate over rights, over universalism, over government and empire . . . [,]" and to "understand the Atlantic as an integrated intellectual space" (2005, 3, 13).

20. Which is not to say Europeans and North Americans did not try desperately to do so by branding Haitians "barbaric" while conveniently ignoring the depravity of both slavery itself and the horrifying terrorist tactics of General Rochambeau.

21. Archives Nationales, AF/III/210.

22. CAOM, Bibliothèque Moreau de St. Mery, 2eme serie, vol. 32, bobine no. 25. 87 MIOM 57.

23. Oral tradition informs us, however, that Toussaint never worked in the cane fields, but was instead always a domestic servant. We also know that after he was freed in 1776, he was himself a slaveowner (Pluchon 57).

24. *Bulletin Officiel de St. Domingue*, Feb. 12, 1797; May 18, 1979. CAOM Bibliothèque Moreau de St. Mery, 2ème série, Vol. 32, bobine no. 25. 87 MIOM 57.

25. In the preface to Sala-Molins's *Les misères des Lumières,* the author rightly asserts that "lire les Lumières sans eux [les "nègres" esclaves], c'est . . . limiter la philanthropie universelle à l'universalité de mon quartier" (15) and calls on readers to "lire les Lumières en se situant du côté des esclaves noirs" (17). The bulk of his text is preoccupied precisely, however, with the white European thinkers of the Enlightenment; although Sala-Molins ventriloquizes the black slaves, he tends to reduce them to the role of reactive victims, "ceux qui doivent . . . souffrir dans leurs âmes et leurs corps" (26). While he intentionally remains within the same Francocentric perspective as Sala-Molins, Benot offers a compelling critique of Sala-Molins's failure to examine the historico-economic structure underlying the Enlightenment critique of slavery (105).

26. In this sense I think that Aravamudan's argument, in its focus on what he calls "tropicopolitan . . . metaliteracy," does not go far enough in demonstrating the slaves' active participation in a transnational dialogue on universal (and not merely "tropical") human rights. Instead, the author's more limited project is to reconstruct imaginatively the way the reception of Raynal's *Histoire des deux Indes* may have "refut[ed] and extend[ed] Western Enlightenment assumptions" as it was read in "a context outside its European purview."

27. Laurent Dubois' *A Colony of Citizens* (2004) is a salutary exception to this tendency.

28. It is not only historians of the Haitian Revolution who have tended to downplay the role of ideas; as Dale Van Kley points out, leftist historians of the French Revolution have as well: "In reaction to conservative historiography's indictment of the Enlightenment and Rousseau, both liberal and socialist histories of the Revolution have tended to minimize the role of ideas in general to the benefit of concrete events and contingent 'circumstances'" (73).

29. Where I differ from Scott's assessment is in his tendency to locate these forces of modernity only in "the regime of [the] slave plantation," and not, as I am underscoring, in the Radical Enlightenment ideology of universal human rights (115). I would only add, in response to Scott's Foucauldian emphasis on the social determination of subjectivity, that in order for "new choices [to be] constructed" by these rebel slaves, one must consider as well the ontological horizon of their possible reconstruction of their world, their universal potentiality of singularization (122).

30. Fick's more recent article, "The French Revolution in Saint Domingue: A Triumph of a Failure" (1997), continues to discount the power of Enlightenment ideas in Saint-Domingue as "relatively benign [philosophy]" (52). The article nonetheless complexifies our understanding of the idea of freedom in revolutionary Saint-Domingue, articulating the vast range of implications that the single term "freedom" bore depending on one's position in that society (54, 57). For reflection on this diversity of meanings according to geography and culture from a contemporary of the Haitian Revolution, see Stephen (26–27).

31. To claim as I am that the slaves of Saint-Domingue were *participants* in this transnational public sphere does not, of course, imply that they were *equal* participants in an ideal instance of Habermasian communicative rationality. For their contribution to the debate to be heard, they had to resort to violence, the negation of civil public discourse. They were nonetheless heard loud and clear: by Sonthonax in 1793, the French Assembly in 1794, and the North Atlantic slaveholding powers in their 1804 defeat of Napoleon. On the distortion of communicative rationality in situations of colonial violence, see Henry (179).

32. This becomes clear in his famous 1971 debate with Chomsky on human nature (Chomsky and Foucault).

33. Benot explicitly rejects any denigration of the slave's capacity for reflection as "la vision des colons" (139); I wish merely to point out that his book is little concerned with searching out the surviving traces of this autonomous thought.

34. On such a critique of Habermas's primarily linguistic conception of communicative action, see Gould (27).

35. The following critique of Habermas and Kant in light of the events in Saint-Domingue draws upon Warren Montag's trenchant and illuminating article "The Pressure of the Street: Habermas' Fear of the Masses." See also Perry Anderson, "Arms and Rights."

36. The following chapter analyzes this text.

37. Weil 69. See also Hegel 1991.

38. "The public sphere demoted [by Hegel] to a 'means of education' counted no longer as a principle of enlightenment and as a sphere in which reason realized itself. The public sphere served only to integrate subjective opinions into the objectivity assumed by the spirit in the form of the state" (Habermas 1962, 120).

39. Kant at least allowed that "it is, I admit, somewhat difficult to determine

what is required in order to be able to claim the rank of a human being who is his own master" (1996, 295).

40. Peter Sloterdijk is trenchant: Habermas "ne pouvait pas utiliser la diversité réelle des cultures dans son modèle de consensus. Ses 'situations idéales de parole' sont totalement prétraitées par la monoculture, 'l'intégration de l'autre' s'arrête précisément au point où il faudrait dépasser les frontières culturelles pour se retrouver face à l'autre réel" (82).

41. I discuss Laclau's theory more fully in its relevance to Saint-Domingue in chapter 4.

42. Nancy Fraser describes how other, nonbourgeois publics (primarily women, for Fraser) forced their way into the public sphere or, conversely, created alternative, nonbourgeois spheres—what she terms "subaltern counterpublics"—that gave them access to discussion of political questions of common interest: "Virtually from the beginning, counterpublics contested the exclusionary norms of the bourgeois public, elaborating alternative styles of political behavior and alternative norms of public speech" (1992, 116). Fraser rehearses the argument that the function of this new public sphere was in fact ideologically repressive, insofar as "this new mode of political domination, like the older one, secures the ability of one stratum of society to rule the rest" (117). The case of public discourse on universal rights in Saint-Domingue is interesting precisely because it is one case in which exactly the opposite occurred: the public use of reason by private individuals (slaves) led to their emancipation. Unlike Fraser, I am arguing that Saint-Domingue was an active participant in a single, variegated transnational public sphere, not a mere segregated "counterpublic."

43. Scott describes the profound level of identification British sailors shared with the African slaves they brought to the New World (137–42).

44. The Bibliothèque Moreau de St. Méry in the Centre des archives d'outre mer (CAOM) in Aix-en-Provence preserves a wide variety of these publications from the 1790s.

45. Pluchon cites further evidence of this rapid spread of news to Saint-Domingue in a letter of Oct. 1, 1789, by the free colored landowner François Raimond, who writes to his brother in France: "With talk of the oppressed and humanity, the troubles in France have become known here" (40).

46. CAOM, Bibliothèque de Moreau de St. Méry, 87 MIOM 13.

47. CAOM, Bibliothèque de Moreau de St. Méry, 87 MIOM 13.

48. *Courrier politique et littéraire du Cap-Français,* July 15, 1791. CAOM, Bibliothèque de Moreau de St. Méry, 87 MIOM 13.

49. Jacob 1993, 114; Bell 2007, 63, 77; de Cauna 198.

50. Maximin 26; Laguerre 45. "Never did they preach submission of the slaves to the colonists: rather they exhorted them to revolt against their masters and to sabotage their properties, and they incited numberless slaves to leave the plantations and to join the maroon settlements. The underlying idea was that,

without political freedom, there could be no possibility for cultural and religious freedom" (Laguerre 52).

51. *Moniteur Universel,* Oct. 31, 1790.

52. Because of their desire to inflame public opinion against the abolitionists, such comments certainly need to be read critically, and Benot dismisses such attacks on the *Amis des noirs* as "grotesque" (138). Ironically, though, it is often the defenders of slavery and the plantation order who tell us the most about the circulation of such discourse, since abolitionists sought to blame the colonists' violence and blindness, rather than the ideas of the revolution, for the unrest in Saint-Domingue.

53. "All decrees of the Assembly . . . uniformly purport, *that all regulations* [on slavery] *should originate with the Planters themselves.* After having declared that all mankind were born equal, . . . they sanctioned a decree that gave the lie to the first principles of their constitution" (2).

54. Similarly, the Terror and the laws of 22 Prarial became admissible for Robespierre only when he abandoned in practice, if not concept, his previous, principled fidelity to the universal cultivation of human freedom and singularity to the climate of paranoia and political expediency.

55. Michel DeGraff remarks that the suffix *-té* "is an abstraction marker par excellence: it derives nouns of quality from adjectives that describe qualities. This contradicts the oft-repeated claims . . . that Creoles are languages 'in which you don't think abstractly'" (9). See also Dayan 4–5. Aimé Césaire famously articulated this sentiment in an interview with Jacqueline Leiner: "le niveau de la langue, de la créolité . . . qui est resté . . . au stade de l'immédiateté, incapable de s'élever, d'exprimer des idées abstraites" (1978, xi). More recently, Raphaël Confiant restated this assertion in the June 6, 2000, edition of the *Chronicle of Higher Education:* "The problem [with Creole] is . . . dealing with a language in which you don't think abstractly" (cited by DeGraff 7).

56. David Scott figures the fundamental contradiction of the Haitian Revolution and Toussaint in particular as a tragic narrative of a figure caught between his Enlightenment vision of a radically new, positive liberty in "confrontation with the ideas and institutions of slavery" that had "made him what he [Toussaint] was" (133). "In that moment of tragic conflict with Moïse," Scott writes, "we are made to recognize, with a startling and humbling clarity, the arrogant simplicity of Toussaint's sophisticated and cosmopolitan world of value. . . . It is hard not to reach the conclusion that Toussaint's brilliant enlightenment is merely the condition of his surpassing blindness" (206).

### 3. Penser la Révolution Haïtienne

1. The previous chapter called attention to the thirteenth-century Malian *Charte du Mande* as a predecessor unknown to modern European parochialism, both in the Enlightenment and today.

2. On Lukacs, see Žižek 2001, 117.

3. Readers interested in the history of natural rights would do well to consult Bloch's *Natural Law and Human Dignity,* Sériaux (1993), and Leo Strauss's *Natural Right and History.* The latter unsurprisingly suffers from the author's Neoplatonic, elitist anthropology ("not all men are equally equipped by nature for progress toward perfection" [134]). More surprising is the degree to which much of Strauss's analysis echoes themes in contemporary post-Marxian philosophy—in particular, that of Castoriadis: It is only when a society first questions the fundamental ontological coordinates that regulate its constitution (what Strauss calls "convention") that modernity (for Castoriadis, the possibility of an "autonomous society") arises. Substantially, that is, each equates philosophy with the critique of norms (Strauss 83).

4. "Naturel: Qui se trouve dans la nature, n'est pas le fruit de la pensée" (*Dictionnaire Robert*).

5. Sériaux 21–41; Trigeaud 161; Bloch 39.

6. Aristotle, *Politics* 1.5. Cited in Davis 1984, 3; my emphasis.

7. Aristotle "could never think of *this man* [*tel homme*], but simply humanity" (Trigeaud 163).

8. See also chapter 2 of the *Tractatus Politicus:* "The right whose enjoyment belongs to God extends to everything, without restriction. . . . Thus, under the name of natural right [*jus naturae*], I designate the actual laws or rules of nature itself in virtue of which all things come to be, that is to say, the actual power of nature itself" (1958, 267, translation modified).

9. "Nature is not limited by the laws of human reason which aim only at the true interest and the preservation of the species" (Spinoza 2007, 197, translation modified).

10. Spinoza, *Ethics* 3.12, cited in Misrahi 53.

11. Spinoza, forever the "anomaly," as Negri has called him, fits clearly in neither of these categories with his simultaneous ontological insistence on universal causality and his undivided, moraline-free ethics of natural rights.

12. Reproduced in Hunt 1996, 72.

13. The article goes on to derive these rights, in distinctly un-Spinozian fashion, from a "God, whose power over creatures is always immediate" (cited in Proust 384).

14. Or, one could say in a Marxist vein, by means of a *false* universal that in fact simply articulated the "bourgeois" class interests of the Encyclopedists (on the latter, see Proust, ch. 1 and 4).

15. The article "liberté naturelle" is theoretically identical to the critique of slavery in the *Esprit des lois,* where Montesquieu wrote: "Literally, slavery is the establishment of a right that renders a man so much the property of another man that he is the absolute master of his life and goods" (cited in Proust 349).

16. The 1760 essay *A System of Principles in the Law of Scotland* by the Scottish jurist George Wallace was an important predecessor and influence for the *Encyclopédie*'s critique of slavery: "Every one of those unfortunate men, who are

pretended to be slaves," Wallace wrote, "has a right to be declared free, for he has never lost his liberty; he could not lose it; his prince had no power to dispose of him. . . . This right he carries about with him, and is entitled every where to get it declared" (cited in Davis 1975, 269).

17. Vernière elaborates in detail the profound similarities (to the point of virtual plagiarism in some passages of the *Contrat social*) between the political philosophies of Rousseau and Spinoza, whom Rousseau still dared not cite affirmatively, a century after the former's death (481–86). Their profound differences lie elsewhere: in Rousseau's steadfast, dualist faith in a transcendent divinity and in his refusal of Spinoza's systematic natural determinism.

18. Rousseau's critique of Grotius and Diderot is not a critique of natural rights per se, but rather the unmasking of their manipulation of a logical category (the "natural") as mere ideology (the domination of the weak by the strong called the "natural right to property" or the defense of monarchy the right to "security"). Although Rousseau does ground his understanding of human nature via the "natural" qualities of self-preservation and pity, understood as universal human attributes, this human nature can only be more than a logical possibility in the modern world if it is developed as "political right," as the subtitle to the *Contrat social* puts it, since the state of nature is forever lost to us (cited in Hulliung 68; see also Proust 368).

19. Rousseau "created, as it were, a new subject of responsibility, of 'imputability.' This subject is not individual man, but human society" (Cassirer 75).

20. On this dimension of Spinoza's political philosophy, see Misrahi: "The free man of the *Ethics*, just as for the citizen of the *Political Treatise*, only truly realizes the power [*puissance*] of his desire through *rational unification*: . . . man is freer in the City where he lives according to communal law, than in solitude, where he obeys only himself" (31, 29; italics in original).

21. For Spinoza, "The efforts of an isolated man . . . would be doomed to failure." The natural rights of human beings, unlike animals ("fish," says Spinoza [2007, 195]), are only realizable in society: "The natural rights of the human species are only conceivable under precise conditions: men must accept general laws . . . and live in accordance with the common judgment of all" (1958, 277, translation modified). Rousseau's debt to Spinoza in the conceptualization of the General Will is, here as elsewhere, palpable.

22. Spinoza's logic is unequivocal on the necessity of a universal emancipation. Quite simply, "Chacun jouira d'un droit d'autant moins considerable, que l'ensemble des autres par rapport à lui incarnera plus de puissance" (1954, 91).

23. Such a reading, stemming from Hegel's analysis of the Terror, finds eloquent expression in Blanchot's "Literature and the Right to Death," and dominates Carolyn Weber's more recent reading of the *Contrat social*.

24. These are Caroline Weber's glosses in her interpretation of the passage (8).

25. Who is the subject of universal human rights, Toussaint asked? "A false universalism has accustomed us to so many excuses and pretexts, the rights of

man have so often been reduced to no more than the rights of European man, that the question is not superfluous" (1960, 343). And Césaire's conclusion is magnificent: "When Toussaint Louverture came on the scene, it was to take the Declaration of the Rights of Man at its word; it was to show that there is no pariah race; that there is no marginal country; that there can be no excepted peoples. It was to incarnate and particularize a principle; that is to say, to vivify it. In history and in the domain of the rights of man, he was for blacks the architect [*opérateur*] and intermediary [*intercesseur*].... Toussaint Louverture fought for the transformation of formal rights into real rights, his was a combat for the *recognition* of man, and that is why he inscribed himself and the revolt of the black slaves of Saint-Domingue within the history of universal civilization" (344).

26. See for example his defense of the American Revolution (315–36).

27. An anonymous pamphlet, published in London in 1760, stands as an important predecessor to Diderot's call for slave revolt: "All the black men now in our plantations, who are by unjust force deprived of their liberty, and held in slavery, as they have none upon earth to appeal to, may lawfully repel that force with force, and to recover their liberty, destroy their oppressors" (cited in Davis 1975, 270).

28. While we have no historical indication whether Toussaint had read Raynal when he joined the Revolution in 1791, by 1801 there can be no doubt of his familiarity with the text, as he had by then placed a bust of Raynal in his residence (Descourtilz).

29. This Lockean property-based view of human freedom would remain predominant at least until Kant (who based human freedom on reason acting independently of the empirical) and Hegel (who, as I will argue in the following section, explicitly refuted the property-based critique of slavery to articulate an explicit condemnation of slavery based on this Kantian understanding of human freedom).

30. Reproduced in Hunt 1996, 150.

31. Kant does not speak here of "slaves" (*Sklaven*), but rather euphemistically of a "master [who] uses the powers of his subject as he pleases" (472).

32. Israel describes the many responses to Spinozianism of European church and state, including the struggle to destroy Spinoza's posthumous *Ethics* before it could be published (285–94), pan-European censorship (97–118), the persecution and imprisonment of Adrian and Johannes Koerbagh in Amsterdam (185–96), and the many and varied counteroffensives of a Catholic church eager to counter the Spinozian refutation of the soul's immortality, miracles, and divine Providence (173).

33. Cited in Israel 259. On this aspect of the *Encyclopédie*, see Israel 516.

34. On the relation of Kant to Spinoza, see Macherey (226–46), who ultimately argues for their fundamental dissimilarity: "For Spinoza, there are not two orders of reality, one substantial and infinite, the other modal and finite, but a single, self-same reality, continuous and indivisible, determined by a single law

of causality, through which law the finite and infinite are linked indissolubly" (246).

35. Adorno was not thinking only of Kant when he argued that an ideological distortion of the concept of freedom occurs in "all the propositions that assert that freedom originally consisted in nothing other than voluntarily accepting a compulsion that human beings cannot escape anyway. Wherever it is maintained that the substance of freedom is that you are free when you freely accept what you have to accept anyway, you can be certain that the concept of freedom is being abused and is being twisted into its opposite" (2006, 197). Žižek reproduces this line of thought in *Violence* (2008).

36. Of course, to call slaves a "contracting party" already demonstrates the absurdity of such a proposition.

37. Without entering into further discussion at this point, suffice it to say that I will problematize in my concluding chapter what I present here as the simple elision of "individual" and "community," to question to what degree the singularization of a community such as that of *Bossale* Haiti (as an example of an actually existing, centuries-old egalitarian society functioning within Western modernity) has depended upon the internal suppression of the process of singularization of its individual members.

38. Cited in Alan Wood 2003, 51. Condorcet described what he understood to be the "general laws . . . of the progress of human intellect," laws that would lead to "the improvement of the human faculties" and which he thought prove that "the perfectibility of man is absolutely indefinite" (cited in Kramnick 388).

39. If this is so, then Heidegger's Kant is a mere straw man, the latter's radically open practical philosophy schematically reduced to the "domain of present things" in putative opposition to Heidegger's concern for "the future in its possibility" (2002, 147).

40. Dates such as 1789, 1917, 1956, and 1968 for Alain Badiou.

41. As with so many other dimensions of his moral thought, Kant developed his notion of personality from Rousseau, as Cassirer has shown (1989, 56).

42. I would follow Alan Wood in arguing that within a philosophy of immanence two centuries after Kant, the fact that we can longer accept the absolute Kantian transcendental distinction between the realm of nature and a supernatural freedom need not condemn Kantian practical philosophy as a whole. "If we are capable of rationally recognizing that people are free and equal self-governing beings and ends in themselves, then we do not have to bow down to anything supernatural in order to sustain our commitment to treating them as their dignity requires. . . . Of course we are animals—namely animals that have somehow evolved capacities to direct their lives according to principles of reason" (2002, 176–77).

43. In a contemporary turning of Kant's transcendental distinction between nature and freedom, Alain Badiou has attempted to refound ethical thought upon an understanding of the human as double: man for Badiou is at once both a "living

animal" and "immortal singularity" (2003, 26). The humanistic and moralistic defense of "human rights"—putatively derived from Kant—that Badiou castigates as a contemporary nihilism, is, as Badiou himself implies, a mere (false) popular "image" of Kantian ethics (23). Instead, Badiou's Kantian call for an ethics of singular "situations," of "maximal possibility" (31), is Kantian through and through.

44. In this, Kant rejoined Spinoza, whose conception of the immanent power of natural beings—including their power of reason—drew no ontological distinction (such as that of Hobbes) between the rights and powers of humans and other beings (Lazzeri 134). On the other hand, since Kant tended *in practice* (that is, in his empirical observations) to maintain a strict separation between the freedom of human reason and instinctual animal behavior, drastically underestimating the mental capabilities of nonhuman animals (Alan Wood 2003, 59), it would be left to anthropologists and the science fiction of writers such as Stanislaw Lem (*Solaris*) to develop the implications of this Kantian notion of a nonhuman, universal reason.

45. In contrast to Fichte's speciesism: "A sure criterion has been established for determining which sensuous beings are to have rights ascribed to them, and which are not. Everyone who has a human shape is internally compelled to recognize every other being with the same shape as a rational being, and therefore as a possible subject of right. But everything that does not have this shape is to be excluded from the sphere of this concept, and there can be no talk of the rights of such beings" (84). Such a criterion opens the door not only to a justification of slavery but also to nineteenth-century racialism, that is, the specious scientific attempt to "prove" that African morphology lay closer to that of apes then putatively "higher" races, and so on.

46. In his 1930 lecture course on Kant and the problem of freedom, Heidegger figures this ontological ground of human freedom in terms of pure passivity, announcing already the turn of the *Letter on Humanism*: "*Freedom must itself, in its essence, be more primordial than man.* Man . . . . can only let-be the freedom which is accorded to him. . . . Human freedom now no longer means freedom as a property of man, but *man as a possibility of freedom*" (2002, 93). The problem here seems to be that Heidegger attributes (temporal?) priority to the ontological ground of freedom, radically separating this ground from its possible instantiations. I wish to argue instead for the *immanence* and *virtuality* of this ground in relation to any "human" (in the Kantian sense of autonomously rational) existence.

47. Paul Patton offers a succinct and lucid analysis of Deleuze's distinction between the possible and the virtual in *Deleuze and the Political* (35–40).

48. Thus Benhabib's salutary call in the concluding pages of *Critique, Norm, and Utopia* for an ethics that mediates the defense of human dignity with the claims of singular specificity (342).

49. This is the limitation of a Kantian-Habermasian understanding of the public sphere and the intersubjective use of discussion and reason that I will address in the following chapter.

50. On this point see Adorno's discussion of Kantian formalism in the lecture notes published as *History and Freedom* (252).

51. The fascinating 1971 debate on Dutch television between Michel Foucault and Noam Chomsky on the subject of human nature is emblematic of such a anarchist understanding of universal human nature. Somewhat surprisingly, their exchange reveals these thinkers as something less than implacable adversaries. Instead, we witness the extraordinary and surprising coincidence of their aims, to, as Foucault states, "account for fact that with a few rules or definite elements, unknown totalities, never even produced, can be brought to light by individuals" (1997, 117).

52. One of the few exceptions to the widespread contemporary condemnation of slave violence was Garran's *Rapport sur les troubles de Saint-Domingue*.

53. See Fischer (24–33) for a nuanced discussion of Hegel's silence regarding the Haitian Revolution. Fischer concludes that "Hegel fell silent [regarding the Saint-Domingue revolution] at the end of the master-slave dialectic," never looking beyond that text to the *Philosophy of Right* to question whether that later volume might have more to say, and more explicitly, on actual slave revolutions in the Age of Enlightenment.

54. Were there any doubt following Buck-Morss's rigorous demonstration, she reminds us that Hegel in fact "mentions the Haitian Revolution by name" in the 1830 *Encyclopedia* (854).

55. Buck-Morss considers Hegel a "cultural racist" and not "a biological one" (864). My reading of the *Philosophy of Right* in what follows sustains just such an interpretation: African slaves are perfectly able to and indeed must overthrow slavery to enter into a historical, autonomous existence.

56. In her footnotes Buck-Morss explicitly acknowledges her "disagreement" with Hyppolite's overall reading of the *Phenomenology* without offering any details on this difference of interpretation (2000, 67, n. 96).

57. Many thanks to David Durst for proposing this analysis of the master-slave dialectic.

58. Buck-Morss briefly mentions Hegel's discussion of slavery in the *Philosophy of Right* in a note to her article (67, n. 87).

59. A shift that Buck-Morss herself registers in her citation from Hegel's lectures on Right from 1817–18 (55).

60. Alan Wood, editor's introduction to Hegel's *Elements of the Philosophy of Right*, ix.

61. Cited in Bloch, 123, 127, 125. In contrast, Bloch celebrates the *Critique of Natural Law* of Anselm Feuerbach, a lone voice among European Enlightenment legal theorists in its analysis of "law as the sum of rights, not of prohibitions" and duties (90).

62. Thanks to Alberto Moreiras for drawing my attention to this point.

63. On the subsequent philosophical history of this Hegelian denigration of the possibility of populist reason, see Laclau 2005, pt. 1.

64. That said, the precise degree and evolution of Hegel's "liberalism" remains a point of scholarly debate—the so-called battle of letters (*Kampf um den Buchstaben*)—surrounding the publication between 1973 and 1983 of transcripts of Hegel's various lectures on the Philosophy of Right from 1817 to 1830 (Deranty 12).

65. It is Hegel's dismissal of the possibility of a global ethical society as "not real" (cited in Alan Wood's introduction, xxv) that limits the otherwise radical *Philosophy of Right* (*PR*). Certainly, a global ethical society does not yet exist, yet progress toward it since Kant's "Idea for a Universal History" has been enormous. In refusing to consider this movement of history in deference to the more limited nation-state (*PR* §344), in dismissing it because it doesn't *yet* exist, Hegel suddenly places an absolute block on the human possibility of instantiating a determinate universal, the very block he had dismissed as a mere figment of the imagination in his critique of the Kantian thing-in-itself. Eric Weil, however, catches a glimpse even of this possibility in a paragraph of the *Encyclopedia* (77).

66. Hegel's was here as elsewhere a distinctly Spinozian understanding of the inalienability of natural right, for the latter derived those rights not, as did Hobbes and Locke, from the preservation of biological life, but rather from true human life understood "not by the mere circulation of blood and other vital processes common to all animals, but above all by reason, the true measure of value" (Spinoza 1958, 311, translation modified; see also Lazzeri 173). On Locke's critique of slavery, see Buck-Morss (2002, 45).

67. The fundamental difference between Spinoza and the later idealism of Kant and Hegel, as Pierre Macherey has shown, lies in Spinoza's refusal to attribute any moral or teleological priority to human reason within the whole of Being (Substance) (92).

68. Alain David, in *Racisme et antisémitisme: Essai de philosophie sur l'envers des concepts,* rightly takes the most recent French translators of the *Phenomenology* to task for abandoning Hyppolite's *esclave* in favor of the far weaker *valet.* While it may be, as Pierre-Jean Labbarière puts it, that "the *knecht* is the individual who, in a domestic setting [*au sein d'une domesticité*], finds himself owing [*redevable*] his force of labor to a master," this is to ignore that, in David's words, "it is here a matter of life and death, which is manifestly not the case . . . in a domestic setting" (Labarrière, cited in David 294).

69. Andrew Cole's article "What Hegel's Master/Slave Dialectic Really Means" is an important exception. Cole sharply and usefully distinguishes between *Knechtschaft* and *Sklaverei,* but limits the domain of the latter to the slavery of classical antiquity. Cole misleadingly focuses his attention only on the momentary invocation of *Knecht* and the *Phenomenology* in §57, passing over the section's overall focus on *Sklaverei.* Cole rejects out-of-hand Buck-Morss's evidence and simultaneously ignores the problem of modern, postfeudal slavery, with which Hegel is explicitly grappling in this paragraph, as the latter's references to Caribbean revolution and *les droits de l'homme* indicate. It may well be

that Greco-Roman freedom "is peculiar to the individual" and bore no relation to the universal, but this is clearly not the case—as Hegel's explicit invocation of *les droits de l'homme* indicates—for the post-1789 institution of *Sklaverei*. Moreover, Cole's subsequent analysis of feudal labor and its alienated relation to property holds at least as true for the Caribbean slave labor of Hegel's time (593). Thanks to David Durst for his helpful insights into this problem.

70. Thanks to Susan Buck-Morss for pointing out to me that Hegel had also used the term *Sklave* in the earlier, pre-*Phenomenology* "Jena" manuscripts, that is to say, precisely at the time he was reading of the Haitian Revolution in the German paper *Minerva* (see also Buck-Morss 2000, 846–47).

71. The Idea (*Idee*), it will be recalled, is distinct in Hegel's usage from the more limited and abstract concept (*Begriff*). The latter is a mere mental abstraction, while the Idea designates the full development of a concept as it unfolds and reveals itself in historical reality through the movement of historical human development via concrete, reflective social action.

72. Césaire will write in *Toussaint Louverture*: "[La part de Toussaint], c'est tout le domaine qui sépare le *seulement pensé* de la réalité concrete" (343).

73. This is where I would disagree somewhat with Susan Buck-Morss, who sees Hegel's usage of *Knecht* and *Sklave* from the "Jena" manuscripts to the 1830 *Philosophy of Subjective Spirit* as "interchangeable" (2000, 854). While this may be true for these bracketing texts, in the *Phenomenology* and *Philosophy of Right*, they are used quite precisely. My thesis is that the *Phenomenology* sustains the radicality of the earlier Jena manuscripts in the substance of its argument (the fight to the death that only a slave, and not a bondsman or "valet," must confront) while becoming more conservative on the surface of this published text in its terminological and diagetical refusal to confront the modern institution of slavery. In the *Philosophy of Right*, this differentiation is then made quite explicit, as the term *Knecht* appears *only* when Hegel refers his listeners back to the earlier *Phenomenology*.

74. See Macherey's extraordinary *Hegel ou Spinoza* on Hegel's complex dependency—expressed as denial—upon Spinoza. For all their affinities, Hegel lags behind Spinozianism in the idealist priority the former gives to Spirit, triumphant in the teleological goal of its own self-realization. In contrast, Spinoza posits thought as simply another mode of universal Substance, an open-ended "procès sans fin" bearing no universal priority beyond its essential utility for human beings (Macherey 75, 92, 94).

75. Spinoza defines an essence, Deleuze observes, as "an internal difference, a difference of intensity. So much so that each finite being must be said to express the absolute, according to the intensive quantity that constitutes its essence, that is to say, according to its degree of power [*puissance*]" (1968, 180).

76. Insofar as the miraculous indicates not a faith in divine intervention or the suspension of natural law, but mere human ignorance of the causes of an unpredicted incident, the Haitian Revolution is a properly Spinozian sequence:

"The word miracle can only indicate the opinions of men and signifies nothing other than a phenomenon whose natural cause cannot be explained" (2007, 84, translation modified).

### 4. Beyond Jacobinism

1. Although my conclusions are markedly different from his focus on a tragic narrative of "emancipationist redemption" that is "enfeebled and exhausted," I share with David Scott the primary challenge of his analysis of *The Black Jacobins:* to analyze the relation between the events of the Haitian Revolution and the predicaments of our present age (30).

2. See Fischer (11–24) for a nuanced and insightful overview of the debate over the "modernity" of Saint-Domingue and the Haitian Revolution that has taken place since James's *Black Jacobins,* as well as her conclusion that structures the whole of her groundbreaking study: that "heterogeneity is a congenital condition of modernity, and that the alleged purity of European modernity is an a posteriori theorization or perhaps even part of a strategy that aims to establish European primacy" (24).

3. Though Haiti no longer plays the economically dominant role in the world-system it enjoyed in the eighteenth century, the country is no isolated backwater, but instead remains thoroughly imbricated in that world-system. This not only is true of its predatory elite, skimming surplus profits from the export of peasant production (Trouillot 1990, Fatton, Lundahl), but also extends down to the smallest daily transactions of the peasant economy itself (Lundahl 1979, ch. 2).

4. Wallerstein, speaking to Africa's integral place in the world-system, argues that this division of labor is fundamental to the structure of global capitalism: "A capitalist world-economy is based on a division of labor between its core, its semiperiphery, and its periphery in such a way that there is unequal exchange between the sectors but dependence of all the sectors, both economically and politically, on the continuance of this unequal exchange" (2000, 56). It is this differentiated, tension-filled state of equilibrium that Haiti called into question.

5. See Paget Henry and Paul Buhle's volume *C. L. R. James' Caribbean* on this dimension of James's legacy.

6. Beside James's study itself, the most notable exception to this neglect is Robin Blackburn's *The Overthrow of Colonial Slavery* (258–59), as well as the author's shorter study of *The Black Jacobins,* "*The Black Jacobins* and New World Slavery," where the author pays particular attention to the "risks and costs" of the Assembly's contingent decision in 1794 to abolish slavery (94).

7. The following description of Laclau's concept of hegemony draws upon Simon Critchley's characterization in the introduction to the edited volume *Laclau: A Critical Reader,* as well as David Howarth's article on hegemony in that same volume.

8. On this process in the case of Schoelcher and the abolition of 1848, see Nesbitt (2008).

9. Analogously, Žižek and Laclau modestly overlook the participation of their own theories in the active displacement of hegemony from the self-satisfied bearers of rights to the disenfranchised.

10. Yes, the universal "announces, as it were, its 'non-place,'" but more than that, it *progresses,* as Judith Butler herself points out, "precisely when challenges to its *existing* formulation emerge from those who are not covered by it [women, slaves], who have no entitlement to occupy the place of the 'who,' but nevertheless demand that the universal as such ought to be inclusive of them" (Butler 39; italics in original). In Butler's poststructuralist formulation of the universal, universal incompletion and progressive historical instantiations of the universal remain abstractly separated categories; attention to the particularity of events such as the Haitian Revolution, as an at-once incomplete, contradictory, *and* progressive, concrete universal, can serve to mediate the radical abstraction of Butler's formulation.

11. Fischer goes on to develop this insight in her analysis of the 1805 Constitution's discourse on race, in which she observes that "the paradox that the universal is typically derived through a generalization of one of the particulars" holds true in Dessaline's prescription that all Haitians, regardless of skin color, be referred to as "black" (233).

12. Žižek, in dialogue with Judith Butler and Ernesto Laclau, delineates this theoretical process of a strategic reformulation of ontological categories precisely: "Universality is unavoidable. . . . While of course each determinate historical figure of universality involves a set of inclusions/exclusions—universality simultaneously opens up and sustains the space for questioning these inclusions/exclusions, for 'renegotiating' the limits of inclusion/exclusion as part of the ongoing ideologico-political struggle for hegemony. . . . The reference to universality can serve precisely as a tool that stimulates [the renegotiation of the notion of human rights]. . . . Universality becomes 'actual' precisely and only by rendering thematic the exclusions on which it is grounded, by continuously questioning, renegotiating, displacing them, that is, by assuming the gap between its own form and content, by conceiving itself as unaccomplished in its very notion" (2000, 102).

13. The phrase is Rancière's (1995, 129).

14. Following Deborah Jenson's brilliant rendering of mimesis as the *social* process, not of imitation and representation, but instead of the very construction of the social itself, the mimetic refashioning of the French Declaration of the Rights of Man and Citizen that occurred in Saint-Domingue can be understood to have engendered a total reconstruction of social reality (2001, 6–7).

15. In contrast, the critique of events in Saint-Domingue as the failure to sustain a becoming-minoritarian and to avoid recapture as a new majoritarianism would dramatically underscore the shortcomings of the Haitian Revolution, both of Toussaint's dictatorial authoritarianism (1797–1802) and that of the Haitian state itself after 1804. A Deleuzian analysis of the Haitian Revolution might draw attention as well to the rebel slaves' functioning as a "war-machine" in the precise

sense Deleuze and Guattari give to the term in *Milles plateaux,* via the constant creation of smooth space opposed to the striated space of the plantation, through lines of maroon flight that escape the plantation.

16. See also Laclau 2005, 140.

17. This view of the Enlightenment as an opportunity for a radical productivity on the part of disenfranchised, colonized subjects has been made by Spivak in a number of different contexts (2004, 565, n. 3). The author's analysis in *Critique of Postcolonial Reason,* however, while subtly taking Kant and other master discourses to task from the perspective of the subaltern, remains enthralled to that master discourse. In other words, Spivak ably deconstructs the *Critique of Judgment* to show how "Kant's philosophical project, whether sublime or bourgeois, operates in terms of an implicit cultural difference" that distinguishes the "Master Subject" from the "raw man" of nature; she does not, however, take the next step, which would be to ask whether that subaltern subject herself can refuse Kant's parochialism and, in lands far from Königsberg, make anything of Kant to address her own particular needs (26–32).

18. This struggle for hegemony over a *symbolic* human product points to yet another way in which the Haitian Revolution is only now becoming thinkable, as struggle over information and communication networks replaces industrial production as the determinant mode of production in postmodern "Empire." On the latter, see Dean (277).

19. On the exclusion of Jews, women, and slaves from the emancipatory process of 1789, see Singham.

20. Césaire (188) describes Marat's uncompromising attacks on colonialism, while Gauthier shows how Robespierre attacked the institution of slavery well into the summer of 1793. Far from being the compromise with bourgeois property interests some have seen in it, Robespierre's rejection of the Girondists' May 1791 attempt to institutionalize slavery in Saint-Domingue is a systematic rejection of the institution of slavery based upon the principled application of Declaration of the Rights of Man: "Dès le moment où, dans un de vos décrets, vous aurez prononcé le mot *esclave,* vous aurez prononcé votre propre déshonneur et le renversement de votre constitution" (2000, 97). As so often prior to 1793, Robespierre was here far in the minority, and attempted to sway opinion by a politics of dissidence that would hold the majority to account under the terms of its own founding document.

21. Reproduced in Hunt 1996, 104; my emphasis.

22. This adds a certain nuance to Carolyn Fick's otherwise correct assertion that "during these early struggles, the slaves never demanded outright the absolute abolition of slavery" (1990, 141).

23. CAOM, 87 MIOM 13.

24. CAOM, 87 MIOM 13.

25. "Récit historique sur les événements qui se sont succèdes dans les camps de la grande-rivière, du dondon, de ste-suzanne et autres, depuis le 26 Octobre

1791 jusqu'au 24 décembre de la même année, par M. Gros, fait prisonnier par Jeannot, chef des brigands" (CAOM, 87 MIOM 13).

26. AN, DXXV 1, folder 4, no. 6. Carolyn Fick is overly generous, I think, when she interprets this gesture as "the best Jean-François could do . . . under the circumstances" (1990, 115).

27. AN, DXXV 1, folder 4, nos. 14 and 19.

28. The term "générale" in French refers to the universal characteristic of any abolition, its nonexclusivity: "Qui intéresse, réunit sans exception tous les individus, tous les éléments d'un ensemble" (*Dictionnaire Robert*).

29. David Geggus has suggested that the letter may in fact be a forgery by the royalist Colonel Cambefort, designed to "discredit his radical critics" (Geggus cited by Jeremy Popkin, personal correspondence, from Geggus 2007).

30. Bell's 2007 biography skillfully weighs the many complexities and obscurities surrounding Toussaint's life and thought through the author's familiarity with both the traditional and a number of striking, newly discovered documents. See the conclusion of the book's fourth and seventh chapters for Bell's analysis of Toussaint's complex persona.

31. "Far from considering the world of the slaves as closed and devoid of any relation to the Revolution, we can observe that the slaves responded to the words 'Liberty' and 'Equality' with an uprising. It therefore appears that the slaves were in no case lacking the faculty of thought that [slavemasters] had tried to take from them, the better to dehumanise them. On the contrary, as early as 1792, a group of the leaders of the insurgent slaves showed itself to be enlightened, and to a far greater degree than the legislative assembly itself!" (Piquionne 139).

32. Reproduced in Bell 2007, 39.

33. Madiou 102; de Cauna 191–93; Fick 92.

34. AN II/1375.

35. *Journal Politique de Saint Domingue*, Sept. 20, 1792. CAOM, 87 MIOM 80.

36. AN DXXV 23, 231.

37. Reproduced in Bell 2007, 40.

38. In calling Haitian revolutionaries such as Toussaint the "first dissidents," I mean this in the particularly modern sense of a generalizable methodology of political contestation against the state that bases its actions upon universal norms of human rights. Of course, dissidence as a protest of individual conscience against injustice extends far back, beyond Jan Hus to figures of antiquity such as Antigone and the Hebrew midwives Shiphra and Puah.

39. I am not, of course, claiming any fundamental degree of similarity here between events in Haiti and the 1989 "Velvet" Revolution Havel would go on to lead. The degree of subjective violence in the two sequences was incomparable (and this violence, though necessary in Saint-Domingue, is to be distinguished from the process of positing dissident claims I am describing). Rather, I am following Havel's much earlier theoretical analysis of dissidence to make the

historical claim that this logic was first adopted by the former slaves of Saint-Domingue.

40. The latter is the name of the Czechoslovak rock group whose trial initiated the Charter 77 dissidence movement.

41. "People who live in the post-totalitarian system know only too well that the question of whether one or several political parties are in power, and how these parties define and label themselves, is of far less importance than the question of whether it is possible or not to live like a human being [*zda lze či nelze lidsky žít*]" (Havel 1991, 161, translation modified).

42. "People who have simply decided to live within truth," Havel writes, refuse "to define their own original and positive position negatively, in terms of something else, . . . [but] simply as people who *are* what they are" (1991, 167).

43. "Because the system cannot do without the law, because it is hopelessly tied down by pretending the laws are observed, . . . demanding that the laws be upheld is precisely an act of living within the truth that threatens the whole structure of lies precisely in its point of maximum mendacity" (1991, 190; translation modified). "Dovolávání se zákona je totiž přesně tím aktem 'života v pravdě,' který potenciálně ohrožuje celou prolhanou stavbu právě v její prolhanosti" (300).

## 5. Toussaint Louverture, the *Moun andeyo*, and the Transcendental Conditions of Political Autonomy

1. Stephen's *The Crisis of the Sugar Colonies,* as Laurent Dubois points out, is a contemporary account that repeatedly attests to the enormous transformations in mentality, the "change in ideas" that occurred among the former slaves of Saint-Domingue in the 1790s (Stephen 75, also 48, 54; Dubois 2004a, 191). Among the most interesting aspects of Stephen's 1802 commentary on events in Saint-Domingue is his clear insight into the nature of the conflict pitting Toussaint against Napoleon, which he calls a "contest . . . between France and negro freedom in the West Indies" (63).

2. CAOM, 87 MIOM 13.

3. CAOM Bibliotheque Moreau de St. Mery, 2ème série, Vol 32, bobine no 25. 87 MIOM 57.

4. Cornelius Castoriadis defines an autonomous society in such a fashion, as one which gives itself "[its] own laws, and [which] can change them when the need or desire is felt" (123).

5. CAOM CC9B, 217 MIOM/12.

6. "Procès verbal de la cérémonie au Cap-Francais . . . [le] jour de la Proclamation de la Constitution" (CAOM CC9B, 217 MIOM/12).

7. Article 34 of Toussaint's Constitution states that "the Governor confirms [*scelle*] and promulgates the laws."

8. The only exceptions are those few articles that develop the Constitution's basic ground, such as Article 63, assuring freedom from unwarranted intrusion of the police in one's home.

9. CAOM CC9B, 217 MIOM/12.

10. "Art. 28.—La Constitution nomme Gouverneur le citoyen Toussaint Louverture, général en chef de l'armée de Saint-Domingue, et en considération des importants services que ce général a rendus à la colonie, dans les circonstances les plus critiques de la révolution, et sur le vœu des habitants reconnaissants, les rênes lui en sont confiées pendant le reste de sa glorieuse vie."

11. Article 63 is of special note in light of the constant insecurity Haitians have known in their own homes in recent years: "La maison de toutes personnes est un asile inviolable. Pendant la nuit, nul n'a le droit d'y entrer que dans le cas d'incendie, d'inondation ou de réclamation de l'intérieur. Pendant le jour, on peut y entrer pour un objet spécial déterminé ou par une loi ou par un ordre émané d'une autorité publique." On the partially successful implementation of justice and the rule of law following the Raboteau massacre, see Fatton 155.

12. The Constitution's first two articles simply define the object of consideration—the territory of Saint-Domingue and its formal structure: "Art. 1er.—Saint-Domingue dans toute son étendue, et Samana la Tortue, la Gonâve, les Cayemites, l'île-à-Vache, la Saône, et autres îles adjacentes, forment le territoire d'une seule colonie, qui fait partie de l'empire français, mais qui est soumise à des lois particulières. Art. 2.—Le territoire de cette colonie se divise en départements, arrondissements et paroisses."

13. Ernst Bloch traces the systematic legal protection of property back to Roman law (18).

14. This is the case even in the otherwise highly progressive constitution of 1793, which only defended "les droits de l'homme *en société*" (Gauthier 99). Here, in the most radical constitution of the period, natural rights predating any specific social implementation were already reduced to mere goods, an object given to citizens by governments, rather than being possessed a priori by all humans in accord with their nature.

15. Gauthier draws attention to Robespierre's repeated support of abolition as late as June 1793, putting the lie to the historiographic myth of his abandonment of the cause of abolition (220–25).

16. On this point as well, the Haitian Revolution stands as the culmination of the Spinozian Radical Enlightenment, for it was Spinoza who stood in distinct contrast to the many thinkers from Hobbes and Locke to the framers of the Thermidorian constitution of 1795 and beyond, who gave ontological priority to the rights of property before those of human freedom. In the *Tractatus politicus,* Spinoza maintains that in a free society, "the fields, the totality of the land, and, if possible, the houses must belong to public property" (1965, 124). Were we to miss this fundamental and radical dimension of Spinozian (political) freedom, he reiterates his point, not once, but twice more: "It is very important as well that no citizen possess real estate" (144, and again, 152).

17. In addition to its assertion of the unlimited authority of Toussaint himself, the Constitution was profoundly undemocratic: the representatives of the

assembly it calls for are simply appointed by municipal administrations. "Art. 23.—L'Assemblée est renouvelée tous les deux ans par moitié ; nul ne peut être membre pendant six années consécutives. L'élection a lieu ainsi : les administrations municipales nomment, tous les deux ans, au 10 ventôse (1er mars), chacune un député, lesquels se réunissent, dix jours après, aux chefs-lieux de leurs départements respectifs où ils forment autant d'assemblées électorales départementales, qui nomment chacune un député à l'Assemblée Centrale."

18. Most conspicuously in their successful refusal of President Boyer's authoritarian 1826 *Code rural* (Lundahl 1979, 298). See Trouillot (1980) for a critique of Lundahl's study.

19. "Land reform also contributed to an almost hermetic separation of the masses from the elite. [The former] withdrew into subsistence cultivation (gradually supplemented by production for the market) and expressed no desire to take part in national politics. . . . The upper class, for their part, lost all interest in agriculture, except as a source of taxes" (Lundahl 1979, 289).

20. The ongoing effort to describe and bring into being such an autonomous society is the subject of Cornelius Castoriadis's voluminous writings. Castoriadis's writings constitute a remarkably prescient vision that is only now, since the collapse of the Cold War political structure and the rise of a transnational culture of the Multitude, becoming fully comprehensible in its originality. The widespread refusal of work on the Saint-Domingue plantations from 1793 on (Fick 1990, 171–82) serves as a perfect historical illustration of one of Castoriadis's main critiques of theoretical Marxism: that labor is never a passive quantity fully exploited by the capitalist, but is instead *living* labor, constantly resisting its exploitation and striving to create the conditions of its own autonomy (2005, 46).

21. Barthélemy has underscored certain more progressive aspects of Polverel's work code—its recognition of agrarian corporatism—in comparison with both the previous slave regime and the later codes of Toussaint and Christophe (93).

22. Bell 2007, 123, 130. See Jean-Godefroy Bidima on the political and theoretical implications of the traditional African practice of the *palabre*.

23. Bell 2007, 212. See Bell (219–20, 267) on the astounding implications, both for French power and for the possible global abolition of slavery in the nineteenth century, had such a federation between France and Saint-Domingue, Napoleon and Toussaint, been constructed. It is also of note that a model for such a decentralized imperial confederation was first proposed (and perhaps Toussaint had this model in mind) by Robespierre in his "Projet de confédération entre la France et la Corse" (April 26, 1790) (2000, 94).

24. This is not to claim, of course, that no comparable social structures have existed in the modern world. The best known of such stateless egalitarian systems is perhaps the Russian *mir*, which survived well into the twentieth century in rural Russia, until Stalin's forced collectivization and artificial famines of 1929–34 killed some thirteen million peasants (Skirda 124). The *mir* was a "democratic regime in its simplest and purest form, without intermediaries and

without representation. It is a regime of direct democracy in which each member personally takes part in all deliberations and all decisions . . . without hereditary, individual, or oligarchic authority" (Anatole Leroy-Beaulieu, cited in Skirda 31). Like the Haitian *moun andeyo*, the world of the Russian *mir* "constituted a closed-off world, separated from that of the cities. . . . Since the time of the Muscovite Tsars, two societies lived superposed one upon the other: that of the true country [*le pays réel*], the peasants, the living force of productive labor, and that of the State power and its predatory clientele" (Skirda 34).

25. This is true with the exception of short- and medium-term labor in the Dominican Republic by those in the twenty to thirty-five year age group, stays that allow for the accumulation of a minimum of capital without endangering the internal balance of the community.

26. 1999, 42; see also Barthélemy 29.

27. See Spivak (2004, 534–35) for a defense of a responsibility not to dispensing rights from above to the subaltern, but, instead, to a responsibility to learning and self-transformation through a shared engagement to education outside the narrow networks of the elite university system. More generally, this process occurs as an imperative to become human that we receive, before our will (545), an imperative that I have called in this book the ontological ground of the process of singularization.

### Conclusion

1. Hardt and Negri address this point, to some degree, in the more recent *Multitude,* and rightly point to events such as the revolt in Chiapas and the protests against the Sardar Sarovar dam project in India as moments in a struggle that transcends the borders of the first-world nations (286).

2. Badiou makes a similar theoretical point in his call for an ethics figured not as a Levinassian respect for difference, but as the "recognition of the Same" (2003, 43). The singularization of human rights in Saint-Domingue, in light of Badiou's point, occurred not as an incorporation of slaves under the purview of an a priori notion of "humanity," but rather through the singularization of Right within a Truth that is "indifferent to differences . . . , a truth is *the same for all*" (46; emphasis in original). Whether or not Peter Hallward is correct in his observation that "Badiou's ethics is incommensurable with the whole Kantian register of legality, duty, obligation, and conformity," I think he too quickly accepts Badiou's explicitly caricatural reading of Kantian morality (Badiou 2003, 23) to assert that "what sets Badiou's ethics clearly apart from Kant's is his unwavering insistence on the singular and exceptional character of every ethical imperative" (Hallward 2003, 267). Both Kant and Badiou actually offer a remarkably similar ethics of universal singularization. Badiou could hardly be more Kantian in asserting that ethics has "nothing to do with the 'interests' of the animal, is indifferent to its perpetuation, and has eternity as its destiny" (cited in Hallward 2003, 258).

3. Wargny retraces the substantial efforts to end impunity and create a legal and human rights infrastructure in 1990s Haiti, as well as the systematic destruction of these efforts exemplified by the brutal assassination of the journalist Jean Dominique in 2000 (148–60).

4. This process was theorized by Carl Schmitt and implemented by the National Socialists. Schmitt's classic (and analytically brilliant) attacks on rational law, parliamentarism, and "lifeless" universalism occur in works such as *The Crisis of Parliamentary Democracy* and *The Concept of the Political*. See William Scheuerman's *Between the Norm and the Exception*, his study of Schmitt's Frankfurt School critics Otto Kirchheimer and Franz Neumann, for a defense of rationalized universalistic law as an unfinished project of modernity. For an overview of Schmitt's thought, see Gopal Balakrishnan, *The Enemy: An Intellectual Portrait of Carl Schmitt,* and Giorgio Agamben's *State of Exception* for a historical and philosophical critique of the tendency of all modern political orders, whether democratic or totalitarian, toward the deformalization of the legal order through the generalization of the state of exception.

5. See Lazzeri 306, 329.

6. On French support for the overthrow of Aristide, see Hallward, 2007, xxx.

7. See Hallward's *Damming the Flood* (2007) for a global inquiry into the United States' systematic attempts to undermine Haitian democracy from 1990 to 2004.

8. Paul Farmer documents and summarizes the extensive, and ongoing, efforts of the "Land of Liberty" to destroy the process of democratization in Haiti from well before the first U.S. invasion in 1914 to the 1990s (Chomsky, Farmer, and Goodman, 1995, 11–36).

9. Chomsky (1999) extensively documents such failures on the part of the United States since the adoption of the Universal Declaration of Human Rights on Dec. 10, 1948.

10. It is important not to conflate Heidegger's insightful and original (Jameson calls it "thrilling") critique of modern subjectivity as *Vorstellung,* as representation, with his critique of technological modernity. In the former, objects are made available *for* (*Vor-*) a subject, a subject that itself only comes into existence, finds an opening for its existence, in this arranging of an object world (Jameson 45–48). In Heidegger's critique of technological modernity, however, from *Being and Time* through later essays such as "The Question Concerning Technology," he extends this insight only to make a crude and naïve (which is not to say incorrect) condemnation of (what the Frankfurt School will call) "instrumental reason," of the creation of a world in which every object exists merely in its use value *for* the autonomous subject (a forest becomes timber, a river hydroelectric power). Even cruder is his reactionary solution to this dilemma; thanks to his refusal to engage with the complexities of modern society, he can only withdraw into the *Heimat* of the Black Forest, philosophically stylized as the turn from beings to Being.

11. For description of such acts in the final and most violent period of the revolution, see Fick 1990, 220–21, and on Rochambeau's particularly sadistic violence, 229.

12. Deleuze makes a similar point in *Negotiations*, arguing that to "say revolutions turn out badly . . . [confuses] two different things, the way revolutions turn out historically and people's revolutionary becoming"; in Deleuze's complex understanding of the relation between becoming and history, the former indicates the break with the past, the event that allows the emergence of the New (cited in Žižek 2004, 12).

13. "In the revolutionary explosion as an Event," says Žižek of the French Revolution, "another utopian dimension shines through, the dimension of universal emancipation, which, precisely, is the excess betrayed by the market reality that takes over 'the day after'—as such, this excess is not simply abolished, dismissed as irrelevant, but, as it were, *transposed into the virtual state,* continuing to haunt the emancipatory imaginary as a dream waiting to be realized" (2004, 31).

14. See Arthur and Dash (80–110) on the destruction of the Haitian forest.

15. On this Franco-French debate, see Hunt 1996.

16. For more information, see *Hidden Slaves: Forced Labor in the United States,* available online at http://www.freetheslaves.net/. See also http://www.antislavery.org/index.htm.

17. Trouillot 1990, 215; Arthur and Dash 105, 232; Dupuy 2007; Hallward 2007.

18. Hallward 2007; Dupuy 2007, 101–34; Farmer 161, 183, 185, 187.

19. "Empires, unlike states, are under an informal pressure to assume primacy in every sphere in which power, prestige and performance can be measured and compared" (Münkler 31). Since the end of the Cold War, Münkler argues, the American empire has become unable to tolerate even the smallest threats to its imperial prestige (32). Though I accept this aspect of Münkler's analysis, the consequences I would draw from it are directly opposite to his rehabilitation of empire, the interventionist imperative, and the claim that we can divorce such an analysis from the ethical claims of a critique of imperialism. See Teschke for a detailed critique of *Empires.*

20. Though Dupuy is fulminous in his condemnation of Aristide's putative messianism, the author's account is fundamentally tendentious, repeatedly contradicting itself, as when he will point out that (a mere five days before he was deposed) Aristide was in fact calling for "the decentralization of the political structures to increase popular participation in decision making at the rural, communal, departmental, and national levels" (110).

21. Dupuy 2007, 146–75. Both Dupuy and Hallward (2007) extensively document Aristide's repeated concessions to the increasingly unrealistic demands of the Bush administration during his second term as an elected official; at each new overture, the latter simply upped the demands. Clearly, both the CD and the Bush administration had no desire to see Aristide continue in office. Colin Powell's

message to Haiti was as clear as it was impossible for Aristide to accept without total capitulation of his long-held democratic principles: "Either negotiate an agreement that satisfied the demands of the United States, the [international financial institutions], and the CD, or your government will continue to be denied legitimacy and financial asistance" (149).

22. On *Tropicalia,* see Dunn, as well as Caetano Veloso's memoir *Tropical Truth.*

### Appendix

1. The following summary of the events of the Haitian Revolution draws upon the recent narratives of Geggus (2002, 5–29), Dubois (2004a), and Bell (2007; 1995, 504–23).

# Works Cited

Adorno, Theodor W. 1973. *Negative Dialectics*. New York: Continuum.
———. 1998. "Progress." In *Critical Models: Interventions and Catchwords*. Trans. Henry Pickford. New York: Columbia University Press. 143–60.
———. 2006. *History and Freedom: Lectures, 1964–1965*. Trans. Rodney Livingstone. Cambridge: Polity Press.
Agamben, Giorgio. 2005. *State of Exception*. Chicago: University of Chicago Press.
Alquié, Ferdinand. 2003. *Leçons sur Spinoza*. Paris: La Table Ronde.
Anderson, Perry. 2005. "Arms and Rights." *New Left Review* 31 (Jan.–Feb.): 5–40.
Aravamudan, Srinivas. 1999. *Tropicopolitans: Colonialism and Agency, 1688–1804*. Durham, NC: Duke University Press.
Arendt, Hannah. 1963. *On Revolution*. New York: Viking.
———. 1968. "What Is Freedom?" In *Between Past and Future: Eight Exercises in Political Thought*. New York: Viking. 143–71.
———. 1971. *The Life of the Mind: Thinking*. New York: Harcourt Brace Jovanovich.
———. 1982. *Lectures on Kant's Political Philosophy*. Ed. Ronald Beiner. Chicago: University of Chicago Press.
———. 1998. *The Human Condition*. Chicago: University of Chicago Press, 1958.
Arthur, Charles, and Michael Dash, eds. 1999. *Libète: A Haiti Anthology*. London: Latin American Bureau.
Badiou, Alain. 1988. *L'être et l'événement*. Paris: Seuil.
———. 1998. *Abrégé de métapolitique*. Paris: Seuil.
———. 2003. *L'éthique: Essai sur la conscience du mal*. Paris: Nous.
Baker, Keith Michael. 1994. "The Idea of a Declaration of Rights." In *The French Idea of Freedom: The Old Régime and the Declaration of the Rights of 1789*. Stanford, CA: Stanford University Press. 154–98.
Baker, Keith Michael, and Peter Hanns Reill, eds. 2001. *What's Left of Enlightenment?* Stanford, CA: Stanford University Press.

Balakrishnan, Gopal. 2000. *The Enemy: An Intellectual Portrait of Carl Schmitt.* New York: Verso.
Balibar, Étienne. 2000. "What Makes a People a People? Rousseau and Kant." In *Masses, Classes, and the Public Sphere.* Ed. Mike Hill and Warren Montag. New York: Verso. 105–31.
Barthélemy, Gérard. 1990. *L'univers rural Haïtien: Le pays en dehors.* Paris: L'Harmattan.
Beaud, Olivier. 2003. "Souveraineté." In *Dictionnaire de philosophie politique.* Ed. Philippe Raynaud and Stéphane Rials. 2nd ed. Paris: Presses Universitaires de France. 735–42.
Bell, Madison Smartt. 1995. *All Souls' Rising.* New York: Vintage.
———. 2007. *Toussaint Louverture: A Biography.* New York: Pantheon Books.
Bellegarde-Smith, Patrick. 1990. *Haiti: The Breached Citadel.* Boulder, CO: Westview Press.
Benhabib, Seyla. 1986. *Critique, Norm, and Utopia: A Study of the Foundations of Critical Theory.* New York: Columbia University Press.
———. 1992. "Models of Public Space: Hannah Arendt, the Liberal Tradition, and Jürgen Habermas." In *Habermas and the Public Sphere.* Cambridge, MA: MIT Press. 73–99.
Benjamin, Walter. 1968. *Illuminations.* New York: Schoken.
Benot, Yves. 2004. *La révolution française et la fin des colonies, 1789–1794.* Paris: La Découverte, 1987.
Bidima, Jean-Godefroy. 1997. *La palabre: Une juridiction de la parole.* Paris: Michalon.
Blackburn, Robin. 1988. *The Overthrow of Colonial Slavery: 1776–1848.* New York: Verso.
———. 1995. "*The Black Jacobins* and New World Slavery." In *C. L. R. James: His Intellectual Legacies.* Ed. Selwyn R. Cudjoe and William E. Cain. Amherst: University of Massachusetts Press. 81–97.
———. 2004. "Of Human Bondage." *Nation,* 4 Oct., 26–32.
Blanchot, Maurice. 1994. "Literature and the Right to Death." In *The Work of Fire.* Trans. Charlotte Mandell. Stanford, CA: Stanford University Press.
Bloch, Ernst. 1987. *Natural Law and Human Dignity.* Trans. Dennis J. Schmidt. Cambridge, MA: MIT Press.
Blumrosen, Alfred W., and Ruth G. Blumrosen. 2005. *Slave Nation: How Slavery United the Colonies and Sparked the American Revolution.* Naperville, IL: Sourcebooks.
Bobbio, Norberto. 1990. *L'età dei diritti.* Torino: Giulio Einaudi.
Bourgeois, Bernard. 1990. *Philosophie et droits de l'homme de Kant à Marx.* Paris: Presses Universitaires de France.
Brière, Jean-François. 2004. "Abbé Grégoire and Haitian Independence." *Research in African Literatures* 35, no. 2: 34–43.

Bronner, Stephen Eric. 2004. *Reclaiming the Enlightenment: Toward a Politics of Radical Engagement*. New York: Columbia University Press.
Buchanan, Ruth, and Sundhya Pahuja. 2004. "Legal Imperialism: *Empire's* Invisible Hand?" In *Empire's New Clothes: Reading Hardt and Negri*. Ed. Paul A. Passavant and Jodi Dean. New York: Routledge. 73–94.
Buck-Morss, Susan. 2000. "Hegel and Haiti." *Critical Inquiry* 26, no. 4 (Summer): 821–65.
———. 2002. "Globalization, Cosmopolitanism, Politics, and the Citizen." *Journal of Visual Culture* 1, no. 3: 325–40.
———. 2003. *Thinking Past Terror: Islamism and Critical Theory on the Left*. London: Verso.
Butler, Judith. 2000. "Restaging the Universal: Hegemony and the Limits of Formalism." In *Contingency, Hegemony, Universality: Contemporary Dialogues on the Left*. Ed. Judith Butler, Ernesto Laclau, and Slavoj Žižek. London: Verso. 10–43.
Carpentier, Jean, and François Lebrun. 2000. *Histoire de France*. Paris: Éditions du Seuil.
Cassirer, Ernst. 1968. *The Philosophy of the Enlightenment*. Princeton, NJ: Princeton University Press.
———. 1989. *The Question of Jean-Jacques Rousseau*. Trans. Peter Gay. New Haven, CT: Yale University Press, 1932.
Castoriadis, Cornelius. 1997. *The Castoriadis Reader*. Ed. David Ames Curtis. New York: Blackwell.
———. 2005. *Une société à la dérive: Entretiens et débats 1974–1997*. Paris: Seuil.
Cauna, Jacques de, ed. 2004. *Toussaint Louverture et l'indépendence de l'Haïti: Témoignages pour un bicentenaire*. Paris: Kathala.
Césaire, Aimé. 1960. *Toussaint Louverture: La révolution française et le problème colonial*. Paris: Présence Africaine.
———. 1978. "Entretien avec Aimé Césaire par Jacqueline Leiner." In *Tropiques*. Paris: Jean-Michel Place. v–xxxviii.
Chakrabarty, Dipesh. 2000. *Provincializing Europe: Postcolonial Thought and Historical Difference*. Princeton, NJ: Princeton University Press.
Charlesworth, Hilary. 1997. "Human Rights as Men's Rights." In *Key Concepts in Critical Theory: Gender*. Ed. Carol C. Gould. Atlantic Highlands, NJ: Humanities Press. 384–93.
Chartier, Roger. 1990. *Origines culturelles de la révolution française*. Paris: Seuil.
Chomsky, Noam. 1999. *The Umbrella of U.S. Power: The Universal Declaration of Rights and the Contradictions of U.S. Policy*. New York: Seven Stories Press.
Chomsky, Noam, Paul Farmer, and Amy Goodman. 2004. *Getting Haiti Right This Time: The U.S. and the Coup*. Monroe, ME: Common Courage Press.

Chomsky, Noam, and Michel Foucault. 1997. "Human Nature: Justice Versus Power." In *Foucault and His Interlocutors*. Ed. Arnold I. Davidson. Chicago: University of Chicago Press. 107–45.

Cissé, Youssouf Tata, and Jean-Louis Sagot-Duvauroux, trans. 2003. *La charte du Mandé et autres traditions du Mali*. Paris: Albin Michel.

Clastres, Pierre. 1989. *Society against the State: Essays in Political Anthropology*. New York: Zone Books.

Cole, Andrew. 2004. "What Hegel's Master/Slave Dialectic Really Means." *Journal of Medieval and Early Modern Studies* 34, no. 3 (Fall): 577–610.

Condorcet, Jean-Antoine-Nicolas, Marquis de. 2000. *Réflexions sur l'esclavage des Nègres*. Paris: Mille et une nuits.

Corcuff, Philippe. 2006. "Vers des Lumières tamisées-contre des Lumières aseptisées, contre des Lumières totales." *Contretemps* 17 (September): 85–94.

Cormack, William S. 2005. "Communications, the State, and Revolution in the French Caribbean." *French Colonial History* 6: 45–54.

Damas, Léon-Gantran. 1939. "89 et nous, les noirs." *Europe* (July): 511–16.

Danticat, Edwidge. 2007. *Brother I'm Dying*. New York: Alfred A. Knopf.

Dash, J. Michael. 2006. "Haïti chimère: Revolutionary Universalism and its Caribbean Context." In *Reinterpreting the Haitian Revolution and its Cultural Aftershocks*. Ed. Martin Munro and Elizabeth Walcott-Hackshaw. Kingston: University of the West Indies Press. 9–19.

David, Alain. 2001. *Racisme et antisémitisme: Essai de philosophie sur l'envers des concepts*. Paris: Ellipses.

Davis, David Brion. 1975. *The Problem of Slavery in the Age of Revolution, 1770–1823*. Ithaca, NY: Cornell University Press.

———. 1983. "American Slavery and the American Revolution." In *Slavery and Freedom in the Age of the American Revolution*. Ed. Ira Berlin and Ronald Hoffman. Charlottesville: University Press of Virginia. 262–80

———. 1984. *Slavery and Human Progress*. New York: Oxford University Press.

Dayan, Joan. 1995. *Haiti, History, and the Gods*. Berkeley: University of California Press.

Dean, Jodi. 2004. "The Networked Empire." In *Empire's New Clothes: Reading Hardt and Negri*. Ed. Paul A. Passavant and Jodi Dean. New York: Routledge. 265–88.

Debien, Gabriel. 1956. "Les débuts de la Révolution à Saint-Domingue vus des plantations de Bréda." *Notes d'histoire coloniale* 45: 143–73.

———. 1966. *Les affranchissements aux Antilles françaises aux XVIIe et XVIIIe siècles*. Sevilla: Anuario de estudios americanos.

Debien, Gabriel, M. A. Menier, and J. Fouchard. 1977. "Toussaint Louverture avant 1789: Légendes et réalités." *Conjonction, revue franco-haïtienne* 134 (Juin–Juillet): 66–80.

Debray, Régis. 2004. *Haïti et la France*. Paris: La Table Ronde.

DeGraff, Michel. 2004. "Three Centuries of Transnational (Anti-) Utopias in Creole Studies." Public lecture, University of Columbia, MO, Nov. 4.
Deleuze, Gilles. 1968. *Différence et répétition*. Paris: PUF.
———. 2002. *L'île déserte et autres textes*. Paris: Les Éditions de Minuit.
Deleuze, Gilles, and Félix Guattari. 1987. *A Thousand Plateaus*. Minnesota: University of Minnesota Press.
Descourtilz, Michel-Étienne. 1935. *Voyage d'un naturaliste en Haïti: 1799–1803*. Paris: Plon.
Deranty, Jean-Philippe. 2002. Translator's introduction in *G. W. F. Hegel: Leçons sur le droit naturel et la science de l'état (Heidelberg, semester d'hiver 1817–1818)*. Paris: Vrin. 9–43.
Donnelly, Jack. 1989. *Universal Human Rights in Theory and Practice*. Ithaca, NY: Cornell University Press.
———. 2003. *Universal Human Rights in Theory and Practice*. 2nd ed. Ithaca, NY: Cornell University Press.
Dorsinville, Roger. 1965. *Toussaint Louverture, ou La vocation de la liberté*. Paris: René Julliard.
Doyle, William, and Colin Hayden, eds. 1999. *Robespierre*. London: Cambridge University Press.
Dubois, Laurent. 2004a. *Avengers of the New World: The Story of the Haitian Revolution*. Cambridge, MA: Harvard University Press.
———. 2004b. *A Colony of Citizens: Revolution and Slave Emancipation in the French Caribbean, 1787–1804*. Chapel Hill: University of North Carolina Press.
———. 2005. "An Enslaved Enlightenment: Or, Voltaire and the Ibo Zaïre in the French Atlantic." Paper presented to the Seminar of the Dept. of History, Johns Hopkins University, Baltimore, MD, Sept. 19.
Dubois, Laurent, and John D. Garrigus, eds. 2006. *Slave Revolution in the Caribbean, 1789–1804: A Brief History with Documents*. Boston: Bedford St. Martin's.
Duboys. *Précis historique des annales de la colonie française de Saint-Domingue depuis 1789*. BN Nouvelles acquisitions françaises 14878–14879.
Dubroca. 1983. *La vie de Tousaint Louverture*. Port-au-Prince: Éditions Fardin, 1802.
Duchet, Michèle. 1977. *Anthropologie et histoire au siècle des lumières*. Paris: Flammarion.
Dumorier. 1791. *Sur les troubles des colonies, et l'unique moyen d'assurer la tranquillité, la prospérité et la fidéilté des ces dépendances de l'Empire*. Paris: Didot Jeune.
Dunn, Christopher. 2001. *Brutality Garden: Tropicalia and the Emergence of a Brazilian Counterculture*. Chapel Hill: University of North Carolina Press.
Dupuy, Alex. 1995. "Toussaint Louverture and the Haitian Revolution: A Reassessment of C. L. R. James' Interpretation." In *C. L. R. James: His Intellectual*

*Legacies.* Ed. Selwyn R. Cudjoe and William E. Cain. Amherst: University of Massachusetts Press. 106–17.

———. 2004. "Class, Race, and Nation: Unresolved Contradictions of the Saint-Domingue Revolution." *Journal of Haitian Studies* 10, no. 1 (Spring): 6–21.

———. 2007. *The Prophet and Power: Jean-Bertrand Aristide, the International Community, and Haiti.* Lanham, MD: Rowman and Littlefield.

Durand, Guy. 2004. *Pour une éthique de la dissidence.* Montreal: Libeer.

Dussel, Enrique. 1998. "Beyond Eurocentrism: The World-System and the Limits of Modernity." In *The Cultures of Globalization.* Ed. Fredric Jameson and Masao Miyoshi. Durham, NC: Duke University Press. 3–31.

*Encyclopédie de Diderot et D'Alembert.* 2003. DVD-ROM, version 1.0.0. Marsane: Éditions Redon.

Eze, Emmanuel Chukwudi. 1997. *Race and the Enlightenment: A Reader.* Cambridge: Blackwell.

Farge, Arlette. 1994. *Subversive Words: Public Opinion in Eighteenth Century France.* Trans. Rosemary Morris. Philadelphia: Pennsylvania State University Press.

Farmer, Paul. 2006. *The Uses of Haiti.* Monroe: Common Courage Press, 1994.

Fatton, Robert. 2002. *Haiti's Predatory Republic: The Unending Transition to Democracy.* Boulder, CO: Lynn Rienner Publishers.

Fauchois, Yann, Thierry Grillet, and Tzvetan Todorov. 2006. *Lumières! Un héritage pour demain.* Paris: Bibliothèque nationale de France.

Fichte, J. G. 2000. *Foundations of Natural Right According to the Principles of the Wissenschaftslehre.* Trans. Michael Baur. London: Cambridge University Press, 1796.

Fick, Carolyn. 1990. *The Making of Haiti: The Saint-Domingue Revolution from Below.* Knoxville: University of Tennessee Press.

———. 1997. "The French Revolution in Saint-Domingue: A Triumph or Failure?" In *A Turbulent Time: The French Revolution and the greater Caribbean.* Ed. David Barry Gaspar and David Patrick Geggus. Bloomington: Indiana University Press.

Finkelman, Paul. 2001. *Slavery and the Founders: Race and Liberty in the Age of Jefferson.* 2nd ed. Armonk, NY: M. E. Sharpe.

Fischer, Sibylle. 2004. *Modernity Disavowed: Haiti and the Cultures of Slavery in the Age of Revolution.* Durham, NC: Duke University Press.

Foucault, Michel. 1972. *The Archeology of Knowledge.* Trans. A. M. Sheridan Smith. New York: Pantheon Books.

———. 1977. "Nietzsche, Genealogy, History." In *Language, Counter-memory, Practice.* Ed. Donald Bouchard. Ithaca, NY: Cornell University Press. 139–64.

———. 2001. "Qu'est-ce que les Lumières?" In *Dits et écrits II, 1976–1988.* Paris: Gallimard Quarto. 1498–1507.

Fraser, Nancy. 1992. "Rethinking the Public Sphere: A Contribution to the Critique of Actually Existing Democracy." In *Habermas and the Public Sphere*. Cambridge, MA: MIT Press. 109–42.

Frey, Sylvia R. 1991. *Water from the Rock: Black Resistance in a Revolutionary Age*. Princeton, NJ: Princeton University Press.

Furet, François. 1978. *Penser la révolution française*. Paris: Gallimard.

———. 1992. "Jacobinisme." In *Dictionnaire critique de la révolution française: Idées*. Ed. François Furet and Mona Ozouf. Paris: Flammarion. 233–51.

Furet, François, and Denis Richet. 1965. *La révolution française*. Paris: Hachette.

Garran, Jean-Phillippe. 1797–99. *Rapport sur les troubles de Saint-Domingue, fait au nom de la Commission des colonies, des Comités de salut public, de legislation de la marine, réunis*. Paris: BNF, electronic document: FRBNF37228586; Cote: NUMM-49245-8. Accessed April 16, 2008.

Gauchet, Marcel. 2002. *La démocratie contre elle-même*. Paris: Gallimard.

———. 2006. "De la critique à l'auto-critique." In *Lumières! Un héritage pour demain*. Ed. Yann Fauchois, Thierry Grillet, and Tzvetan Todorov. Paris: Bibliothèque nationale de France. 38–45.

Gauthier, Florence. 1992. *Triomphe et mort du droit naturel en Révolution: 1789–1795–1802*. Paris: Presses Universitaires de France.

Geggus, David, ed. 2001. *The Impact of the Haitian Revolution in the Atlantic World*. Columbia: University of South Carolina Press.

———. 2002. *Haitian Revolutionary Studies*. Bloomington: Indiana University Press.

Genovese, Eugene. 1979. *From Rebellion to Revolution: Afro-American Slave Revolts in the Making of the Modern World*. Baton Rouge: Louisiana State University Press.

Girard, Philip R. 2005. "*Liberté, Egalité, Esclavage:* French Revolutionary Ideals and the Failure of the Leclerc Expedition to Saint Domingue." *French Colonial History* 6: 55–78.

Glissant, Edouard. 1990. *Poétique de la relation*. Paris: Gallimard.

Gordon, Daniel. 1994. *Citizens without Sovereignty: Equality and Sociability in French Thought, 1670–1789*. Princeton, NJ: Princeton University Press.

Gough, Hugh. 1999. "Robespierre and the Press." In *Robespierre*. Ed. Colin Hayden and William Doyle. London: Cambridge University Press. 111–26.

Gould, Carol L. 2004. *Globalizing Democracy and Human Rights*. Cambridge: Cambridge University Press.

Grégoire, Abbé. 1791. "Lettre aux citoyens de couleur et nègres libres de Saint-Domingue." Paris: Imprimerie du patriote François, place du Théâtre Italien.

Groethuysen, Bernard. 1956. *Philosophie de la révolution française*. Paris: Gallimard.

Gros. 1793. *Isle de Saint Domingue: Précis historique*. Paris: n.p.

Habermas, Jürgen. 1991. *The Structural Transformation of the Public Sphere: An Inquiry into a Category of Bourgeois Society*. Trans. Thomas Burger. Cambridge, MA: MIT Press.

———. 1998. *Between Facts and Norms: Contributions to a Discourse Theory of Law and Democracy*. Trans. William Rehg. Cambridge, MA: MIT Press.

Hallward, Peter. 2003. *Badiou: A Subject to Truth*. Minneapolis: University of Minnesota Press.

———. 2004a. "Option Zero in Haiti." *New Left Review* 27 (May–June): 23–47.

———. 2004b. "Haitian Inspiration: On the Bicentenary of Haiti's Independence." *Radical Philosophy* 123 (January/February). Available online at http://www.radicalphilosophy.com/default.asp?channel_id=2187&editorial_id=14344. Accessed April 27, 2008.

———. 2006. *Out of This World: Deleuze and the Philosophy of Creation*. London: Verso.

———. 2007. *Damming the Flood: Haiti, Aristide, and the Politics of Containment*. London: Verso.

Hardt, Michael, and Antonio Negri. 2000. *Empire*. Cambridge, MA: Harvard University Press.

———. 2004. *Multitude: War and Democracy in the Age of Empire*. New York: Penguin.

Hartman, Saidiya V. 1997. *Scenes of Subjection: Terror, Slavery, and Self-Making in Nineteenth Century America*. Cambridge, MA: Harvard University Press.

Havel, Václav. 1989. *Eseje a jiné texty z let, 1970–1989: Dálkový Výslech* Vol. 4. Praha: Torst.

———. 1991. *Open Letters: Selected Prose, 1965–1990*. Ed. Paul Wilson. Boston: Faber and Faber.

Hegel, G. W. F. 1970. *Grundlinien der Philosophie des Rechts*. Stuttgart: Philipp Reclam.

———. 1973. *Naturrecht und Staatswissenschaft: Nach der Verlesungsnachschrift von C. G. Homeyer 1818/19*. Ed. Karl-Heinz Ilting. In *Vorlesungen über Rechtsphilosophie: 1818–1831. Edition und Kommentar in sechs Bänden von Karl-Heinz Ilting*. Vol. 1. Stuttgart-Bad Cannstatt: Friedrich Frommann Verlag.

———. 1975. *Lectures on the Philosophy of World History: Introduction*. Cambridge: Cambridge University Press.

———. 1977. *Hegel's Phenomenology of Spirit*. Trans. A. V. Miller. Oxford: Oxford University Press.

———. 1991. *Elements of the Philosophy of Right*. Ed. Allen Wood. Trans. H. B. Nisbet. Cambridge: Cambridge University Press.

———. 1999. *Political Writings*. Ed. Laurence Dickey and H. B. Nisbet. Trans. H. B. Nisbet. New York: Cambridge University Press.

Heidegger, Martin. 1977. *Basic Writings*. Ed. David Farrell Krell. New York: Harper and Row.

———. 1996. *Being and Time: A Translation of Sein und Zeit*. Trans. Joan Stambaugh. Albany: State University of New York Press.

———. 2002. *The Essence of Human Freedom: An Introduction to Philosophy*. Trans. Ted Sadler. New York: Continuum.

Henry, Paget. 2000. *Caliban's Reason: Introducing Afro-Caribbean Philosophy.* New York: Routledge.
Henry, Paget, and Paul Buhle, eds. 1992. *C. L. R. James' Caribbean.* Durham, NC: Duke University Press.
Hibbert, Christopher. 1981. *The Days of the French Revolution.* New York: Quill.
Higgonet, Patrice. 1998. *Goodness beyond Virtue: Jacobins during the French Revolution.* Cambridge, MA: Harvard University Press.
Hill, Mark, and Warren Montag, eds. 2000. *Masses, Classes, and the Public Sphere.* New York: Verso.
Hulliung, Mark. 1998. *The Autocritique of the Enlightenment: Rousseau and the Philosophes.* Cambridge, MA: Harvard University Press.
Hunt, Lynn, ed. 1996. *The French Revolution and Human Rights: A Brief Documentary History.* Boston: Bedford/St. Martin's.
Hutchings, Kimberly. 1996. *Kant, Critique, and Politics.* New York: Routledge.
*Inquiry into the Causes of the Insurrection of the Negroes in the Island of St. Domingo.* 1792. London: J. Johnson.
Isaac, Jeffrey C. 1996. "A New Guarantee on Earth: Hannah Arendt on Human Dignity and the Politics of Human Rights." *American Political Science Review* 90, no. 1 (March): 61–73.
Israel, Jonathan I. 2001. *Radical Enlightenment: Philosophy and the Making of Modernity, 1650–1750.* Oxford: Oxford University Press.
Jacob, Margaret C. 1981. *The Radical Enlightenment: Pantheists, Freemasons, and Republicans.* London: Allen and Unwin.
———. 1993. "Money, Equality, Fraternity: Freemasonry and the Social Order in Eighteenth Century Europe." In *The Culture of the Market: Historical Essays.* Cambridge: Cambridge University Press. 102–35.
James, C. L. R. 1989. *The Black Jacobins: Toussaint Louverture and the San Domingo Revolution.* New York: Vintage.
Jameson, Fredric. 2002. *A Singular Modernity.* London: Verso Books.
Jenson, Deborah. 2001. *Trauma and Its Representations: The Social Life of Mimesis in Post-Revolutionary France.* Baltimore, MD: Johns Hopkins University Press.
———. 2005. "From the Kidnapping(s) of the Louvertures to the Alleged Kidnapping of Aristide: Legacies of Slavery in the Post/Colonial World." In "The Haiti Issue: 1804 and Nineteenth-Century French Studies." Ed. Deborah Jenson. Special issue. *Yale French Studies* 107 (Spring): 162–86.
———. 2008. "Toussaint Louverture, Spin Doctor? Launching the Haitian Revolution in the French Media." In *Tree of Liberty: Legacies of the Haitian Revolution in the Atlantic World.* Ed. Doris Garraway. Charlottesville: University of Virginia Press. 41–62.
Jordan, Winthrop D. 1968. *White over Black: American Attitudes toward the Negro, 1550–1812.* Chapel Hill: University of North Carolina Press.
Kant, Immanuel. 1968. *Kants Werke (VII): Der Streit der Fakultäten; Anthropologie in pragmatischer Hinsicht.* Berlin: Walter de Gruyter.

———. 1974. *Anthropology from a Pragmatic Point of View.* Trans. Mary J. Gregor. The Hague: Martinus Nijhoff.

———. 1996. *Practical Philosophy.* Trans. and ed. Mary J. Gregor. Cambridge: Cambridge University Press.

———. 1997. *Critique of Pure Reason.* Trans. Paul Geyer and Alan W. Wood. Cambridge: Cambridge University Press.

Kley, Dale Van. 1994. "From the Lessons of French History to Truths for All Times and All People: The Historical Origins of an Anti-Historical Declaration." In *The French Idea of Freedom: The Old Régime and the Declaration of the Rights of 1789.* Stanford, CA: Stanford University Press. 72–113.

Knight, Franklin W. 2005. "The Haitian Revolution and the Notion of Human Rights." *Journal of the Historical Society* 3 (Fall): 391–416.

Kramnick, Isaac, ed. 1995. *The Portable Enlightenment Reader.* New York: Penguin.

Labica, Georges. 1990. *Robespierre: Une politique de la philosophie.* Paris: Presses Universitaires de France.

Laclau, Ernesto. 1996. *Emancipation(s).* New York: Verso.

———. 2000. "Identity and Hegemony: The Role of Universality in the Constitution of Political Logics." In *Contingency, Hegemony, Universality: Contemporary Dialogues on the Left.* London: Verso. 44–89.

———. 2004. "An Ethics of Militant Engagement." In *Think Again: Alain Badiou and the Future of Philosophy.* Ed. Peter Hallward. New York: Continuum. 120–37.

———. 2005. *On Populist Reason.* London: Verso.

Laclau, Ernesto, and Chantal Mouffe. 1985. *Hegemony and Socialist Strategy: Towards a Radical Democratic Politics.* London: Verso.

Laguerre, Michel. 1989. *Voodoo and Politics in Haiti.* New York: St. Martin's Press.

Latour, Bruno. 1983. "Give Me a Laboratory and I Will Raise the World." In *Science Observed: Perspectives on the Social Study of Science.* Ed. Karin Knorr and Michael Mulleny. London: Sage. 258–75.

Laurent, Gérard M. 1953. *Toussaint Louverture à travers sa correspondance (1794–1798).* Madrid.

Lazzeri, Christian. 1998. *Droit, pouvoir, et liberté: Spinoza critique de Hobbes.* Paris: PUF.

Leibniz, Gottfried. 1995. *Discours de métaphysique, suivi de Monadologie.* Paris: Gallimard.

Lem, Stanislaw. 1961. *Solaris.* Trans. Joanna Kilmartin and Steve Cox. London: Faber and Faber.

Levinas, Emmanuel. 1998. "The Rights of Man and Good Will." In *Entre Nous: On the Thinking of the Other.* Trans. Michael B. Smith and Barbara Harshav. New York: Columbia University Press. 155–58.

Linebaugh, Peter, and Marcus Rediker. 2000. *The Many-Headed Hydra: Sailors,*

*Slaves, Commoners, and the Hidden History of the Revolutionary Atlantic.* Boston: Beacon Press.

Locke, John. 1965. *Two Treatises of Government.* New York: Mentor. Reprint; Cambridge: Cambridge University Press, 1960.

Louis, Abel. 2002. "Franc-maçonnerie, libres de couleur et abolitionisme à la Martinique (1738–1848)." *Bulletin de la société d'histoire de la Guadeloupe* 132 (May–August): 13–30.

Lundahl, Mats. 1979. *Peasants and Poverty: A Study of Haiti.* New York: St. Martin's Press.

———. 1997. "The Haitian Dilemma Reexamined: Lessons From the Past in Light of Some New Economic Theory." In *Haiti Renewed: Political and Economic Prospects.* Ed. Robert I. Rotberg. Washington, DC: Brookings Institution Press. 60–92.

Macherey, Pierre. 1990. *Hegel ou Spinoza.* Paris: Éditions la Découverte, 1979.

MacKinnon, Catherine A. 1993. "Crimes of War, Crimes of Peace." In *On Human Rights: The Oxford Amnesty Lectures 1993.* Ed. Stephen Shute and Susan Hurley. New York: Basic Books. 83–109.

MacLeod, Duncan J. 1974. *Slavery, Race and the American Revolution.* Cambridge: Cambridge University Press.

Madiou, Thomas. 1981. *Histoire d'Haïti: Tome 1 (1492–1799).* Port-au-Prince: Éditions Fardin, 1847.

Marchart, Oliver. 2004. "Politics and the Ontological Difference: On the 'Strictly Philosophical' in Laclau's Work." In *Laclau: A Critical Reader.* Ed. Simon Critchley and Oliver Marchart. New York: Routledge. 54–72.

Maximin, Daniel. 2006. *Les fruits du cyclone: Une géopolitique de la Caraïbe.* Paris: Éditions du Seuil.

May, Todd. 2004. "Badiou and Deleuze on the One and the Many." In *Think Again: Alain Badiou and the Future of Philosophy.* Ed. Peter Hallward. New York: Continuum. 67–76.

Mignolo, Walter. 2000. *Local Histories/Global Designs: Coloniality, Subaltern Knowledges, and Border Thinking.* Princeton, NJ: Princeton University Press.

Mill, John Stuart. 1997. *On Liberty.* New York: W. W. Norton.

Millet, Kethly. 1978. *Les paysans haïtiens et l'occupation américaine, 1915–1930.* La Salle: Collectif Paroles.

Mintz, Sidney. 1986. *Sweetness and Power: The Place of Sugar in Modern History.* New York: Penguin Books.

Misrahi, Robert. 1978. Preface to *Traité de l'autorité politique* by Benedict de Spinoza. Paris: Gallimard.

Montag, Warren. 1999. *Bodies, Masses, Power: Spinoza and His Contemporaries.* London: Verso.

———. 2000. "The Pressure of the Street: Habermas' Fear of the Masses." In *Masses, Classes, and the Public Sphere.* Ed. Mike Hill and Warren Montag. New York: Verso. 132–45.

Morange, Jean. 2002. *La declaration des droits de l'homme et du citoyen.* Paris: Presses Universitaires de France.

Moreau, Pierre-François. 2003. *Spinoza et le spinozisme.* Paris: Presses Universitaires de France.

Moreau de St. Méry. 1958. *Description topographique, physique, civile, politique, et historique de la partie française de l'isle Saint-Domingue.* Vols. 1–3. Paris: Société de l'histoire des colonies françaises.

Moreiras, Alberto. 2001. *The Exhaustion of Difference: The Politics of Latin American Cultural Studies.* Durham, NC: Duke University Press.

Mornet, Daniel. 1967. *Les origines intellectuelles de la révolution française, 1715–1787.* Paris: Colin, 1933.

Mourgeon, Jacques. 2002. *Les droits de l'homme.* Paris: Presses Universitaires de France, 1978.

Münkler, Herfried. 2005. *Empires: The Logic of World Domination from Ancient Rome to the United States.* Trans. Patrick Camiller. Cambridge: Polity.

Muthu, Sankar. 2003. *Enlightenment against Empire.* Princeton, NJ: Princeton University Press.

Negri, Antonio. 1999. *Insurgencies: Constituent Power and the Modern State.* Minneapolis: University of Minnesota Press.

———. 2004. *Negri on Negri: In Conversation with Anne Dufourmentelle.* Routledge.

Nesbitt, Nick. 2003. *Voicing Memory: History and Subjectivity in French Caribbean Literature.* Charlottesville: University of Virginia Press.

———. 2004. "Troping Tousssaint, Writing Revolution." In "Haiti, 1804–2004." Ed. Abiola Irele. Special issue. *Research in African Literatures.* 35, no. 2 (Summer): 18–33.

———. 2005a. "A Singular Revolution." In *Memory, Empire and Postcolonialism: Legacies of French Colonialism.* Ed. Alec Hargreaves. Lanham, MD: Lexington. 37–50.

———. 2005b. "The Idea of 1804." In "The Haiti Issue: 1804 and Nineteenth-Century French Studies." Ed. Deborah Jenson. Special issue. *Yale French Studies* 107 (Spring): 6–38.

———. 2006. "Penser la révolution haïtienne." *Critique* 711–12 (Aug.–Sept.): 652–64.

———. 2008. "The Haitian Revolution and the Globalization of the Radical Enlightenment." In *Carribean(s) on the Move: Archipiélagos literarios del Caribe.* Ed. Ottmar Ette. Peter Lang: Frankfurt am Main. 39–59.

Nemours, Général. 1945. *Histoire des relations internationals de Toussaint Louverture, avec documents inédits.* Port-au-Prince: Imprimerie du Collège Vertières.

Neuhouser, Frederick. 2000. *Foundations of Hegel's Social Theory.* Cambridge, MA: Harvard University Press.

Niang, Mangoné. 2006. "The Kurukan Fuga Charter: An Example of an Endogenous Governance Mechanism for Conflict Prevention." Club du Sahel et de l'Afrique de l'Ouest (Ouagadougou). Available at http://www.oecd.org/dataoecd/60/55/37341473.pdf. Accessed May 2007.

Nietzsche, Friedrich. 1968. *Humain, trop humain II.* Trans. Robert Rovini. Paris: Gallimard.

Ogle, Gene E. 2003. "'The Eternal Power of Reason' and 'The Superiority of Whites': Hilliard d'Auberteuil's Colonial Enlightenment." *French Colonial History* 3: 35–50.

Parham, Althéa. 1959. *My Odyssey: Experiences of a Young Refugee from Two Revolutions. By a Creole of Saint Domingue.* Baton Rouge: Louisiana State University Press.

Patterson, Orlando. 1995. "Freedom, Slavery, and the Modern Construction of Rights." In *Historical Change and Human Rights: The Oxford-Amnesty Lectures, 1994.* Ed. Olwen Huft. New York: Basic Books. 131–78.

Patton, Paul. 2000. *Deleuze and the Political.* New York: Routledge.

Piquionne, Nathalie. 1998. "Lettre de Jean-François, Biassou et Belair, Juillet 1792." *Annalles historiques de la révolution française* 311 (Janvier–Mars): 132–39.

Pluchon, Pierre. 1989. *Toussaint Louverture: Un révolutionnaire noir d'ancien régime.* Paris: Fayard.

Popkin, Jeremy. 2008. *Facing Racial Revolution: Eyewitness Accounts of the Haitian Revolution.* Chicago: University of Chicago Press.

Porter, Ray, and Mikulás Teich, eds. 1981. *The Enlightenment in National Context.* Cambridge: Cambridge University Press.

Proust, Jacques. 1995. *Diderot et l'Encyclopédie.* Paris: Albin Michel, 1962.

Rai, Milan. 1995. *Chomsky's Politics.* London: Verso.

Rancière, Jacques. 1987. *Le maître ignorant: Cinq leçons sur l'émancipation intellectuelle.* Paris: Fayard.

———. 1995. *La mésentente: Politique et philosophie.* Paris: Galilée.

———. 2004. "Who Is the Subject of the Rights of Man?" *South Atlantic Quarterly* 103, nos. 2–3: 297–310.

Rasch, William. 2003. "Human Rights as Geopolitics: Carl Schmitt and the Legal Form of American Supremacy." *Cultural Critique* 54 (Spring): 120–47.

Raynal, Abbé G. Th. 2001. *Histoire philosophique et politique des deux Indes.* Ed. Yves Bénot. Paris: La Découverte.

Ritter, Joachim. 1982. *Hegel and the French Revolution: Essays on the Philosophy of Right.* Cambridge, MA: MIT Press.

Robespierre, Maximilien. 1965. *Discours et rapports à la Convention.* Paris: Union Générale d'Éditions.

———. 2000. *Pour le bonheur et pour la liberté: Discours.* Paris: La Fabrique-Éditions.

Robinson, Donald L. 1971. *Slavery in the Structure of American Politics, 1765–1820.* New York: Harcourt Brace Jovanovich.

Rogozinski, Jacob. 1999. *Le don de la loi: Kant et l'énigme de l'éthique.* Paris: Presses Universitaires de France.

Romulus, Marc. 1991. *Les cachots de Duvalier.* Port-au-Prince: Imprimerie Kopirapid.

Rose, Erik. 2005. "Kant, J. G. Fichte, and the Politics of Decapitation in Lazarus Bendavid's *Etwas zur Charakteristick der Juden.*" Unpublished essay.

Saint-Remy. 1982. *Mémoires du général Toussaint Louverture, écrits par lui-même, suivis d'une étude historique et critique.* Paris: Pagnerie, 1853.

Sala-Molins, Louis. 1992. *Les misères des Lumières: Sous la raison, l'outrage.* Paris: Laffont.

Scheuerman, William E. 1994. *Between the Norm and the Exception: The Frankfurt School and the Rule of Law.* Cambridge, MA: MIT Press.

Scott, David. 2004. *Conscripts of Modernity: The Tragedy of Colonial Enlightenment.* Durham, NC: Duke University Press.

———. "Interview with Stuart Hall." 2004–5. *Bomb. Special Americas Issue: Tribute to Haiti* (Winter): 55–59.

Scott, Julius S. 1986. "The Common Wind: Currents of Afro-American Communication in the Era of the Haitian Revolution." PhD diss., Duke University, Durham, NC.

Sepinwall, Alyssa Goldstein. 2005. *The Abbé Grégoire and the French Revolution: The Making of Modern Universalism.* Berkeley: University of California Press.

Sériaux, Alain. 1999. *Le droit naturel.* Paris: Presses Universitaires de France.

Sieyès, Emmanuel Joseph. 1963. *What Is the Third Estate?* Trans. M. Blondel. London: Pall Mall Press.

Singham, Shanti Marie. 1994. "Betwixt Cattle and Men: Jews, Blacks and Women, and the Rights of Man." In *The French Idea of Freedom: The Old Régime and the Declaration of the Rights of 1789.* Stanford, CA: Stanford University Press. 114–53.

Skirda, Alexandre. 2000. *Les anarchistes russes, les soviets, et la révolution de 1917.* Paris: Les Éditions de Paris.

Sloterdijk, Peter. 2003. *Ni le soleil ni la mort: Jeu de piste sous forme de dialogues avec Hans-Jürgen Heinrichs.* Trans. Olivier Mannoni. Paris: Fayard.

Spinoza, Benedict de. 1956. *Traité de l'autorité politique.* Trans. Madeleine Francès. Paris: Gallimard.

———. 1958. *The Political Works.* Ed. and trans. A. G. Wernham. Oxford: Clarendon Press.

———. 1965. *Traité théologico-politique.* Trans. Charles Appuhn. Paris: Gallimard.

———. 1994. *A Spinoza Reader.* Ed. Edwin Curley. Princeton, NJ: Princeton University Press.

———. 1999. *Éthique*. Édition bilingue latin-français. Trans. Bernard Pautrat. Paris: Éditions du Seuil.
———. 2007. *Theological-Political Treatise*. Trans. Michael Silverthorne and Jonathan Israel. Cambridge: Cambridge University Press. 1965.
Spivak, Gayatri Chakravorty. 2004. "Righting Wrongs." *South Atlantic Quarterly* 103, nos. 2–3 (Spring/Summer): 523–82.
Stark, Werner. 2003. "Historical Notes and Interpretive Questions about Kant's Lectures on Anthropology." In *Essays on Kant's Anthropology*. Ed. Brian Jacobs and Patrick Kain. Cambridge: Cambridge University Press. 15–37.
Stein, Robert Louis. 1985. *Léger Félicité Sonthonax: The Lost Sentinel of the Republic*. London: Associated University Press.
Stephen, James. 1969. *The Crisis of the Sugar Colonies; or, An enquiry into the objects and probable effects of the French expedition to the West Indies*. New York: Negro Universities Press, 1802.
Strauss, Leo. 1953. *Natural Right and History*. Chicago: University of Chicago Press.
Tallett, Frank. 1999. "Robespierre and Religion." In *Robespierre*. Ed. Colin Hayden and William Doyle. London: Cambridge University Press. 92–108.
Tavoillot, Pierre-Henri. 2006. "L'idée d'universalité." In *Lumières! Un héritage pour demain*. Ed. Yann Fauchois, Thierry Grillet, and Tzvetan Todorov. Paris: Bibliothèque nationale de France. 94–101.
Teschke, Benno. 2006. "Imperial Doxa from the Berlin Republic." *New Left Review* 40: 128–40.
Thornton, John K. 1993. "'I am the Subject of the King of Kongo': African Ideology and the Haitian Revolution." *Journal of World History* 4, no. 2: 181–214.
Todorov, Tzvetan. 2006. "L'héritage des Lumières." In *Chroniques de la Bibliotheque nationale de France* 34 (Printemps): 6–11.
Trigeaud, Jean-Marc. 2003. "Droit." In *Dictionnaire de philosophie politique*. Ed. Philippe Raynaud and Stéphane Rials. 2nd ed. Paris: Presses Universitaires de France. 159–69.
Trouillot, Michel-Rolph. 1980. "Review of *Peasants and Poverty* by Mats Lundahl." *Journal of Peasant Studies* 8, no. 1: 112–16.
———. 1990. *Haiti: State against Nation: The Origins and Legacy of Duvalierism*. New York: Monthly Review Press.
———. 1995. *Silencing the Past: Power and the Production of History*. Boston: Beacon.
———. 1997. "A Social Contract for Whom? Haitian History and Haiti's Future." In *Haiti Renewed: Political and Economic Prospects*. Ed. Robert I. Rotberg. Washington, DC: Brookings Institution Press. 47–59.
Vastey, Baron de. 1969. *An Essay on the Causes of the Revolution and Civil Wars of Hayti*. New York: Negro Universities Press, 1823.
Vernière, Paul. 1954. *Spinoza et la pensée française avant la revolution*. 2 vols. Paris: Presses Universitaires de France.

Virno, Paolo. 2004. *A Grammar of the Multitude: For an Analysis of Contemporary Forms of Life.* Los Angeles: Semiotext(e).
Wallerstein, Immanuel. 2000. "Africa in a Capitalist World." In *The Essential Immanuel Wallerstein.* New York: The New Press, 1973. 39–68.
Wargny, Christophe. 2004. *Haiti n'existe pas. 1804–2004: Deux cents ans de solitude.* Paris: Autrement.
Weber, Caroline. 2003. *Terror and Its Discontents: Suspect Words in Revolutionary France.* Minneapolis: University of Minnesota Press.
Weil, Eric. 2002. *Hegel et l'état: Cinq conferences.* Paris: Vrin, 1950.
Wilder, Gary. 2005. *The French Imperial Nation-State: Negritude and Colonial Humanism between the Two World Wars.* Chicago: University of Chicago Press, 2005.
Willis, Susan. 2006. "Guantánamo's Symbolic Economy." *New Left Review* 39 (May/June): 123–31.
Wolfe, Carry. 1998. "Old Orders for New Ecology, Animal Rights, and the Poverty of Humanism." *Diacritics* 28, no. 2: 21–40.
Wood, Alan. 2002. "What Is Kantian Ethics?" In *Groundwork for the Metaphysics of Morals.* Ed. Allen W. Wood. New Haven, CT: Yale University Press. 157–82.
———. 2003. "Kant and the Problem of Human Nature." In *Essays on Kant's Anthropology.* Ed. Brian Jacobs and Patrick Kain. Cambridge: Cambridge University Press. 38–59.
Wood, Ellen Meiksins. 2003. *Empire of Capital.* London: Verso.
Wood, Gordon S. 1991. *The Radicalism of the American Revolution.* New York: Vintage Books.
Žižek, Slavoj. 2000. "Class Struggle or Postmodernism? Yes, Please!" In *Contingency, Hegemony, Universality: Contemporary Dialogues on the Left.* London: Verso. 90–135.
———. 2001. *Did Somebody Say Totalitarianism? Five Interventions on the (Mis)use of a Notion.* New York: Verso.
———. 2004. *Organs without Bodies: Deleuze and Consequences.* New York: Routledge.
———. 2005. "Against Human Rights." *New Left Review* 34 (July–August): 115–31.
———. 2008. *Violence. Six Sideways Reflections.* London: Profile Books.
Zuckert, Michael. 2000. "Natural Rights in the American Revolution: The American Amalgam." In *Human Rights and Revolution.* Ed. Jeffrey N. Wasserstrom, Lynn Hunt, and Marilyn B. Young. New York: Rowman and Littlefield.
Zupancic, Elena. 2000. *Ethics of the Real: Kant, Lacan.* London: Verso.

# Index

Adams, John, 28
Adorno, Theodor, 210n25, 224n35, 226n50
*Agronomist*, 183-87
American Revolution, 13, 208-9n8; and abolition, 13; and property, 13, 14. *See also* French Revolution, and nationalism; Haitian Revolution
Aquinas, Thomas, 85, 86
Aravumudan, Srinivas, 61, 217n26
Arendt, Hannah, 125-28; and the Haitian Revolution, 126. *See also* Haitian Revolution
Aristide, Jean-Bertrand, 39, 46, 179, 186-87, 194-95, 238n20
Aristotle, 221n7; and slavery, 84-85

Badiou, Alain, 27, 125, 211n31, 214n5, 224-25n43, 236n2
Barnave, Antoine, 17
Barthélemy, Gérard, 169-71, 235n21
Beaubrun, Ardouin, 113
Bell, Madison Smartt, 147, 168, 232n30, 235n23
Benhabib, Seyla, 71, 100, 110, 225n48
Benjamin, Walter, 179
Benot, Yves, 64-65, 76, 92, 217n25
Biassou, Georges, 143-44, 155
Bidima, Jean-Godefroy, 235n22
Black Jacobinism, concept of, 131-33
*Black Jacobins*. *See* James, C. L. R.
Blanchot, Maurice, 222n23
Bloch, Ernst, 116, 226n61, 234n13
Blumrosen, Alfred W., 209n14
Borgella, 156
*Bossale* community, 165; and the Radical Enlightenment, 169, 172; and singularization, 175; and stateless egalitarianism, 169-71. *See also* Louverture, Toussaint
Boukman, Dutty, 142
Buck-Morss, Susan, 228n70; "Hegel and Haiti," 114-16, 226nn55-56, 228n73
Burke, Edmund, 187
Butler, Judith, 70, 208n4, 230n10

Cadusch, P. de, 143
Cambefort, Colonel, 232n29
Cassirer, Ernst, 29, 31, 32, 101, 222n19
Castoriadis, Cornelius, 112, 221n3, 233n4, 235n20
Césaire, Aimé, 63, 91, 145, 220n55, 223n25, 231n20
Chanlatte, Juste, 59
Chartier, Roger, 64, 211n32
Chomsky, Noam, 226n51, 237n9
Christianity, 43
Clastres, Pierre, 170
Club Massiac, 18, 77
Cole, Andrew, 227n69
Condillac, Étienne Bonnot de, 212n39
Condorcet, Marquis de, 15, 33, 137, 208n6, 224n38
Confiant, Raphaël, 220n55
constitution(s): of Haiti, 19; French (1793), 19
Cooper, John, 14
*Courier politique et littéraire du Cap-Français*, 73, 74
Critchley, Simon, 229n7

David, Alain, 227n68
Davis, David Brion, 15, 208-9n8, 214-15n6

Dayan, Joan, 30, 61, 77
Debray Report, 181–82
Declaration of the Rights of Man and Citizen, 18; and Saint-Domingue, 36, 53, 62, 81, 94. See also French Revolution, and nationalism; Haitian Revolution; Robespierre, Maximilien
DeGraff, Michel, 220n55
Deleuze, Gilles, 27, 107, 180, 238n12; interpreting the Haitian Revolution in light of, 230–31n15; and Spinoza, 24, 31, 228n75. See also singularization; virtual
Demme, Jonathan. See Dominique, Jean
democracy, 49
democratization, 39
de Penier, 73
Descartes, René, 23
Diderot, Denis, 221n13; critique of slavery, 92; and *Histoire des deux Indes,* 91–92; and Spinoza, 22; theories of natural law, 87–88. See also *Encyclopédie,* and natural law; Enlightenment, the; Haitian Revolution; Radical Enlightenment, the; slavery, and social contract; Spinoza, Benedict de
dissidence, 148–52, 185, 232n38. See also Havel, Václav
Dominican Republic, 236n25
Dominique, Jean, 183–87
Donnelly, Jack, 208n2
Dubois, Laurent, 216–17n19, 233n1
Duchet, Michele, 216n19
Dumorier, 77
Dunn, Christopher, 239n22
Duport, Adrien, 17
Dupuy, Alex, 195, 238nn20–21
Duvalier, Jean-Claude, 213–14n51

education, 33. See also Enlightenment, the
emancipation, gradual vs. immediate, 14. See also general emancipation; Haitian Revolution; Louverture, Toussaint; Sonthonax, Léger-Félicité
*Encyclopédie,* and natural law, 87. See also Diderot, Denis
Enlightenment, the: Radical vs. Moderate, 21; and reason, 31
enlightenment, concept of, 80
Eze, Emmanuel, 216n19

Farmer, Paul, 193, 237n8
Fatton, Robert, 39

Feurbach, Anselm, 226n61
Fichte, J. G., 93, 225n45
Fick, Carolyn, 30, 62, 133, 146, 153, 154, 164, 218n30, 231n22, 232n26
Fischer, Sybille, 78, 107–9, 158–60, 226n53, 229n2, 230n11
Foucault, Michel, 106, 211n34, 226n51
France, and slavery, 15
Franklin, Benjamin, 13
Fraser, Nancy, 219n42
Freemasonry: and Toussaint Louverture, 76; and universalism, 76
French Revolution, and nationalism, 19. See also American Revolution; Declaration of the Rights of Man and Citizen; Haitian Revolution; Louverture, Toussaint; Robespierre, Maximilien
Furet, François, 37, 78

Garran, Jean-Phillippe, 74–75, 226n52
Gauchet, Marcel, 190–91
Gauthier, Florence, 161, 231n20, 234n15
Geggus, David, 62, 214n3, 232n29
general emancipation, 145. See also emancipation, gradual vs. immediate
Genovese, Eugene, 133
Gil, Gilberto, 196
Gilligan, Carol, 110
Glissant, Edouard, 41
Godwin, William, 33
Gouge, Olympe de, 111
Grégoire, Abbé, 56, 90; and education, 34; and gradual emancipation, 15–16, 61
Groethuysen, Bernard, 153
Gros, 59, 154–55
Grotius, Hugo, 93
Guadeloupe, 12

Habermas, Jürgen, 218n38; and the French Revolution, 41–42; on public sphere, 69
Haiti: and democracy, 39; and public sphere, 192; and rule of law, 180–81
Haitian Revolution: and autonomy, 20; causes of, 30, 42, 63; and communicative reason, 70; and Declaration of Rights of Man and Citizen, 42, 47, 62; and democracy, 37, 213n48; and early-modern world-system, 82, 131; and the Enlightenment, 20, 28, 33, 35, 54; and epistemology, 36; and faculty of judgment, 29; and the French Revolution, 10, 34, 56, 64; and global capitalism,

25; historiography of, 41; and human rights, 191; and Kant, 56, 107; and land reform, 38, 163; legacy of, 179–83; and Mande Charter, 45; miraculous status of, 124–28; and modernity, 9; and neocolonialism, 9; and political philosophy, 32; and progress, 10; and the Radical Enlightenment, 21, 24; reception of, 11; and Rights of Man, 11; and rule of law, 180–81; and singularization, 20, 24; and truth, 31; and the "Velvet" Revolution, 232n39; and violence, 11
Hallward, Peter, 211n30, 214n2, 236n2, 237n7, 238n21
Hardt, Michael, 210n29
Havel, Václav, 69, 150–52, 232n39
Hegel, G. W. F.: critique of Locke, 119; and the Haitian Revolution, 113–24; and human rights, 121; *Phenomenology of Spirit*, 115–16; *Philosophy of Right*, 113–24; and postcolonial theory, 118; and public sphere, 68; and social normativity, 117; and Spinoza, 121, 123, 227n66
hegemony, 134, 138
Heidegger, Martin, 105, 187, 225n46, 237n10
Helvétius, Claude Adrien, 32
historiography, and the Haitian Revolution, 37
Holbach, Baron d', 22
human rights, 81, 137, 176; vs. natural right, 82–95; as positive rights, 10. *See also* natural right/law
Humboldt, Wilhelm von, 81
Hyppolite, Jean, 115, 116

Israel, Jonathan, 96, 210n26, 223n32

James, C. L. R., 113, 129–33, 145; and modernity, 129
Jean-François (Papillon), 143–44
Jefferson, Thomas, 209n10
Jenson, Deborah, 59, 78, 208n7, 230n14
judgment, faculty of, 30, 35, 36, 93, 212n40; and sensation, 29

Kant, Immanuel, 33, 53, 218–19n39; *Anthropology*, 100; and dignity, 97; and enlightenment, 63; and freedom, 55; and the French Revolution, 188; and the Haitian Revolution, 111; and human action, 54; and human rights, 93; and imperialism, 100; limitations of, 109–11; as Moderate Enlightenment thinker, 96, 97; and perfectibility, 101; and personality, 102, 103; political philosophy of, 95–113; and production-based subjectivity, 110; and progress, 40, 188; on public sphere, 67; and revolution, 95–99; and singularization, 99–107; and slavery, 102; and Spinoza, 47–48, 223n34, 225n44; and universal law, 98, 101; and violence, 98
Keita, Soundiata. *See* Mande Charter
Kirchheimer, Otto, 237n4
Kongo kingdom, 43
Kreyol, 185, 186, 220n55; and abstraction, 79

Laclau, Ernesto, 70, 133; chain of equivalence, 134; *Hegemony and Socialist Strategy*, 134; theory of populist reason, 139–40
Lafarge, Arlette, 70
La Fayette, Marquis de, 86
Laguerre, Michel, 215n8, 219–20n50
Lameth, Alexandre, 17
La Mettrie, Julien Offray de, 22
Laplaine, Dodo, 76
La Révellière-Lépeaux, Louis-Marie de, 90
Lavalas, 195
Laveaux, Etienne, 59, 155
*liberté/libete*, 29, 74, 79, 138, 140, 141, 142. *See also* emancipation, gradual vs. immediate
Linebaugh, Peter, 72
Locke, John, 33, 34, 216n14
Lord Kames, 51
Louverture, Toussaint, 217n23; and Abbé Raynal, 223n28; and African culture, 154; concept of freedom, 164–67; critique of, 167–69; 1801 constitution of, 108–9, 155–60, 234nn10–12; and forced labor, 162, 189; and Freemasonry, 76; and the French Revolution, 57, 91; and human rights, 93; letter to Directory, 28, 57; political philosophy of, 153–62; as public intellectual, 59; and public sphere, 59, 74; and the Radical Enlightenment, 43, 58; and rebels of Port-de-Paix, 166–67; and Republicanism, 57; role in beginnings of revolt, 146; and Rousseau, 91; and rule

Louverture, Toussaint (*continued*)
  of law, 154, 157; and symbolic capital, 78; and universalism, 60, 79, 94, 168
Lundahl, Mats, 163, 207n1 (chap. 1), 208n7, 211–12n36, 235n19

Macaya, 44
Macherey, Pierre, 213n45, 228n74
Madiou, Thomas, 113
Mande Charter, 45–46, 215n9
Marat, Jean-Paul, 231n20
maroons: and anarchist social structure, 76; and public sphere, 76
Mason, George, 28
Meslier, Jean, 22
Mignolo, Walter, 81
*mir* (Russian), 235–36n24
Mirabeau, Comte de, 215n11
Misrahi, Robert, 209n23
Moderate Enlightenment, the, 96. *See also* Enlightenment, the; Radical Enlightenment, the
Montag, Warren, 173, 218n35
Montesquieu, Baron de, 22, 221n15
Mornet, Daniel, 27
*Moun andeyo*, 140. *See also* Louverture, Toussaint
Mourgeon, Jacques, 190
Münkler, Herfried, 238n19
Muthu, Sankar, 100, 209n22

Napoleon Bonaparte, 12
natural right/law, 82–95; as conservative ideology, 84; definition of, 83. *See also* human rights
Negri, Antonio, 210–11n29
Neumann, Franz, 214n53, 237n4
"Nicoleau," 142
Nietzsche, Friedrich, 107

Ogé, Vincent, 77, 142
Otis, James, 13

Parks, Rosa, 149
Pascal (secretary general to Toussaint), 158
Patton, Paul, 225n47
Pechmeja, 92
Péralte, Charlemagne, 152
perfectibility, 15, 107. *See also* Diderot, Denis; Kant, Immanuel; Rousseau, Jean-Jacques
Piquionne, Natelie, 144–45, 232n31

Pluchon, Pierre, 133, 145, 154, 219n45
Polverel, Etienne, 164–66
Popkin, Jeremy, 213n47
progress, 40; and human rights, 187–93. *See also* Kant, Immanuel
Provincial Assembly of Saint-Domingue, and defense of slavery, 18
public sphere, 60, 64–71, 192, 218n31; and Black Atlantic, 65; contemporary Haitian, 183–87; definition of, 66; and Habermas, 65; and oral culture, 66, 184; in Saint-Domingue, 61, 71–78. *See also* Habermas, Jürgen; Haitian Revolution; Kant, Immanuel; Louverture, Toussaint

Quakers, 14

Radical Enlightenment, the, 96, 174; and universal emancipation, 23. *See also* Enlightenment, the; Moderate Enlightenment, the
Rancière, Jacques, 41, 212n44
Raynal, Abbé de, 217n26
Rediker, Marcus, 72
Ritter, Joachim, 116
Robespierre, Maximilien, 209n17, 216nn15–16, 234n15; and civil rights, 51; as dissident, 50, 216n13, 231n20; and freedom of the press, 52; and the Haitian Revolution, 48; political philosophy of, 48–52; Project for a declaration of the rights of man and citizen (1793), 90, 161; and property rights, 51; and Spinoza, 50; and violence, 99; and women, 52. *See also* dissidence; French Revolution, and nationalism; Haitian Revolution; Louverture, Toussaint; Radical Enlightenment, the
Rogozinski, Jacob, 103
Rousseau, Jean-Jacques, 33, 222nn17–19; *Contrat social*, 89; critique of *philosophes*, 88; and education, 34; on freedom, 88; on property, 91; and Spinoza, 89, 222n21; and state of nature, 90. *See also* Haitian Revolution; Kant, Immanuel, Louverture, Toussaint
rule of law, 38, 214n53. *See also* Louverture, Toussaint
Rush, Benjamin, 13

Saint-Domingue. *See* Haiti; Haitian Revolution; Louverture, Toussaint

Saint-Just, Louis de, 37
Sala-Molins, Louis, 61, 208n6, 217n25
Scheuermann, William, 237n4
Schmitt, Carl, 187, 237n4
Schoelcher, Victor, 113
Scott, David, 218n29, 219n43, 220n56, 229n1
Scott, Julius, 76
Sièyes, Abbé, 141
singularization, 25, 27; relation to Kant, 99–113; relation to Spinoza, 25. See also Deleuze, Gilles; Haitian Revolution; Kant, Immanuel; Radical Enlightenment, the; Spinoza, Benedict de
slavery, and social contract, 99. See also American Revolution; Diderot, Denis; French Revolution, and nationalism; Haitian Revolution; Hegel, G. W. F.; Kant, Immanuel; Louverture, Toussaint
Sloterdijk, Peter, 70, 219n40
Société des amis des noirs, 18
Sonthonax, Léger-Félicité, 36, 146–48; and Declaration of Rights of Man and Citizen, 77
sovereignty, 49, 181. See also Spinoza, Benedict de
Spinoza, Benedict de: and adequate idea, 23, 47; and common notions, 94; and contemporary philosophy, 26; and democracy, 23, 212n38; and freedom, 173, 222n22; and the French Enlightenment, 22; and the Haitian Revolution, 35; and human rights, 22, 221n11; and natural right/law, 21, 85–86, 221nn8–9; and perfectibility, 22; and property, 234n16; and the Radical Enlightenment, 96, 210n26; and reason, 35, 86, 213n46; and rule of law, 23; and slavery, 23, 123; and society, 222n21; and sovereignty, 31. See also Diderot, Denis; Enlightenment, the; Haitian Revolution; Louverture, Toussaint; Radical Enlightenment, the; Robespierre, Maximilien
Spivak, Gayatri, 231n17, 236n27
Stephen, James, 233n1
Strauss, Leo, and natural law, 83
Suffrard, Charles, 186
sugar, 128

Terror (French Revolutionary), 220n54; and deformalization of law, 37; and revolution, 38. See also Robespierre, Maximilien
Thornton, John K., 43–44, 112
Thucydides, 195
Toussaint Louverture. See Louverture, Toussaint
Trouillot, Michel-Rolph, 54, 158, 163, 207n1 (chap. 1), 214n52
truth, living in, 150–52. See also Havel, Václav; Kant, Immanuel; Spinoza, Benedict de

United States, relation to Haiti, 193–94
universal emancipation, 152, 208n7; as concept, 36, 141; and history, 26. See also Haitian Revolution; Louverture, Toussaint; slavery, and social contract
universality, 24, 79, 135–36, 138; critique of, 163, 230n12
universal rights, 10, 197

Vattel, Emeric de, 51
Veloso, Caetano, 196, 239n22
Vernière, Paul, 22, 209–10n23, 222n17
Villevaleix, Seguy de, 77
Vincent, Colonel, 169
violence, 98, 193; and human rights, 79; subjective vs. objective, 12, 137. See also Kant, Immanuel; Louverture, Toussaint; Robespierre, Maximilien
virtual, 104–6. See also Deleuze, Gilles
Vodun, 30; and the Haitian Revolution, 43. See also Haitian Revolution; Louverture, Toussaint
Voltaire, 22

Wallace, George, 221–22n16
Wallerstein, Immanuel, 130, 229n4
Wargny, Christophe, 237n3
Weber, Carolyn, 222n23
Weil, Eric, 118
Wimpfenn, Baron de, 74
Wollstonecraft, Mary, 136
Wood, Allen, 224n42
Wood, Gordon, 208n8
Wordsworth, William, 82
world-system, 130. See also Wallerstein, Immanuel

Žižek, Slavoj, 136, 230n12, 238n13

www.ingramcontent.com/pod-product-compliance
Lightning Source LLC
Chambersburg PA
CBHW021806220426
43662CB00006B/197